W9-BOB-995

FIX-IT and FORGET-IT®
SLOW COOKER
Surprises

Fix-It and Forget-It

SLOW COOKER
Surprises

335+ FUSS-FREE FAMILY RECIPES
INCLUDING COMFORT CLASSICS AND EXCITING NEW DISHES

Good Books

New York, New York

Copyright © 2019 by Good Books

Photographs by: Jeremy Hess, Timothy W. Lawrence, Bonnie Matthews, Oliver Parini, Oxmoor House, Dalila Tarhuni, Jason Varney

Book design by Chris Gaugler

All rights reserved. No part of this book may be reproduced in any manner without the express written consent of the publisher, except in the case of brief excerpts in critical reviews or articles. All inquiries should be addressed to Good Books, 307 West 36th Street, 11th Floor, New York, NY 10018.

Good Books books may be purchased in bulk at special discounts for sales promotion, corporate gifts, fund-raising, or educational purposes. Special editions can also be created to specifications. For details, contact the Special Sales Department, Good Books, 307 West 36th Street, 11th Floor, New York, NY 10018 or info@skyhorsepublishing.com.

Good Books is an imprint of Skyhorse Publishing, Inc.®, a Delaware corporation.

Visit our website at www.goodbooks.com.

10 9 8 7 6 5 4 3 2 1

Library of Congress Cataloging-in-Publication Data is available on file.

Cover photo by Oliver Parini. Styling by Natalie Wise.

Print ISBN: 978-1-68099-534-3
Ebook ISBN: 978-1-68099-545-9

Printed in China

CONTENTS

Delicious Dishes

Slow cooker meals guarantee delicious food with minimal effort. When you have a busy day ahead, it's so simple to toss ingredients in the pot and go. The slow cooker does the hard work for you while you're not home, giving you a flavorful meal for the family. Cleanup is a breeze with just one dish to clean, allowing even more time with family and friends! Even when whipping up a feast for company, your slow cooker can be an essential tool, offering more cooking space while the oven is full. And of course it's perfect on hot days when you want to keep the house cool.

All of these reasons and more are why slow cookers should have a place in every home. And if you're looking for some new, exciting recipes, switch them up with *Fix-It and Forget-It Slow Cooker Surprises*. Here you'll find 325 recipes you never thought could come from a slow cooker. From savory bone-in turkey breasts to delicious cakes and brownies, you'll be sure to please your loved ones with these mouthwatering recipes.

WHAT MAKES THESE RECIPES A SURPRISE?

Stews, soups, and chili come to mind when you think of slow cooker recipes. Your slow cooker is capable of a lot more than you might imagine. So don't be shy about what you ask of it—like cooking burgers, steaks, and breads. It can even prepare breakfast while you sleep. It is a near-miracle appliance, if you understand a little bit about how it works. Take what you already know and try something new.

Forget the oven! Cook a whole chicken in the slow cooker, like our Sunny Chicken (page 132). Even flavorful fish dishes can be done in the slow cooker without overcooking, like Teriyaki Salmon (page 179). Burger in the slow cooker? It's possible! Try the Pita Burgers (page 100) or the Pizzaburgers (page 99) for juicy burgers without a grill. Other handheld dishes like Cheese-Stuffed Pizza (page 216) will have your family thinking it came straight from the brick oven. Savory dishes are just the beginning, though.

❧ SAVE ROOM FOR DESSERT ❧

Cakes, pies, muffins, and 100+ more desserts can all be made without turning on the oven. Easy recipes like Chocolate Bread Pudding (page 334) or a classic Double-Crust Cherry Pie (page 310) will become after-dinner staples. And you'll never worry about drying out your cakes, especially with the Best Pineapple Cake on page 257 that's so moist and wonderfully tender. Have a hard time caramelizing the sugar on your flan? With our Spanish Flan (page 346), the slow cooker does it for you!

Make sure all these sweet recipes are a success by having the right equipment. Oven mitts are common to have in the kitchen, though when baking with your slow cooker, make sure to have ones that are well insulated but not too thick. This makes it easier to lift baking dishes, ramekins, and loaf pans out of the slow cooker. Sturdy tongs with a bear-jaw grip are also handy for lifting ramekins out of a hot slow cooker. And it's good to have a baking or cooling rack ready when your slow cooker has finished its job. Placing the hot container on the cooling rack will keep your treats from getting soggy.

❧ DISCOVER NEW TIPS AND TRICKS ❧

Still can't believe you can make so many tasty treats in your slow cooker? Packed within these pages are helpful hints for foolproof dishes every time. Keep brownies and pies safe from unwanted lid moisture by using the "swoop" technique! A lot of moisture gathers on the inside of your slow cooker lid when you use it. Simply grip the handle of the lid firmly, and with a swift and firm move, lift the lid and turn it right-side up in a take-charge motion.

Find tips for savory dishes too! Learn the right time to add fresh herbs or sour cream to a dish to get maximum flavor. Don't want your pasta to turn into mush in the slow cooker? If it's on low, just add it 30 minutes before the end of cooking time for perfectly cooked pasta. Use these tips and many more while whipping up fun, new recipes.

❧ MAKE MEAL PREP A BREEZE ❧

The recipes in this cookbook are not only surprising, but also easy to put together. The moist Lemony Turkey Breast (page 169) only has six ingredients, and can sit in the slow cooker for up to 8 hours while you're out running errands. And our mouthwatering Italian Sausage, Peppers, and Potatoes (page 115) has just four ingredients—all are probably in your kitchen right now. It's important to know your slow cooker too, so that you have a perfect meal each time.

Consider buying a cooker that allows you to program the cooking time and then switches to warm automatically so you don't have to worry about being home the moment it stops cooking.

If you are home while the slow cooker is on, remember there are consequences to lifting the lid. To compensate for the lost heat you should plan to add on 15 to 20 minutes of cooking time for each time the lid was lifted off.

It's helpful to know your slow cooker and how it cooks at different settings so that meals come out perfect each time. Here are approximate slow cooker temperatures. Remember, each slow cooker is different.

- High—212°F–300°F

- Low—170°–200°F

- Simmer—185°F

- Warm—165°F

⁐ PICK THE RIGHT SLOW COOKER ⁑

To assure your recipes come out perfect every time, you'll need the right-size vessel. For baking, make sure to have a 5- or 6-quart round slow cooker, and since they are reasonably priced, adding a 6-quart oval slow cooker lets you make every baking recipe. A 1-quart round baking dish with a lid, a 6½" or 7" springform pan, as well as a 2-quart round baking dish with a lid will fit into your 5- or 6-quart round slow cooker, and four or five 3" (6-ounce) ramekins will fit in a 6-quart oval slow cooker without having them touch each other. You can even set a bread or loaf pan (9¼" x 5¼" x 2¾") on the floor of a 6-quart oval slow cooker. If it doesn't fit, let it hang onto the top edge of the oval cooker.

As for all the other exciting, savory dishes in this cookbook, you'll want a cooker that's at least 3 to 4 quarts. And for showstopper recipes, like the Leg of Lamb with Rosemary and Garlic (page 126), opt for a 6- to 7-quart oval cooker.

⁐ ENDLESS POSSIBILITIES ⁑

Cooking and baking are much easier when they're done in the slow cooker, and with hundreds of recipes to choose from you'll never run out of ideas. Whip up a batch of Apple Granola (page 42) for a quick breakfast treat, or make a Creamy Garden Quiche (page 10) for a relaxing Sunday brunch. From cheesy Baked Ziti (page 198) to the decadent Deep and Dark Chocolate Cake (page 230), you'll have a hard time choosing what to put on the table next!

BREAKFASTS

and Brunches

WELSH RAREBIT

SHARON TIMPE, MEQUON, WI

Makes: 6–8 servings
PREP. TIME: 10 MINUTES
COOKING TIME: 1½–2½ HOURS
IDEAL SLOW-COOKER SIZE: 3- OR 4-QUART

- 12 oz. can beer
- 1 Tbsp. dry mustard
- 1 tsp. Worcestershire sauce
- ½ tsp. salt
- ⅛ tsp. black or white pepper
- 1 lb. American cheese, cubed
- 1 lb. sharp cheddar cheese, cubed
- English muffins or toast
- tomato slices
- bacon, cooked until crisp
- fresh steamed asparagus spears

1. In slow cooker, combine beer, mustard, Worcestershire sauce, salt, and pepper.
2. Cover and cook on High 1–2 hours, until mixture boils.
3. Add cheese, a little at a time, stirring constantly until all the cheese melts.
4. Heat on High 20–30 minutes with cover off, stirring frequently.
5. Serve hot over toasted English muffins or over toasted bread cut into triangles. Garnish with tomato slices, strips of crisp bacon, and steamed asparagus spears.

TIP

This is a good dish for brunch with fresh fruit, juice, and coffee. It also makes a great lunch or late-night light supper. Serve with a tossed green salad, especially fresh spinach and orange slices with a vinaigrette dressing.

HUEVOS RANCHEROS IN THE CROCK

PAT BISHOP, BEDMINSTER, PA

Makes: 6 servings
PREP. TIME: 25 MINUTES
COOKING TIME: 1 HOUR 40 MINUTES
IDEAL SLOW-COOKER SIZE: 4-QUART

3 cups salsa, room temperature

2 cups cooked beans, drained, room temperature

6 eggs, room temperature

salt and pepper to taste

⅓ cup grated Mexican-blend cheese, optional

6 tortillas, for serving

1. Grease interior of slow cooker crock. Mix salsa and beans in slow cooker.

2. Cook on High 1 hour, or until steaming.

3. With a spoon, make 6 evenly spaced dents in the salsa mixture; try not to expose the bottom of the crock. Break an egg into each dent.

4. Salt and pepper eggs. Sprinkle with cheese if you wish.

5. Cover and continue to cook on High until egg whites are set and yolks are as firm as you like them, approximately 20–40 minutes.

6. To serve, scoop out an egg with some beans and salsa. Serve with warm tortillas.

VARIATION

Serve with hot cooked rice instead of tortillas.

TIP
If you want, sprinkle with chopped cilantro or chopped spring onions after cooking.

WESTERN OMELET

MARY LOUISE MARTIN, BOYD, WI
JAN MAST, LANCASTER, PA

Makes: 10 servings
PREP. TIME: 15 MINUTES
COOKING TIME: 4–6 HOURS
IDEAL SLOW-COOKER SIZE: 5-QUART

32	oz. bag frozen hash brown potatoes, divided
1	lb. cooked ham, cubed, divided
1	medium onion, diced, divided
1½	cups shredded cheddar cheese, divided
18	eggs
1½	cups milk
1	tsp. salt
1	tsp. pepper

1. Grease interior of slow-cooker crock. Layer ⅓ each of frozen potatoes, ham, onion, and cheese in bottom of slow cooker.

2. Repeat 2 times.

3. Beat together eggs, milk, salt, and pepper in a large mixing bowl. Pour over mixture in slow cooker.

4. Cover. Cook on Low 4–6 hours, or until potatoes are fully cooked and omelet is firm but not dry or overcooked.

NOTE This is a great breakfast, served along with orange juice and fresh fruit.

SPINACH FRITTATA

SHIRLEY UNTERNAHRER, WAYLAND, IA

Makes: 4–6 servings
PREP. TIME: 15 MINUTES
COOKING TIME: 1½–2 HOURS
IDEAL SLOW-COOKER SIZE: 5-QUART

4 eggs
½ tsp. salt
½ tsp. dried basil
   freshly ground pepper to taste
3 cups chopped fresh spinach, stems removed
½ cup chopped tomato, liquid drained off
⅓ cup freshly grated Parmesan cheese

1. Whisk eggs well in mixing bowl. Whisk in salt, basil, and pepper.
2. Gently stir in spinach, tomato, and Parmesan.
3. Grease interior of slow-cooker crock. Pour mixture into cooker.
4. Cover and cook on High 1½–2 hours, or until middle is set. Serve hot.

VARIATIONS

❧ Add 1 cup browned, crumbled sausage to Step 2.
❧ Add ½ tsp. minced garlic to Step 2.

NOTE Biscuits or hash brown potatoes go well with this recipe.

BREAKFAST CORNBREAD PUDDING

Makes: 10 servings
PREP. TIME: 25 MINUTES
COOKING TIME: 2–3 HOURS
IDEAL SLOW-COOKER SIZE: 6-QUART

4 Tbsp. (½ stick) butter, divided

5 cups cubed cornbread, toasted

5 cups cubed bread

1 cup cooked, crumbled country sausage

2 green onions, diced

¼ cup chopped red bell pepper

½ cup corn

4 cups whole milk

6 eggs

¼ tsp. dried thyme

½ tsp. salt

   pepper, to taste

1. Use 1 Tbsp. butter to grease slow cooker.

2. In the slow cooker, gently stir together cornbread, bread, sausage, onions, peppers, and corn.

3. In a mixing bowl, whisk together milk, eggs, thyme, salt, and pepper.

4. Pour milk mixture over bread mixture, pushing down on bread as needed so it is submerged.

5. Melt remaining 3 Tbsp. butter and drizzle over top.

6. Cover and cook on High for 2–3 hours, until liquid is absorbed and pudding is puffy. Serve hot or warm (although the puffiness will sink down as pudding sits).

NOTE This is a tasty twist on the traditional breakfast casserole. The cornbread gives excellent flavor and texture, and it's a handy way to use up leftover cornbread.

SMOKY BREAKFAST CASSEROLE

SHIRLEY HINH, WAYLAND, IA

Makes: 8–10 servings
PREP. TIME: 15 MINUTES
COOKING TIME: 3 HOURS
IDEAL SLOW-COOKER SIZE: 4-QUART

6 eggs, beaten
1 lb. little smokies (cocktail wieners), or 1½ lbs. bulk sausage, browned and drained
1½ cups milk
1 cup shredded cheddar cheese
8 slices bread, torn into pieces
1 tsp. salt
½ tsp. dry mustard
1 cup shredded mozzarella cheese

1. Mix together all ingredients except mozzarella cheese. Pour into greased slow cooker.

2. Sprinkle mozzarella cheese over top.

3. Cover and cook 2 hours on High, and then 1 hour on Low.

BREAKFAST TORTE

Makes: 8 servings
PREP. TIME: 20 MINUTES
COOKING TIME: 3–4 HOURS
IDEAL SLOW-COOKER SIZE: 4-QUART

2 8-oz. pkgs. refrigerated crescent rolls
1 lb. cooked, crumbled sausage
¾ cup shredded mozzarella
2 green onions, chopped
¾ cup halved grape tomatoes
¼ cup crumbled feta
4 eggs
½ tsp. dried basil

1. Take 1 package of dough and press it into bottom of greased slow cooker.

2. Sprinkle with sausage, mozzarella, green onions, tomatoes, and then feta. Do not mix.

3. In a bowl, beat eggs and basil together.

4. Pour evenly over layers in slow cooker.

5. Take remaining package of dough and flatten it into the shape of the slow cooker. Lay it on top of torte to make a final layer.

6. Cover and cook on High for 3–4 hours until dough is puffy and eggs are set.

TIP

Vary the veggies and meat according to what your family likes and what you have on hand.

CHICKEN AND SPINACH QUICHE

Makes: 6 servings
PREP. TIME: 20 MINUTES
COOKING TIME: 1½–2 HOURS
STANDING TIME: 20–30 MINUTES
IDEAL SLOW-COOKER SIZE: 5-QUART

pastry for 9" pie

1 cup chopped, cooked chicken

1 cup shredded Swiss cheese

½ cup cooked, chopped spinach, drained (about ⅓ of a 10-oz. frozen pkg., thawed)

¼ cup chopped onion

2 eggs

¾ cup mayonnaise

¾ cup milk

⅛ tsp. pepper

1. Take rolled out pastry and fit it into slow cooker crock as you would line a pie plate, bringing it up the sides 1–2" and gently pushing it into the bottom.

2. In a good-sized bowl, mix together chicken, cheese, spinach, and onion.

3. Spoon into crust.

4. In same bowl, stir together eggs, mayonnaise, milk, and pepper until smooth.

5. Pour over chicken-spinach mixture.

6. Cover. Bake on High 1½–2 hours, or until knife inserted into center of quiche comes out clean.

7. Uncover quickly, swooping lid away from yourself so no water drips on quiche from the inside of the lid. Remove crock from cooker and place on baking rack to cool.

8. Let stand 20–30 minutes, or until firm, before slicing to serve.

CREAMY GARDEN QUICHE

Makes: 8 servings
PREP. TIME: 20 MINUTES
COOKING TIME: 1½–2 HOURS
STANDING TIME: 20 MINUTES
IDEAL SLOW-COOKER SIZE: 5-QUART

	pastry for 10" pie
1	lb. feta cheese, crumbled
1½	cups plain yogurt
3	eggs
1	lb. zucchini, grated (no need to peel)
4	cloves garlic, minced
4	oz. can green chilies, drained
2–4	Tbsp. minced fresh dill, or 2–3 tsp. dried dill
2–4	Tbsp. minced fresh parsley, or 2–3 tsp. dried parsley
2–4	Tbsp. minced fresh mint, or 2–3 tsp. dried mint
½	cup chopped pine nuts
	salt and pepper to taste

TIP

For a different look, use your mandoline to slice the unpeeled zucchini. And if you've got both green and yellow summer squash, you'll have a beautiful mixture of colorful rounds.

1. Take rolled out pastry and fit it into slow cooker crock as you would line a pie plate, bringing it up the sides 1–2" and gently pushing it into the bottom.

2. Combine feta, yogurt, and eggs in a food processor or blender. Process until well blended.

3. In a mixing bowl, combine zucchini, garlic, chilies, dill, parsley, mint, pine nuts, salt, and pepper.

4. Pour creamy mixture into vegetables and herbs. Stir together.

5. Pour into pie crust in crock.

6. Cover. Bake on High 1½–2 hours, or until knife inserted into center of quiche comes out clean.

7. Uncover and remove crock from cooker. Place on baking rack for at least 20 minutes before slicing and serving.

ADD-WHAT-YOU-LIKE QUICHE

Photo appears in color section.

Makes: 6–8 servings
PREP. TIME: 15–20 MINUTES
COOKING TIME 1½–2 HOURS
STANDING TIME: 20–30 MINUTES
IDEAL SLOW-COOKER SIZE: 5-QUART

pastry for 9" or 10" pie

2 cups (½ lb.) grated Swiss cheese

½ cup milk

½ cup mayonnaise

2 Tbsp. flour

¼ cup minced onions

2 eggs

Choose 1 Optional Ingredient Listed Below

4 oz. crabmeat

4 oz. fully cooked ham, cubed

6 strips bacon, cooked and crumbled

1½–2 cups chopped fresh spinach

1. Take rolled out pastry and fit it into slow cooker as you would line a pie plate, bringing it up the sides 1–2" and gently pushing it into the bottom.

2. Combine cheese, milk, mayonnaise, flour, onions, eggs, and your choice of one of the optional ingredients in a good-sized bowl.

3. Pour into pie crust.

4. Cover. Bake on High 1½–2 hours, or until knife inserted into center of quiche comes out clean.

5. Quickly remove lid by swooping it away from yourself to prevent water from inside of lid dripping onto quiche. Remove crock from cooker and place on baking rack to cool.

6. Let stand 20–30 minutes, or until firm, before slicing to serve.

NOTE Browned ground beef or cooked and shredded chicken works great here, too.

MEDITERRANEAN QUICHE

Makes: 6–8 servings
PREP. TIME: 30 MINUTES
COOKING TIME: 1½–2 HOURS
STANDING TIME: 20–30 MINUTES
IDEAL SLOW-COOKER SIZE: 5-QUART

pastry for 9" pie

2–3 Tbsp. oil

¼ cup chopped onion

½ a small eggplant, unpeeled and cubed into ½" pieces (about 2 cups)

2 medium tomatoes, seeded and diced

2 Tbsp. chopped fresh parsley

¼ tsp. dried basil or ¾ tsp. chopped fresh basil

½ cup cream or evaporated milk

3 eggs

3 Tbsp. grated Parmesan cheese

¼ tsp. minced garlic

¾ tsp. salt

§ TIP

Evaporated milk is such a great stand-in for cream. Even the low-fat variety does just fine here, especially because the eggs and cheese help bring creaminess.

1. Take rolled out pastry and fit it into slow cooker crock as you would line a pie plate, bringing it up the sides 1–2" and gently pushing it into the bottom.

2. Heat oil in skillet over medium heat. Add onion and eggplant cubes and cook gently, just enough to cook off liquid from the eggplant. (This is to keep your quiche from getting watery.)

3. Add tomatoes and cook a few minutes longer, this time to cook off liquid from tomatoes. Using a slotted spoon, lift mixture out of skillet and into crust in crock.

4. In a bowl, whisk together chopped parsley and basil, cream, eggs, cheese, minced garlic, and salt until well blended.

5. Pour over vegetable mixture in crock.

6. Cover. Bake on High 1½–2 hours, or until a knife inserted into center of quiche comes out clean.

7. Uncover quickly so no water drips from lid onto quiche. Remove crock and place on baking rack to cool.

8. Allow to stand 20–30 minutes, or until quiche firms up in center and can be sliced easily.

SANTA FE QUICHE

Photo appears in color section.

Makes: 6–8 servings
PREP. TIME: 15–20 MINUTES
COOKING TIME: 1½–2 HOURS
STANDING TIME: 20–30 MINUTES
IDEAL SLOW-COOKER SIZE: 5-QUART

pastry for 9" pie
3 cups grated Mexican cheese
4 eggs
½ cup milk
4 oz. can chopped green chilies, drained
1½ cups chopped fresh tomatoes, deseeded

1. Take rolled out pastry and fit it into slow cooker crock as you would line a pie plate, bringing it up the sides 1–2" and gently pushing it into the bottom.

2. Spread cheese over bottom of pie crust.

3. In a medium-sized bowl, beat eggs and milk together.

4. Stir in drained chilies and chopped tomatoes.

5. Pour into pie crust.

6. Cover. Bake on High 1½–2 hours, or until knife inserted into center of quiche comes out clean.

7. Uncover swiftly by swooping lid away from yourself to prevent water from inside of lid dripping onto quiche. Remove crock from cooker and place on baking rack to cool.

8. Let stand 20–30 minutes, or until firm, before slicing and serving.

TIP
It's worth the time to deseed the tomatoes. It helps keep the quiche from getting watery, too.

SPINACH AND TOMATO QUICHE

Photo appears in color section.

Makes: 6 servings
PREP. TIME: 20–30 MINUTES
COOKING TIME: 1½–2 HOURS
STANDING TIME: 30 MINUTES
IDEAL SLOW-COOKER SIZE: 5-QUART

	pastry for 9" pie
2	Tbsp. (¼ stick) butter
½	cup chopped onions
1	tsp. minced garlic
10	oz. pkg. frozen chopped spinach, thawed
1–1½	cups (about 6 oz.) grated Swiss cheese
3	eggs
¾	cup skim milk
½	tsp. salt
1	tsp. dried basil
3	plum tomatoes
1	Tbsp. breadcrumbs
1	Tbsp. Parmesan cheese

1. Take rolled out pastry and fit it into slow cooker crock as you would line a pie plate, bringing it up the sides 1–2" and gently pushing it into the bottom.

2. Melt butter in skillet. Stir in chopped onions and minced garlic. Sauté until veggies just begin to soften.

3. Either squeeze the moisture out of the thawed spinach, or add it to the skillet and cook gently, stirring frequently, until water has evaporated.

4. Stir together spinach and sautéed veggies, grated cheese, eggs, milk, salt, and basil. Pour into pie crust.

5. Slice tomatoes and lay slices over top of filling.

6. Cover cooker. Bake on High 1 hour.

7. Meanwhile, mix together breadcrumbs and Parmesan cheese. At end of first hour of baking, sprinkle quiche with crumb–Parmesan cheese mixture.

8. Return cover to cooker and continue baking another 30–60 minutes, or until a knife stuck into the center of the quiche comes out clean.

9. Swoop cover quickly off cooker so condensation on inside of lid doesn't drip on the quiche. Remove crock from cooker and set on baking rack to cool.

10. Let stand 30 minutes, so quiche can firm up but is still warm. Then slice and serve.

VARIATION

When fresh spinach is in season, you can use it instead of frozen spinach. You'll need about 1½ lbs. fresh spinach to start with. Wash it (leaving some of the water droplets on it for steaming later), chop it, and then put it in a good-sized kettle over medium heat and cover it. Cook gently for a few minutes, and it will cook down to about 1½ cups, or roughly 9–10 oz. When it's cooled, squeeze out any excess water before adding to the quiche mixture.

MUSHROOM QUICHE

Photo appears in color section.

Makes: 6–8 servings
PREP. TIME: 20 MINUTES
COOKING TIME: 1½–2 HOURS
STANDING TIME: 20–30 MINUTES
IDEAL SLOW-COOKER SIZE: 5-QUART

pastry for 9" or 10" pie
1 onion, chopped
½ lb. fresh mushrooms, sliced
4 Tbsp. (½ stick) butter
1 Tbsp. fresh parsley, chopped
dash of salt
freshly ground black pepper
3 eggs
½ cup light cream
1 cup grated cheddar cheese

1. Take rolled out pastry and fit it into slow cooker crock as you would line a pie plate, bringing it up the sides 1–2" and gently pushing it into the bottom.

2. In a large skillet, sauté onions and mushrooms gently in butter for 5 minutes.

3. Remove skillet from heat and drain off cooking liquid.

4. Stir parsley, salt, and pepper into sautéed veggies.

5. In large mixing bowl, beat together eggs and cream.

6. Stir mushroom mixture into eggs and cream. Fold in cheese.

7. Pour into pie crust.

8. Cover. Bake on High 1½–2 hours, or until knife inserted into center of crust comes out clean.

9. Uncover quickly, swooping lid away from yourself to prevent water from inside of lid from dripping on quiche. Remove crock from cooker and place on baking rack to cool.

10. Let stand 20–30 minutes, or until firm in the center, before slicing and serving.

NOTE Remember the vegetarians in your life, but also those who can't get enough mushrooms.

ARTICHOKE PARMESAN QUICHE

Makes: 6–8 servings
PREP. TIME: 15–20 MINUTES
COOKING TIME: 1½–2 HOURS
STANDING TIME: 20–30 MINUTES
IDEAL SLOW-COOKER SIZE: 5- OR 6-QUART

pastry for 9" pie

½ cup grated Parmesan cheese, plus more for garnish

14 oz. can artichoke hearts, drained and chopped

1¼ cups shredded Swiss cheese

3 oz. pkg. cream cheese, softened

½ tsp. nutmeg

⅛ tsp. salt

1 cup + 2 Tbsp. evaporated milk

3 eggs

1. Take rolled out pastry and fit it into slow cooker as you would line a pie plate, bringing it up the sides 1–2" and gently pushing it into the bottom.

2. Sprinkle ½ cup Parmesan cheese over pie crust.

3. Gently squeeze liquid from artichokes, blot them dry, and chop fine.

4. Scatter artichokes over Parmesan cheese.

5. Scatter Swiss cheese over artichokes.

6. In small bowl, beat together cream cheese, nutmeg, and salt.

7. Gradually beat milk and one egg at a time into creamed mixture. Beat well after adding each egg until frothy.

8. Pour over quiche filling.

9. Cover. Bake on High 1½–2 hours, or until knife inserted into center of quiche comes out clean.

10. Uncover quickly, swooping lid away from yourself so no water from the inside of the lid drips on the quiche. Remove crock from cooker and place on baking rack to cool.

11. Let stand 20–30 minutes, or until quiche firms up, before slicing to serve.

12. Sprinkle liberally with Parmesan cheese before serving.

 NOTE This quiche is so creamy and cheesy. The artichokes settle into the mix, and the quiche is a wonderful combination of flavors and textures. You can cut the chokes fairly small or keep the pieces big enough so that you know what you're biting into.

BROCCOLI QUICHE

Makes: 6–8 servings
PREP. TIME: 20–30 MINUTES
COOKING TIME: 1½–2 HOURS
STANDING TIME: 20–30 MINUTES
IDEAL SLOW-COOKER SIZE: 5-QUART

pastry for 9" pie
3 eggs
⅔ cup chicken or vegetable broth
½ cup heavy cream or evaporated milk
½ tsp. salt
¼ tsp. Tabasco
¼ cup grated Parmesan cheese, divided
2 cups chopped fresh broccoli, divided
1 cup grated Swiss cheese, divided
¼ cup sliced scallions, divided

1. Take rolled out pastry and fit it into slow cooker crock as you would line a pie plate, bringing it up the sides 1–2" and gently pushing it into the bottom.

2. Beat eggs with broth, cream, salt, and Tabasco in a bowl. When well mixed, set aside.

3. Sprinkle half the Parmesan cheese over pie crust.

4. Sprinkle half the chopped broccoli over the Parmesan cheese.

5. Sprinkle half the Swiss cheese over the broccoli.

6. Sprinkle half the sliced scallions over the Swiss cheese.

7. Repeat layers of broccoli, Swiss cheese, and scallions.

8. Pour egg mixture over all.

9. Sprinkle with remaining Parmesan cheese.

10. Bake on High 1½–2 hours, or until knife inserted into center of quiche comes out clean.

11. Uncover swiftly, swooping lid away from yourself to prevent condensation from inside of lid dripping on quiche. Remove crock from cooker and place on baking rack to cool.

12. Let stand 20–30 minutes so quiche can firm up, before slicing and serving.

NOTE This quiche fits so many occasions—brunch, supper, or dinner. Pair it with a fresh-veggie salad and good bread.

ASPARAGUS QUICHE

Photo appears in color section.

Makes: 4–6 servings
PREP. TIME: 20 MINUTES
COOKING TIME: 1½–2 HOURS
STANDING TIME: 20–30 MINUTES
IDEAL SLOW-COOKER SIZE: 5-QUART

pastry for a 9" pie

3 cups fresh asparagus, cut in small pieces

2 cups shredded sharp cheddar cheese

1 cup mayonnaise

2 tsp. lemon juice

1. Take rolled out pastry and fit it into slow cooker crock as you would line a pie plate, bringing it up the sides 1–2" and gently pushing it into the bottom.

2. In a mixing bowl, gently combine asparagus, cheese, mayonnaise, and lemon juice.

3. Spoon into pie crust.

4. Cover. Bake on High 1½–2 hours, or until quiche is firm in center.

5. Swoop lid off quickly so no water from the inside of the lid drips on the quiche.

6. Remove crock from cooker and place on wire baking rack to cool.

7. Allow to stand 20–30 minutes, or until firm enough to slice.

Because you don't cook the asparagus ahead of putting it into the crock, it retains its fresh and distinctive flavor. If you want the asparagus to stand front and center, use a milder cheddar so it doesn't compete flavor-wise.

CHEESE GRITS

JANIE STEELE, MOORE, OK

Makes: 6 servings
PREP. TIME: 20 MINUTES
COOKING TIME: 2–3 HOURS
IDEAL SLOW-COOKER SIZE: 3- OR
4-QUART

4 cups water

1 tsp. salt

1 cup regular (not instant) grits, uncooked

3 eggs

¼ cup (½ stick) butter, cut in chunks

1¾ cups grated sharp cheese

¼ tsp. pepper, optional

1. In saucepan, bring water and salt to boil. Slowly add grits, stirring.

2. Cook until grits are thick and creamy, 5–10 minutes.

3. Beat eggs in small bowl. Add spoonful of hot grits to eggs, stirring. This tempers the eggs.

4. Slowly stir egg mixture into rest of hot grits, stirring.

5. Add butter, cheese, and optional pepper. Stir.

6. Grease interior of slow-cooker crock. Pour grits mixture into slow cooker.

7. Cover. Cook on High 2–3 hours, or until grits are set in middle and lightly browned around edges.

VARIATION

Use pepper-jack cheese for a kick.

MEXICAN-STYLE GRITS

MARY SOMMERFELD, LANCASTER, PA

Makes: 10–12 servings
PREP. TIME: 10 MINUTES
COOKING TIME: 2–6 HOURS
IDEAL SLOW-COOKER SIZE: 3-QUART

1½ cups instant grits
1 lb. Velveeta cheese, cubed
½ tsp. garlic powder
2 4-oz. cans diced chilies, drained
1 stick (8 Tbsp.) butter, cut in chunks

1. Prepare grits according to package directions.

2. Stir in cheese, garlic powder, and chilies, until cheese is melted.

3. Stir in butter.

4. Grease interior of slow-cooker crock. Pour mixture into cooker.

5. Cover. Cook on High 2–3 hours, or on Low 4–6 hours, or until grits are firm but not dry.

NOTE Grits are kind of tame on their own, but add some bold seasonings and chilies, and you have a good dish on its own, or as a partner to eggs any style.

HAM AND MUSHROOM HASH BROWNS

EVELYN PAGE, RIVERTON, WY
ANNA STOLTZFUS, HONEY BROOK, PA

Makes: 6–8 servings
PREP. TIME: 15 MINUTES
COOKING TIME: 6–8 HOURS
IDEAL SLOW-COOKER SIZE: 5-QUART

28 oz. pkg. frozen hash brown potatoes
2½ cups cubed cooked ham
2 oz. jar pimentos, drained and chopped
4 oz. can mushrooms, or ¼ lb. sliced fresh mushrooms
10¾ oz. can cheddar cheese soup
¾ cup half-and-half
dash of pepper
salt to taste

1. Combine potatoes, ham, pimentos, and mushrooms in slow cooker.

2. Combine soup, half-and-half, and seasonings. Pour over potatoes.

3. Cover. Cook on Low 6–8 hours. If you turn the cooker on when you go to bed, you'll have a wonderfully tasty breakfast in the morning.

NOTE Don't be afraid to experiment and make changes in recipes. If a recipe calls for an ingredient you don't care for, either substitute something else or leave it out.

CHEESY HASH BROWN POTATOES

CLARICE WILLIAMS, FAIRBANK, IA

Makes: 6–8 servings
PREP. TIME: 10 MINUTES
COOKING TIME: 4–4½ HOURS
IDEAL SLOW-COOKER SIZE: 4-QUART

2 10¾ oz. cans cheddar cheese soup

1⅓ cups buttermilk

2 Tbsp. butter, melted

½ tsp. seasoned salt

¼ tsp. garlic powder

¼ tsp. pepper

2 lb. pkg. frozen, cubed hash brown potatoes

¼ cup grated Parmesan cheese

1 tsp. paprika

1. Combine soup, buttermilk, butter, seasoned salt, garlic powder, and pepper in slow cooker. Mix well.

2. Stir in hash browns. Sprinkle with Parmesan cheese and paprika.

3. Cover. Cook on Low 4–4½ hours, or until potatoes are tender.

CUBED FRENCH TOAST

DONNA SUTER, PANDORA, OH

Makes: 6 servings
PREP. TIME: 20 MINUTES
COOKING TIME: 3¼–5¼ HOURS
IDEAL SLOW-COOKER SIZE: 6-QUART

 1 loaf white bread, cut into 1-inch cubes
 8 eggs
1½ cups milk
 ½ cup heavy cream
 ¼ cup maple syrup
    zest of 1 orange
 ½ cup chopped, toasted pecans
 3 Tbsp. butter, cut into cubes
    maple syrup, for serving
    whipped cream, for serving
    sliced bananas, for serving

1. Place bread cubes on a baking sheet and toast in 400°F oven for 8–10 minutes, or until golden brown. Remove from oven and cool.

2. In large bowl, whisk together eggs, milk, cream, maple syrup, and orange zest.

3. Add in the toasted bread cubes and toss to coat with the egg mixture.

4. Stir in pecans.

5. Grease slow cooker well. Pour bread and egg mixture into cooker. Dot top with cubed butter.

6. Cook on High 3 hours, or on Low 5 hours, or until set.

7. Serve hot, topped with maple syrup, whipped cream, and bananas.

NOTE Toasting the bread cubes before putting them into the slow cooker adds some of the browned flavor of traditional French toast when it's made in a skillet or on a griddle.

PUMPKIN BREAKFAST CUSTARD

AUDREY HESS, GETTYSBURG, PA
Photo appears in color section.

Makes: 4–6 servings
PREP. TIME: 20 MINUTES
COOKING TIME: 1½–2 HOURS
IDEAL SLOW-COOKER SIZE: 2½ OR 3-QUART

2½ cups cooked pumpkin or winter squash
2 Tbsp. blackstrap molasses
3 Tbsp. sugar
¼ cup half-and-half
3 eggs
1 tsp. cinnamon
½ tsp. ground ginger
½ tsp. ground nutmeg
¼ tsp. ground cloves
¼ tsp. salt

1. Purée ingredients in blender until smooth.
2. Grease interior of slow-cooker crock. Pour mixture into cooker.
3. Cook on High 1½–2 hours, or until set in the middle and just browning at edges.
4. Serve warm in scoops over hot cereal, baked oatmeal, or as a breakfast side dish with toast or muffins.

TIPS

Toasted walnuts are a nice topping if you're serving this as a side dish.

Leftover custard will weep a little in the fridge, but it's still fine to use.

This is also good served chilled.

OATMEAL MORNING

BARBARA FORRESTER LANDIS, LITITZ, PA

Makes: 4–5 servings
PREP. TIME: 5 MINUTES
COOKING TIME: 2½–6 HOURS
IDEAL SLOW-COOKER SIZE: 3-QUART

1 cup uncooked steel-cut oats

1 cup dried cranberries

1 cup broken walnuts

½ tsp. salt

1 Tbsp. cinnamon

4 cups liquid—milk, water, or combination of the two

1. Grease interior of slow cooker crock. Combine all dry ingredients in slow cooker. Stir well.

2. Pour in liquid ingredient(s). Mix together well.

3. Cover. Cook on High 2½ hours, or on Low 5–6 hours, or until oats are as tender as you like them.

NOTE
Steel-cut oats have such great body and texture. If you haven't tried them, use this sturdy, flavorful recipe to get acquainted.

VARIATION
If you wish, substitute fresh or dried blueberries or raisins for the dried cranberries.

ADD-WHAT-YOU-LIKE QUICHE ♥ page 11

SANTA FE QUICHE
page 13

SPINACH AND
TOMATO QUICHE
page 14

MUSHROOM QUICHE ♥ page 16

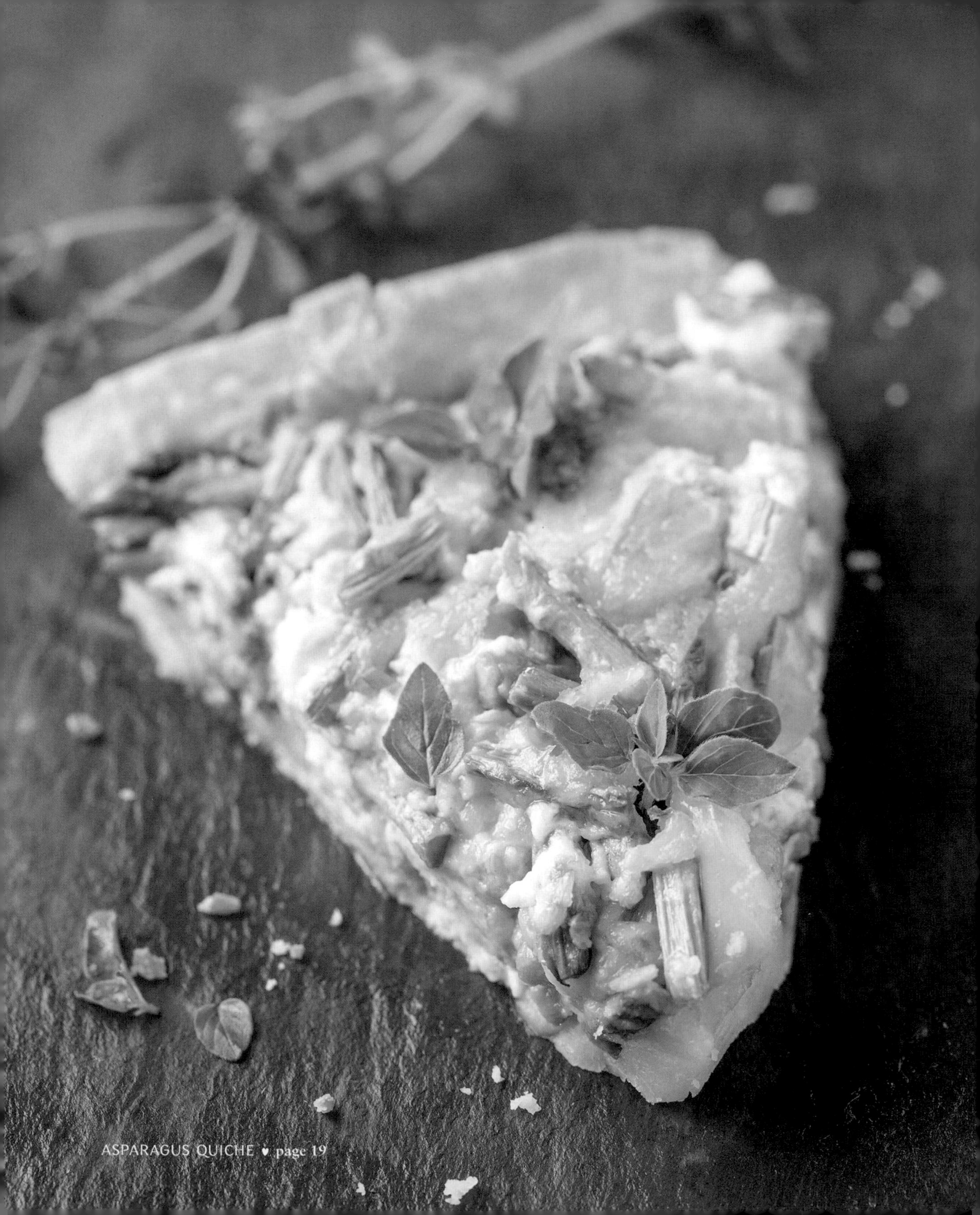

ASPARAGUS QUICHE ♥ page 19

NEW GUINEA GRANOLA ♥ page 31

APPLE GRANOLA ♥ page 42

LOTSA GOOD GRANOLA ♥ page 40

ITALIAN WEDDING SOUP ♥ page 59

SPICED POT ROAST ♥ page 61

BUTTERFLY STEAKS ♥ page 68

CREAMY VEGETABLE BEEF STEW ♥ page 58

ZINGY SHORY RIBS
page 76

ENCHILADA STACK-UP
page 82

NACHOS DINNER ♥ page 80

TEMPTING TORTILLA CASSEROLE ♥ page 81

BIG JUICY BURGERS
page 102

SAVORY SLOW-COOKER
PORK TENDERLOIN
page 107

PULLED PORK WITH DR PEPPER
page 113

GIVE-ME-MORE BARBECUED RIBS
page 115

SLURPING GOOD SAUSAGES ♥ page 116

ITALIAN SAUSAGE, PEPPERS, AND POTATOES
page 117

SAUSAGE TORTELLINI
page 118

APPLE CIDER CINNAMON STEEL-CUT OATMEAL

JENNY UNTERNAHRER, WAYLAND, IA

Makes: 4–6 servings
PREP. TIME: 15 MINUTES
COOKING TIME: 6 HOURS
IDEAL SLOW-COOKER SIZE: 5- OR
6-QUART

- 3 medium Granny Smith apples, peeled and chopped
- 2 cups apple cider
- 1½ cups water
- 1 cup steel-cut oats
- ¼ tsp. ground cinnamon
- ⅛ tsp. salt
- 1 Tbsp. sugar
  maple syrup, optional
  chopped pecans or walnuts, optional

1. Pour a little water in slow cooker crock. Grease a heat-safe baking dish that will fit into your crock.
2. Combine apples, cider, water, oats, cinnamon, salt, and sugar in baking dish.
3. Cover baking dish, either with its lid or aluminum foil, and the slow cooker lid. Cook on Low 6 hours, or until oats are tender. Stir gently before serving.
4. Serve with a drizzle of maple syrup and a sprinkle of nuts over each individual dish, if you wish.

VARIATION

Use 3½ cups apple cider and omit water.

TIP

You can put all of the ingredients into the slow cooker before bed, or program your slow cooker. The oatmeal cooks without effort while you sleep, and in the morning, you will have an aroma that smells like baked apple pie filling your kitchen.

"BAKED" OATMEAL

ELLEN RANCK, GAP, PA

Makes: 4–6 servings
PREP. TIME: 10 MINUTES
COOKING TIME: 2½–3 HOURS
IDEAL SLOW-COOKER SIZE: 3-QUART

⅓ cup oil
½ cup sugar
1 large egg, beaten
2 cups dry quick oats
1½ tsp. baking powder
½ tsp. salt
¾ cup milk

1. Pour the oil into the slow cooker to grease bottom and sides.

2. Add remaining ingredients. Mix well.

3. Bake on Low 2½–3 hours.

NOTE It is a common mistake to add too much liquid when cooking in your slow cooker.

GRAIN AND FRUIT CEREAL

CYNTHIA HALLER, NEW HOLLAND, PA

Makes: 4–5 servings
PREP. TIME: 5 MINUTES
COOKING TIME: 3½ HOURS
IDEAL SLOW-COOKER SIZE: 4-QUART

⅓ cup uncooked quinoa
⅓ cup uncooked millet
⅓ cup uncooked brown rice
4 cups water
¼ tsp. salt
½ cup raisins or dried cranberries
¼ cup chopped nuts, optional
1 tsp. vanilla extract, optional
½ tsp. ground cinnamon, optional
1 Tbsp. maple syrup, optional
½ cup milk

1. Rinse the quinoa, millet, and brown rice well.

2. Grease interior of slow-cooker crock. Place the grains, water, and salt into the crock.

3. Cook on Low about 3 hours, or until most of the water has been absorbed.

4. Add dried fruit, any optional ingredients, and milk.

5. Cover. Cook for 30 minutes more. If the mixture is too thick, add a little more water or milk.

6. Serve hot or cold.

GRANOLA IN THE SLOW COOKER

EARNIE ZIMMERMAN, MECHANICSBURG, PA

Makes: 10–12 servings
PREP. TIME: 10 MINUTES
COOKING TIME: 3–8 HOURS
IDEAL SLOW-COOKER SIZE: 6-QUART

5   cups uncooked rolled oats

1   Tbsp. flaxseeds

¼   cup slivered almonds

¼   cup chopped pecans or walnuts

¼   cup unsweetened shredded coconut

¼   cup maple syrup or honey

4   Tbsp. (½ stick) melted butter or oil of your choice

½   cup dried fruit

1. Grease interior of slow cooker crock. Mix together oats, flaxseeds, almonds, pecans, and coconut in slow cooker.

2. Separately, combine maple syrup and butter. Pour over dry ingredients in cooker and toss well.

3. Place lid on slow cooker with a wooden spoon handle or chopstick venting one end of the lid.

4. Cook on High 3–4 hours, stirring every 30 minutes, or on Low 8 hours, stirring every hour. You may need to stir more often or cook for less time, depending on how hot your cooker cooks.

5. When granola smells good and toasty, pour it out onto a baking sheet to cool.

6. Add dried fruit to cooled granola and store in airtight container.

VARIATION

Add whatever fruit or nuts you like. Dried cranberries, apples, and apricots work in this recipe. Pecans, walnuts, almonds, and sunflower seeds all taste delicious. This is wonderful with milk or yogurt for breakfast.

TIP
Tired of burning granola in the oven? Give your slow cooker a try!

NEW GUINEA GRANOLA

Photo appears in color section.

Makes: 8 servings
PREP. TIME: 15 MINUTES
COOKING TIME: 2–3 HOURS
CHILLING TIME: 1 HOUR
IDEAL SLOW-COOKER SIZE: 5- OR 6-QUART

3 cups dry quick oats

3 cups dry rolled oats

½ cup dry oat bran

½ cup milk powder

⅔ cup honey

⅔ cup vegetable oil

1 tsp. vanilla

¾ cup slivered almonds

½ cup sunflower seeds

¾ cup dried cranberries or raisins

1. Grease interior of slow cooker crock.

2. Mix all ingredients well in crock except almonds, seeds, and cranberries. Stir up from bottom to make sure everything gets incorporated.

3. Cover, but vent the lid by propping it open with a chopstick or wooden spoon handle. Or if you're using an oval cooker, turn the lid sideways.

4. Cook on High for 1 hour, stirring up from the bottom and around the sides every 20 minutes or so. (Set a timer so you don't forget!)

5. Switch the cooker to Low. Stir in almonds, sunflower seeds and cranberries.® Bake another 1–2 hours, still stirring every 20 minutes or so.

6. Granola is done when it eventually browns a bit and looks dry.

7. Pour granola onto parchment or a large baking sheet to cool and crisp up more.

8. If you like clumps, no need to stir it while it cools. Otherwise, break up the granola with a spoon or your hands as it cools.

9. When completely cooled, store in airtight container.

ELLEN'S GRANOLA

Makes: 12 servings
PREP. TIME: 20 MINUTES
COOKING TIME: 2–3 HOURS
CHILLING TIME: 1–1½ HOURS
IDEAL SLOW-COOKER SIZE: 6- OR 7-QUART

1 cup vegetable oil
1 cup honey
8 cups dry rolled oats
1 cup wheat germ
1 cup powdered milk
1 cup shredded unsweetened coconut
½ cup soya flour
1 cup sunflower seeds
1 cup chopped nuts, your favorite
¼ cup sesame seeds
1 cup pumpkin seeds
½ tsp. salt

1. Grease interior of slow cooker crock.

2. Combine oil and honey in a microwave-safe bowl. Heat for 1 minute on High. Stir until well blended.

3. Combine all other ingredients in a big bowl. Stir together well.

4. Pour oil/honey mixture over dry ingredients, mixing thoroughly. Stir up from bottom to make sure everything gets incorporated.

5. Pour everything into the slow cooker crock.

6. Cover, but vent the lid by propping it open with a chopstick or wooden spoon handle. Or if you're using an oval cooker, turn the lid sideways.

7. Cook on High for 1 hour, stirring up from the bottom and around the sides every 20 minutes or so. (Set a timer so you don't forget!)

8. Switch the cooker to Low. Bake another 1–2 hours, still stirring every 20 minutes or so.

9. Granola is done when it eventually browns a bit and looks dry.

10. Pour granola onto parchment or a large baking sheet to cool and crisp up more.

11. If you like clumps, no need to stir it while it cools. Otherwise, break up the granola with a spoon or your hands as it cools.

12. When completely cooled, store in airtight container.

TIP

Here's how Ellen's husband, Keith, likes to eat Ellen's Granola:

1. Fill a large soup bowl ⅓ full of the granola.

2. Add 2–3 large dollops of yogurt.

3. Scoop on a generous topping of applesauce.

4. Add a little honey if you want it sweeter, or a dash of molasses if you're feeling a bit anemic (iron, you know).

5. Add milk and gently mix until it's the right consistency.

6. Skip the milk if you're in the mood for crunchy granola.

CHOCOLATE BUCKWHEAT GRANOLA

Makes: 6–7 servings
PREP. TIME: 20–25 MINUTES
COOKING TIME: 2–3 HOURS
CHILLING TIME: 1 HOUR
IDEAL SLOW-COOKER SIZE: 5- OR 6-QUART

3 cups dry rolled oats

½ cup wheat germ, toasted or not

1 cup buckwheat groats (these are uncooked, shelled buckwheat; they look like little triangular nubbins)

1 cup shredded sweetened coconut

1 cup hazelnuts or other unsalted nuts that you have on hand

¼ cup sesame seeds

⅓ cup honey

⅓ cup vegetable oil

½ tsp. salt

¼ cup dark brown sugar

½ cup unsweetened cocoa powder

1 tsp. vanilla

1. Grease interior of slow cooker crock.

2. In a good-sized bowl, stir together rolled oats, wheat germ, buckwheat groats, coconut, hazelnuts, and sesame seeds.

3. In a microwave-safe bowl, or in a small saucepan, warm together honey, oil, salt, brown sugar, cocoa powder, and vanilla. Stir until smooth.

4. Pour wet ingredients over dry, mixing up from the bottom and around the sides until well combined.

5. Pour into slow cooker crock. Cover, but vent the lid by propping it open with a chopstick or wooden spoon handle. Or if you're using an oval cooker, turn the lid sideways.

6. Cook on High for 1 hour, stirring up from the bottom and around the sides every 20 minutes or so. (Set a timer so you don't forget!)

7. Switch the cooker to Low. Bake another 1–2 hours, still stirring every 20 minutes or so. Granola is done when it eventually browns a bit and looks dry.

8. Pour granola onto parchment or a large baking sheet to cool and crisp up more.

9. If you like clumps, no need to stir it while it cools. Otherwise, continue to break up the granola with a spoon or your hands as it cools.

10. When completely cooled, store in airtight container.

VARIATION

Top this granola with berries and plain yogurt. Or sprinkle on some chocolate chips for a sweet treat!

PECAN GRANOLA

Makes: 6–8 servings
PREP. TIME: 20 MINUTES
COOKING TIME: 2–3 HOURS
CHILLING TIME: 1 HOUR
IDEAL SLOW-COOKER SIZE: 5-QUART

6 cups dry oats, quick or rolled

¾ cup wheat germ

½ cup milk powder

½ cup brown sugar, packed

½ cup unsweetened shredded coconut, optional

¼ cup sesame seeds, optional

1 cup chopped pecans

½ cup + 2 Tbsp. vegetable oil

½ cup + 2 Tbsp. honey

2 Tbsp. water

1½ tsp. vanilla

1 cup raisins

1. Grease interior of slow cooker crock.

2. In a good-sized bowl, mix together all dry ingredients—oats, wheat germ, milk powder, brown sugar, coconut, sesame seeds if you wish, and pecans.

3. In a separate bowl, combine oil, honey, water, and vanilla well.

4. Pour wet ingredients over dry. Stir well, remembering to stir up from the bottom, using either a strong spoon or your clean hands.

5. Pour mixture into crock. Cover, but vent the lid by propping it open with a chopstick or wooden spoon handle. Or if you're using an oval cooker, turn the lid sideways.

6. Cook on High for 1 hour, stirring up from the bottom and around the sides every 20 minutes or so. (Set a timer so you don't forget!)

7. Switch the cooker to Low. Bake another 1–2 hours, still stirring every 20 minutes or so.

8. Granola is done when it eventually browns a bit and looks dry.

9. Pour granola onto parchment or a large baking sheet to cool and crisp up more.

10. Stir in raisins.

11. If you like clumps, no need to stir it while it cools. Otherwise, break up the granola with a spoon or your hands as it cools.

12. When completely cooled, store in airtight container.

VARIATION

If you love pecans, it doesn't hurt to drop the raisins and double the amount of pecans in this recipe!

SUNFLOWER GRANOLA

Makes: 8–10 servings
PREP. TIME: 15–20 MINUTES
COOKING TIME: 2–3 HOURS
CHILLING TIME: 1 HOUR
IDEAL SLOW-COOKER SIZE: 6-QUART

2 cups brown sugar, packed

6 cups dry oats, quick or rolled

2 cups wheat flour

1 cup wheat germ

2 cups unsweetened shredded coconut

1½ cups sunflower seeds

1 cup cooking oil

1 cup water

2 Tbsp. vanilla

1 tsp. salt

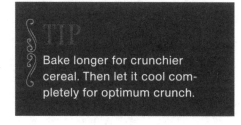

TIP

Bake longer for crunchier cereal. Then let it cool completely for optimum crunch.

1. Grease interior of slow cooker crock.

2. In a large bowl, combine brown sugar, dry oats, wheat flour, wheat germ, coconut, and sunflower seeds.

3. When well mixed, stir in oil, water, vanilla, and salt. Stir well, remembering to stir up from the bottom, using either a strong spoon or your clean hands.

4. Pour mixture into crock. Cover, but vent the lid by propping it open with a chopstick or wooden spoon handle. Or if you're using an oval cooker, turn the lid sideways.

5. Cook on High for 1 hour, stirring up from the bottom and around the sides every 20 minutes or so. (Set a timer so you don't forget!)

6. Switch the cooker to Low. Bake another 1–2 hours, still stirring every 20 minutes or so.

7. Granola is done when it eventually browns a bit and looks dry.

8. Pour granola onto parchment or a large baking sheet to cool and crisp up more.

9. If you like clumps, no need to stir it while it cools. Otherwise, break up the granola with a spoon or your hands as it cools.

10. When completely cooled, store in airtight container.

PEANUT BUTTER GRANOLA SURPRISE

Makes: 9 servings
PREP. TIME: 15 MINUTES
COOKING TIME: 2–3 HOURS
CHILLING TIME: 1 HOUR
IDEAL SLOW-COOKER SIZE: 5- OR 6-QUART

8 Tbsp. (1 stick) butter, cut in chunks
½ cup apple juice concentrate, thawed
1 cup peanut butter, smooth or chunky
¾ cup brown sugar, packed
6 cups dry oats, quick or rolled

1. Put butter, apple juice concentrate, peanut butter, and brown sugar in a microwave-safe bowl.

2. Microwave on High for 45 seconds. Stir. Continue cooking for 30-second intervals, stirring in between, until mixture melts together.

3. Put oats in large bowl and pour melted mixture over top. Stir well, including up from the bottom, until all oats are covered well. Or use your hands to mix.

4. Grease interior of slow cooker crock. Pour in oats mixture.

5. Cover, but vent the lid by propping it open with a chopstick or wooden spoon handle. Or if you're using an oval cooker, turn the lid sideways.

6. Cook on High for 1 hour, stirring up from the bottom and around the sides every 20 minutes or so. (Set a timer so you don't forget!)

7. Switch the cooker to Low and bake another 1–2 hours, still stirring every 20 minutes or so.

8. When granola has eventually browned a bit and looks dry, pour granola onto parchment or a large baking sheet to cool and crisp up more.

9. If you like clumps, no need to stir it while it cools. Otherwise, break it up with a spoon or your hands as it cools.

10. When completely cooled, store in airtight container.

VARIATIONS

❧ Stir in ½ cup raisins and ½ cup sunflower seeds as the granola cools in Step 9.

❧ Serve it with milk or yogurt for breakfast. Or serve it over ice cream as a snack or dessert.

LOTSA GOOD GRANOLA

Photo appears in color section.

Makes: 9–10 servings
PREP. TIME: 15–20 MINUTES
COOKING TIME: 2–3 HOURS
CHILLING TIME: 1 HOUR
IDEAL SLOW-COOKER SIZE: 6-QUART

7 cups dry rolled oats
2½ cups whole wheat flour
½ cup sesame seeds
1 cup shredded unsweetened coconut
½ cup chopped almonds
1 cup wheat germ
¾ cup cooking oil
1 tsp. salt
½ cup brown sugar, packed
½ cup honey
½ cup water
1½ tsp. vanilla
1½ tsp. maple flavoring
1 cup chopped dates
1 cup raisins

1. Grease interior of slow cooker crock.

2. Combine oats, flour, sesame seeds, coconut, almonds, and wheat germ in a large bowl.

3. In a blender or food processor, combine oil, salt, brown sugar, honey, water, vanilla, and maple flavoring. Process until mixture turns to liquid.

4. Pour liquid over dry mixture. Add dates and raisins.

5. Stir well, remembering to stir up from the bottom, using either a strong spoon or your clean hands.

6. Pour mixture into crock. Cover, but vent the lid by propping it open with a chopstick or wooden spoon handle. Or if you're using an oval cooker, turn the lid sideways.

7. Cook on High for 1 hour, stirring up from the bottom and around the sides every 20 minutes or so. (Set a timer so you don't forget!)

8. Switch the cooker to Low. Bake another 1–2 hours, still stirring every 20 minutes or so.

9. Granola is done when it eventually browns a bit and looks dry.

10. Pour granola onto parchment or a large baking sheet to cool and crisp up more.

11. If you like clumps, no need to stir it while it cools. Otherwise, break up the granola with a spoon or your hands as it cools.

12. When completely cooled, store in airtight container.

VARIATION

Swap in another kind of nut or use chopped figs instead of dates. Add dried cranberries or plums for the raisins.

APPLE GRANOLA

Photo appears in color section.

Makes: 6 servings
PREP. TIME: 20 MINUTES
COOKING TIME: 2–3 HOURS
CHILLING TIME: 1 HOUR
IDEAL SLOW-COOKER SIZE: 5-QUART

9	cups unpeeled, sliced apples
1½	tsp. cinnamon
1½	cups dry rolled oats
1½	cups wheat germ
1½	cups whole wheat flour
1½	cups sunflower seeds
1⅓	cups water
¾	cup honey

1. Grease interior of slow cooker crock.

2. Use your food processor to slice the apples. Place slices in crock.

3. Sprinkle apple slices with cinnamon, and then stir together gently.

4. In a good-sized bowl, stir together dry oats, wheat germ, whole wheat flour, and sunflower seeds.

5. When dry ingredients are well mixed, pour in water and honey. Using a sturdy spoon or your clean hands, mix thoroughly until well blended.

6. Spoon over apples.

7. Cover, but vent the lid by propping it open with a chopstick or wooden spoon handle. Or if you're using an oval cooker, turn the lid sideways.

8. Cook on High for 1 hour, stirring up from the bottom and around the sides every 20 minutes or so. (Set a timer so you don't forget!)

9. Switch the cooker to Low. Bake another 1–2 hours, still stirring every 20 minutes or so.

10. Granola is done when it eventually browns a bit and looks dry.

11. Pour granola onto parchment or a large baking sheet to cool and crisp up more.

12. If you like clumps, no need to stir it while it cools. Otherwise, break up the granola with a spoon or your hands as it cools.

13. When completely cooled, store in airtight container.

NOTE If you can't wait to eat until the granola is cooled, help yourself to a bowl while it's still warm and top it with milk or yogurt.

FALL FRUITS GRANOLA

Makes: 6–7 servings
PREP. TIME: 20 MINUTES
COOKING TIME: 2–3 HOURS
CHILLING TIME: 1–2 HOURS
IDEAL SLOW-COOKER SIZE: 5- OR 6-QUART

½ cup honey
⅔ cup applesauce
3½ cups dry rolled oats
½ cup wheat germ
½ cup powdered milk
1 Tbsp. pumpkin pie spice
½ cup shredded unsweetened coconut
¼ cup soy flour
½ cup sunflower seeds
½ cup chopped nuts, your favorite
¼ cup sesame seeds
½ cup pumpkin seeds
¼ tsp. salt

1. Grease interior of slow cooker crock.

2. In a microwave-safe bowl, or in a small saucepan, warm honey and applesauce together until you can easily blend them. Set aside.

3. In a good-sized bowl, mix together oats, wheat germ, powdered milk, pumpkin pie spice, coconut, flour, sunflower seeds, chopped nuts, sesame seeds, pumpkin seeds, and salt.

4. Pour wet ingredients over dry and combine well. Mix up from the bottom and stir in from the sides.

5. Pour mixture into slow cooker crock. Cover, but vent the lid by propping it open with a chopstick or wooden spoon handle. Or if you're using an oval cooker, turn the lid sideways.

6. Cook on High for 1 hour, stirring up from the bottom and around the sides every 20 minutes or so. (Set a timer so you don't forget!)

7. Switch the cooker to Low. Bake another 1–2 hours, still stirring every 20 minutes or so. Granola is done when it eventually browns a bit and looks dry.

8. Pour granola onto parchment or a large baking sheet to cool and crisp up more.

9. If you like clumps, no need to stir it while it cools. Otherwise, continue to break up the granola with a spoon or your hands as it cools.

10. When completely cooled, store in airtight container.

FRUITY GRANOLA

Makes: 7 servings
PREP. TIME: 20 MINUTES
COOKING TIME: 2–3 HOURS
CHILLING TIME: 1 HOUR
IDEAL SLOW-COOKER SIZE: 4- OR 5-QUART

4   cups rolled dry oats
2   cups puffed rice cereal
½   cup shredded sweetened coconut
½   cup oat bran
¼   cup sliced almonds, toasted
¾   cup pineapple juice
½   cup apple juice
½   cup honey
⅓   cup dried blueberries

1. Grease interior of slow cooker crock.

2. In a good sized bowl, stir together dry oats, rice cereal, coconut, oat bran, and toasted sliced almonds.

3. Place pineapple and apple juices in a small saucepan. Heat to a boil, and then simmer until reduced to ⅔ cup. Watch carefully so it doesn't cook dry.

4. Stir honey into reduced juices.

5. Pour over dry ingredients, stirring until well combined.

6. Pour mixture into crock. Cover, but vent the lid by propping it open with a chopstick or wooden spoon handle. Or if you're using an oval cooker, turn the lid sideways.

7. Cook on High for 1 hour, stirring up from the bottom and around the sides every 20 minutes or so. (Set a timer so you don't forget!)

8. Switch the cooker to Low. Bake another 1–2 hours, still stirring every 20 minutes or so. Granola is done when it eventually browns a bit and looks dry.

9. Pour granola onto parchment or a large baking sheet to cool and crisp up more.

10. Stir in dried blueberries when it's almost cool to room temperature. If you like clumps, no need to stir it while it cools. Otherwise, continue to break up the granola with a spoon or your hands as it cools.

11. When completely cooled, store in airtight container.

KEEP IT LOW-FAT GRANOLA

Makes: 5–6 servings
PREP. TIME: 15–20 MINUTES
COOKING TIME: 2–3 HOURS
CHILLING TIME: 1 HOUR
IDEAL SLOW-COOKER SIZE: 5-QUART

2 eggs
1 Tbsp. + 1 tsp. baking powder
2 cups skim milk
2 cups brown sugar, packed
4 cups dry oats, quick or rolled
1 cup dry bran, wheat or oat
1½ cups cornmeal
1 tsp. salt

1. Grease interior of slow cooker crock.

2. Mix all ingredients together in crock, stirring up from the bottom with either a sturdy spoon or your clean hands.

3. Cover, but vent the lid by propping it open with a chopstick or wooden spoon handle. Or if you're using an oval cooker, turn the lid sideways.

4. Cook on High for 1 hour, stirring up from the bottom and around the sides every 20 minutes or so. (Set a timer so you don't forget!)

5. Switch the cooker to Low. Bake another 1–2 hours, still stirring every 20 minutes or so.

6. Granola is done when it eventually browns a bit and looks dry.

7. Pour granola onto parchment or a large baking sheet to cool and crisp up more.

8. If you like clumps, no need to stir it while it cools. Otherwise, break up the granola with a spoon or your hands as it cools.

9. When completely cooled, store in airtight container.

NOTE The eggs add a different consistency to this granola—plus protein. And the cornmeal brings its own flavor. Top your bowl with chopped fresh fruit or berries.

SOY-FLAX GRANOLA

Makes: 10 servings
PREP. TIME: 20 MINUTES
COOKING TIME: 2–3 HOURS
CHILLING TIME: 2 HOURS
IDEAL SLOW-COOKER SIZE: 6-QUART

12 oz. soybeans, roasted with no salt
 4 cups dry rolled oats
 ¾ cup soy flour
 ¾ cup ground flax seed
1¼ cups brown sugar
 1 tsp. salt
 2 tsp. cinnamon
 ⅔ cup coarsely chopped walnuts
 ⅔ cup whole pecans
 ½ cup vegetable oil
 ¾ cup applesauce
 2 tsp. vanilla
    dried cranberries, dried cherries, chopped dried apricots, chopped dried figs, raisins, or some combination of these dried fruits, optional

1. Grease interior of slow cooker crock.

2. Briefly process soybeans in a blender or food processor until coarsely chopped. Place in large bowl.

3. Add oats, flour, flax seed, brown sugar, salt, cinnamon, walnuts, and pecans. Mix thoroughly with spoon, breaking up any brown sugar lumps.

4. In a smaller bowl, combine oil, applesauce, and vanilla well.

5. Pour wet ingredients over dry. Stir well, remembering to stir up from the bottom, using either a strong spoon or your clean hands.

6. Pour mixture into crock. Cover, but vent the lid by propping it open with a chopstick or wooden spoon handle. Or if you're using an oval cooker, turn the lid sideways.

7. Cook on High for 1 hour, stirring up from the bottom and around the sides every 20 minutes or so. (Set a timer so you don't forget!)

8. Switch the cooker to Low. Bake another 1–2 hours, still stirring every 20 minutes or so.

9. Granola is done when it eventually browns a bit and looks dry.

10. Pour granola onto parchment or a large baking sheet to cool and crisp up more.

11. Stir in any of the dried fruits that you want.

12. If you like clumps, no need to stir it while it cools. Otherwise, break up the granola with a spoon or your hands as it cools.

13. When completely cooled, store in airtight container.

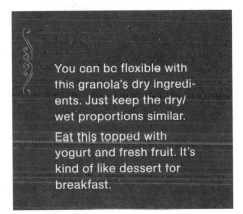

TIPS

You can be flexible with this granola's dry ingredients. Just keep the dry/wet proportions similar.

Eat this topped with yogurt and fresh fruit. It's kind of like dessert for breakfast.

SNACK MIX

YVONNE BOETTGER, HARRISONBURG, VA

Makes: 10–14 servings
PREP. TIME: 10 MINUTES
COOKING TIME: 2 HOURS
IDEAL SLOW-COOKER SIZE: 5-QUART

8 cups Chex cereal, of any combination

6 cups from the following: pretzels, snack crackers, Goldfish, Cheerios, nuts, bagel chips, toasted corn

6 Tbsp. butter, melted

2 Tbsp. Worcestershire sauce

1 tsp. seasoned salt

½ tsp. garlic powder

½ tsp. onion salt

½ tsp. onion powder

1. Combine first two ingredients in slow cooker.

2. Combine butter and seasonings. Pour over dry mixture. Toss until well mixed.

3. Cover. Cook on Low 2 hours, stirring every 30 minutes.

PUMPKIN BUTTER

EMILY FOX, BETHEL, PA

Makes: approximately 6½ cups
PREP. TIME: 5–10 MINUTES
COOKING TIME: 11–12 HOURS
IDEAL SLOW-COOKER SIZE: 3-QUART

6 cups pumpkin purée
2¾ cups light brown sugar
2½ tsp. pumpkin pie spice

1. Grease interior of slow-cooker crock.

2. Mix pumpkin purée, brown sugar, and pumpkin pie spice together in slow cooker.

3. Cook uncovered on Low for 11–12 hours, depending on how thick you'd like the butter to be. Cool.

4. Serve on bread or rolls for seasonal eating.

TIPS

Refrigerate or freeze until ready to use.

You could replace 3 cups pumpkin purée with 3 cups applesauce for a different twist on pumpkin butter.

APPLE BUTTER–FOR YOUR TOAST

ALIX NANCY BOTSFORD, SEMINOLE, OK

Makes: 9 cups
PREP. TIME: 5 MINUTES
COOKING TIME: 4–5 HOURS
IDEAL SLOW-COOKER SIZE: 5- OR 6-QUART

108 oz. can (#8 size) unsweetened applesauce
  2 cups cider
  1 Tbsp. ground cinnamon
  1 tsp. ground ginger
  ½ tsp. ground cloves, or 1 tsp. ground nutmeg, optional

1. Combine applesauce and cider in slow cooker.

2. Cover. Cook on High 3–4 hours.

3. Add spices.

4. Cover. Cook 1 hour more.

5. Sterilize cup- or pint-size jars and lids.

6. Fill jars with apple butter. Clean rim with damp paper towel. Put on lids.

7. Place in canner and cook according to manufacturer's instructions.

NOTE This is better than any air freshener. It also tastes wonderful on plain yogurt!

SLOW-COOKER CHAI

KATHY HERTZLER, LANCASTER, PA

Makes: 18 servings
PREP. TIME: 10 MINUTES
COOKING TIME: 1–1½ HOURS
IDEAL SLOW-COOKER SIZE: 5-QUART

1 gallon water

16 regular black tea bags

8 opened cardamom pods

9 whole cloves

3 Tbsp. gingerroot, freshly grated or chopped fine

3 cinnamon sticks

8 oz. can sweetened condensed milk

12 oz. can evaporated milk (regular or fat-free are equally good)

1. Pour one gallon water into slow cooker. Turn cooker to High and bring water to a boil.

2. Tie tea bag strings together. Remove paper tags. Place in slow cooker, submerging in boiling water.

3. Place cardamom seeds and pods, cloves, and ginger in a tea ball.

4. Place tea ball and cinnamon sticks in boiling water in slow cooker. Reduce heat to Low and steep, along with tea bags, for 10 minutes.

5. After 10 minutes, remove tea bags. Allow spices to remain in cooker. Increase heat to High.

6. Add condensed milk and evaporated milk. Bring mixture just to the boiling point.

7. Immediately turn back to Low. Remove spices 30 minutes later.

8. Serve tea from the slow cooker, but do not allow it to boil.

VIENNESE COFFEE

EVELYN PAGE, GILLETTE, WY

Makes: 4 servings
PREP. TIME: 15 MINUTES
COOKING TIME: 3 HOURS
IDEAL SLOW-COOKER SIZE: 1½- OR
2-QUART

3 cups strong brewed coffee

3 Tbsp. chocolate syrup

1 tsp. sugar

⅓ cup heavy whipping cream

¼ cup crème de cacao, or Irish cream liqueur

   whipped cream, optional

   chocolate curls, optional

1. In a slow cooker, combine coffee, chocolate syrup, and sugar.

2. Cover. Cook on Low 2½ hours.

3. Stir in heavy cream and crème de cacao.

4. Cover. Cook 30 minutes more on Low, or until heated through.

5. Ladle into mugs. Garnish if you wish with whipped cream and chocolate curls.

NOTE This coffee is a special treat for adult dinner parties in the winter. It's so easy, smells delicious, and usually leads to people reminiscing about the coffee they've had and loved.

VANILLA STEAMER

ANITA TROYER, FAIRVIEW, MI

Makes: 8 servings
PREP. TIME: 5–10 MINUTES
COOKING TIME: 2–3 HOURS
IDEAL SLOW-COOKER SIZE: 3-QT.

8 cups milk

⅛ tsp. cinnamon, *or* 2 3-inch-long cinnamon sticks

3 Tbsp. sugar

2 Tbsp. vanilla

pinch of salt

pinch of nutmeg

whipped topping, optional

sprinkling of ground cinnamon, optional

1. Put all ingredients except whipped topping and sprinkling of ground cinnamon in slow cooker.

2. Cover. Cook on Low 2–3 hours, watching near end of cooking time to make sure it doesn't boil.

3. Garnish individual servings with whipped topping and a sprinkling of cinnamon if you wish.

NOTE I found this recipe when my children wanted hot chocolate in the evening, but I didn't want them to get hyper from the chocolate. It's a total hit with them and the adults! Vanilla Steamers are soothing and relaxing and totally delicious.

I usually make a larger recipe than I will need, and then refrigerate the leftovers. We like it either reheated, or as creamer in our coffee.

Meat
MAIN DISHES

TASTY MEATBALL STEW

BARBARA HERSHEY, LITITZ, PA

Makes: 8 servings
PREP. TIME: 1 HOUR (INCLUDES PREPARING
AND BAKING MEATBALLS)
COOKING TIME: 4–5 HOURS
IDEAL SLOW-COOKER SIZE: 4-, 5-, OR
6-QUART

Meatballs

2 lbs. lean ground beef

2 eggs, beaten

2 Tbsp. dried onion

⅔ cup dried bread crumbs

½ cup milk

1 tsp. salt

¼ tsp. pepper

1 tsp. Dijon mustard

2 tsp. Worcestershire sauce

Stew

6 medium potatoes, unpeeled if you wish,
   and diced fine

1 large onion, sliced

8 medium carrots, sliced

4 cups vegetable juice

1 tsp. basil

1 tsp. dried oregano

½ tsp. salt

½ tsp. pepper

1. In a bowl, thoroughly mix meatball ingredients together. Form into 1-inch balls.

2. Place meatballs on a lightly greased jelly-roll pan. Bake at 400°F for 20 minutes.

3. Grease interior of slow-cooker crock.

4. Meanwhile, to make stew, prepare potatoes, onion, and carrots. Place in slow-cooker.

5. When meatballs finish baking, remove them from pan. Blot dry with paper towels to remove excess fat.

6. Place meatballs on top of vegetables in slow-cooker.

7. In a large bowl, combine vegetable juice and seasonings. Pour over meatballs and vegetables in slow-cooker.

8. Cover cooker. Cook on Low 4–5 hours, or until vegetables are as tender as you like them.

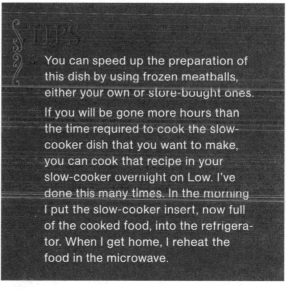

TIPS

You can speed up the preparation of this dish by using frozen meatballs, either your own or store-bought ones.

If you will be gone more hours than the time required to cook the slow-cooker dish that you want to make, you can cook that recipe in your slow-cooker overnight on Low. I've done this many times. In the morning I put the slow-cooker insert, now full of the cooked food, into the refrigerator. When I get home, I reheat the food in the microwave.

CREAMY VEGETABLE BEEF STEW

LORNA RODES, PORT REPUBLIC, VA
Photo appears in color section.

Makes: 6–8 servings
PREP. TIME: 20 MINUTES
COOKING TIME: 5–7 HOURS
IDEAL SLOW-COOKER SIZE: 4-QUART

4 cups tomato juice
½ cup chopped onion
1 cup diced potatoes
1 cup diced carrots
¼ tsp. pepper
½ tsp. dried basil
2 tsp. salt
2–3 cups leftover shredded pot roast

White Sauce
2 Tbsp. butter
2 Tbsp. flour
1⅓ cups milk

1. Place tomato juice, onion, potatoes, carrots, pepper, basil, and salt in slow cooker.

2. Cover and cook on Low 4–6 hours. 1 hour before serving, stir in leftover pot roast. Then, make white sauce.

3. In saucepan, melt butter. Whisk in flour and cook, stirring, until flour and butter are bubbly.

4. Pour in milk gradually, whisking until smooth. Stir over low heat until sauce thickens.

5. Pour white sauce into soup, stirring. Cook an additional hour on Low.

ITALIAN WEDDING SOUP

JANIE STEELE, MOORE, OK
Photo appears in color section.

Makes: 6 servings
PREP. TIME: 30 MINUTES
COOKING TIME: 3–7 HOURS
IDEAL SLOW-COOKER SIZE: 3- TO 4-QUART

2 eggs
½ cup bread crumbs
¼ cup chopped fresh parsley
2 Tbsp. grated Parmesan cheese
3 cloves garlic, minced
¼ tsp. red pepper flakes
½ lb. ground beef or turkey
½ lb. spicy pork sausage, casings removed
2 32-oz. cartons chicken broth
   salt and pepper, to taste
⅔ cup uncooked pasta
1 cup chopped fresh spinach

1. In a large bowl, mix eggs, bread crumbs, parsley, Parmesan, garlic, red pepper flakes, ground meat, and sausage.

2. Form mixture into 1-inch meatballs. Brown in skillet or oven.

3. Transfer meatballs to slow cooker. Add chicken broth, salt, pepper, and pasta.

4. Cook on High for 3–4 hours or Low for 6–7, adding spinach 30 minutes before end of cooking.

SPICY BEEF ROAST

KAREN CENEVIVA, SEYMOUR, CT

Makes: 6–8 servings
PREP. TIME: 15–20 MINUTES
COOKING TIME: 6–8 HOURS
STANDING TIME: 10 MINUTES
IDEAL SLOW-COOKER SIZE: 4- OR 5-QUART

1–2 Tbsp. cracked black peppercorns
2 cloves garlic, minced
3 lb. round tip roast or brisket, trimmed of fat
3 Tbsp. balsamic vinegar
¼ cup reduced-sodium soy sauce
2 Tbsp. Worcestershire sauce
2 tsp. dry mustard

1. Grease interior of slow-cooker crock.

2. Rub cracked pepper and garlic all over roast. Put roast in slow-cooker.

3. Make several shallow slits in top of meat.

4. In a small bowl, combine remaining ingredients. Spoon over meat.

5. Cover. Cook on Low 6–8 hours, or until instant-read meat thermometer registers 145°F when stuck into center of roast.

6. Remove meat from crock. Allow to stand for 10 minutes. Then slice and serve.

SPICED POT ROAST

JANIE STEELE, MOORE, OK
Photo appears in color section.

Makes: 10 servings
PREP. TIME: 30 MINUTES
COOKING TIME: 3–4 HOURS
IDEAL SLOW-COOKER SIZE: 6-QUART

2 lb. boneless beef top round roast
1 Tbsp. olive oil
2 cups apple juice
16 oz. can tomato sauce
2 small onions, chopped
3 Tbsp. white vinegar
1 Tbsp. salt
¾ tsp. ground ginger, or 1 Tbsp. fresh ginger, minced
2–3 tsp. ground cinnamon
¼ cup cornstarch
1 cup water

1. Brown roast in olive oil on all sides in a skillet. Then place in slow cooker.

2. Combine juice, tomato sauce, onions, vinegar, salt, ginger, and cinnamon. Pour over roast.

3. Cook on High 2–3 hours.

4. Mix cornstarch and water until smooth. Remove roast from cooker and keep warm on a platter. Stir cornstarch water into juices in cooker.

5. Return roast to cooker and continue cooking 1 hour on High, or until meat is done and gravy thickens.

WINE TENDER ROAST

ROSE HANKINS, STEVENSVILLE, MD

Makes: 5–6 servings
PREP. TIME: 10 MINUTES
COOKING TIME: 6–8 HOURS
STANDING TIME: 10 MINUTES
IDEAL SLOW-COOKER SIZE: 4- OR 5-QUART

2½–3 lb. beef chuck roast
1 cup thinly sliced onions
½ cup chopped apple, peeled, or unpeeled
3 cloves garlic, chopped
1 cup red wine
salt and pepper

1. Grease interior of slow-cooker crock.

2. Put roast in slow-cooker. Layer onions, apples, and garlic on top of roast.

3. Carefully pour wine over roast without disturbing its toppings.

4. Sprinkle with salt and pepper.

5. Cover. Cook on Low 6–8 hours, or until instant-read meat thermometer registers 145°F when stuck into center of roast.

6. Remove meat from crock. Allow to stand for 10 minutes. Then slice and serve.

NOTE The sweetness of the apple is subtle and lovely in this roast. Thicken the juices left behind in the slow-cooker and serve it as gravy.

READY-WHEN-YOU-GET-HOME DINNER

BEATRICE ORGISH, RICHARDSON, TX

Makes: 6 servings
PREP. TIME: 10–15 MINUTES
COOKING TIME: 4–5 HOURS
IDEAL SLOW-COOKER SIZE: 5-QUART

1 cup uncooked wild rice, rinsed and drained
1 cup chopped celery
1 cup chopped carrots
2 4-oz. cans mushrooms, drained
1 large onion, chopped
1 clove garlic, minced
½ cup slivered almonds
3 beef bouillon cubes
2½ tsp. seasoned salt
2 lb. boneless beef chuck roast, cut into 1½-inch pieces
3 cups water

1. Grease interior of slow-cooker crock.
2. Place ingredients in order listed into slow-cooker.
3. Cover. Cook on Low 4–5 hours or until beef and rice are tender. Stir before serving.

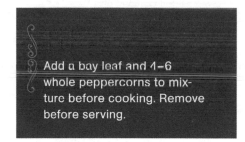

Add a bay leaf and 4–6 whole peppercorns to mixture before cooking. Remove before serving.

BAVARIAN BEEF

NAOMI E. FAST, HESSTON, KS

Makes: 6 servings
PREP. TIME: 15 MINUTES
COOKING TIME: 6–8 HOURS
IDEAL SLOW-COOKER SIZE: 5- OR 6-QUART

3–3½ lb. boneless beef chuck roast
     oil
3 cups sliced carrots
3 cups sliced onions
2 large kosher dill pickles, chopped
1 cup sliced celery
½ cup dry red wine or beef broth
⅓ cup German-style mustard
2 tsp. coarsely ground black pepper
2 bay leaves
¼ tsp. ground cloves
⅓ cup flour
1 cup cold water

1. Grease interior of slow-cooker crock.

2. If you have time, brown roast on both sides in oil in skillet. Place roast in slow-cooker.

3. Distribute carrots, onions, pickles, and celery around roast in slow-cooker.

4. Combine wine, mustard, pepper, bay leaves, and cloves in a bowl. Pour over ingredients in slow-cooker.

5. Cover. Cook on Low 6–8 hours, or until instant-read meat thermometer registers 145°F when stuck into center of roast.

6. Remove meat and vegetables to large platter. Discard bay leaves. Cover to keep warm.

7. Mix flour with 1 cup cold water in bowl until smooth. Turn cooker to High. Stir in flour-water paste, stirring continually until broth is smooth and thickened.

8. Slice meat. Top with vegetables. Serve with broth alongside.

HORSERADISH BEEF

BARBARA NOLAN, PLEASANT VALLEY, NY

Makes: 6–8 servings
PREP. TIME: 10 MINUTES
COOKING TIME: 8–10 HOURS
IDEAL SLOW COOKER SIZE: 4-QUART

3–4 lb. pot roast

2 Tbsp. oil

½ tsp. salt

½ tsp. pepper

1 onion, chopped

6 oz. can tomato paste

⅓ cup horseradish sauce

1. Brown roast on all sides in oil in skillet. Place in slow cooker. Add remaining ingredients.

2. Cover. Cook on Low 8–10 hours.

NOTE Don't salt meat or a roast as you're browning it. Instead, add it to taste at the end of the browning. The meat will stay more moist, since salt draws out moisture.

AUTUMN BRISKET

KAREN CENEVIVA, SEYMOUR, CT

Makes: 8 servings
PREP. TIME: 20–30 MINUTES
COOKING TIME: 6–8 HOURS
STANDING TIME: 10 MINUTES
IDEAL SLOW-COOKER SIZE: 6-QUART

3 lb. boneless beef brisket
   salt to taste
   pepper to taste
1 lb. cabbage, cut into wedges
1 large (¾ lb.) sweet potato, or several small ones, peeled and cut into 1-inch pieces
1 large onion, cut in wedges
1 medium Granny Smith apple, cored and cut into 8 wedges
2 10¾-oz. cans cream of celery soup
1 cup water
2 tsp. caraway seeds, optional

1. Grease interior of slow-cooker crock.

2. Place brisket in slow-cooker.

3. Shake salt and pepper over meat to taste.

4. Top with cabbage, sweet potato, and onion.

5. Season to taste with salt and pepper.

6. Place apple wedges over vegetables.

7. In a medium bowl combine soup, water, and caraway seeds if you wish.

8. Spoon mixture over brisket and vegetables.

9. Cover. Cook on Low 6–8 hours, or until instant-read meat thermometer registers 145°F when stuck into center of roast, and vegetables are fork-tender.

10. Remove meat from cooker and allow to stand 10 minutes. Then slice and top with vegetables and broth before serving.

NOTE When I make this for the first time in chilly weather, my husband says he knows it's really autumn for sure. The scent alone makes the house feel warmer.

SMOKED BEEF BRISKET

JOY MARTIN, MYERSTOWN, PA

Makes: 4–5 servings
PREP. TIME: 5–10 MINUTES
COOKING TIME: 5–6 HOURS
STANDING TIME: 10 MINUTES
IDEAL SLOW-COOKER SIZE: 4-QUART

- 1 Tbsp. liquid smoke
- 1 tsp. salt
- ½ tsp. pepper
- 2½ lb. beef brisket
- ½ cup chopped onion
- ½ cup ketchup
- 2 tsp. prepared Dijon mustard
- ½ tsp. celery seed

1. Grease interior of slow-cooker crock.

2. In a small bowl, mix together liquid smoke, salt, and pepper. Rub brisket with mixture.

3. Place meat in slow cooker. Top with onion.

4. In a small bowl, combine ketchup, mustard, and celery seed. Spread over meat.

5. Cover. Cook on Low 5–6 hours, or until instant-read meat thermometer registers 145°F when stuck into center of roast.

6. Remove meat from cooker and allow to stand 10 minutes.

7. Meanwhile, transfer cooking juices to a blender. Cover and process until smooth. (Cover lid of blender with thick towel and hold it on tightly while using. Hot liquid expands when being processed.)

8. Cut brisket across the grain into thin slices. Top with cooking juices and pass any extra in a separate bowl.

NOTE I love to serve this from the slow cooker to guests—they are always impressed with the flavor I created without using a laborious smoking process outside!

BUTTERFLY STEAKS

MARY LOUISE MARTIN, BOYD, WI
Photo appears in color section.

Makes: 8–10 servings
PREP. TIME: 30 MINUTES
COOKING TIME: 2–4 HOURS
STANDING TIME: 2 HOURS
IDEAL SLOW-COOKER SIZE: 7-QUART OVAL

4 lb. butt beef, or venison, tenderloin
4½ tsp. garlic powder, divided
2 tsp. celery seeds
1 tsp. black pepper
1 Tbsp. salt
½ cup apple cider vinegar
¾ cup canola oil
½ cup soy sauce
⅓ cup olive oil
1 tsp. ground ginger
1 tsp. dry mustard
cooked rice

1. Cut tenderloin into ¾–1-inch-thick slices. Cut each slice through the center but not the whole way through. Flatten into a butterfly-shaped steak and lay in large glass baking dish.

2. In a bowl, mix 4 teaspoons garlic powder, celery seeds, pepper, salt, vinegar, and canola oil for marinade. Pour over steaks in the glass pan.

3. Cover, and marinate in fridge for 2 hours, stirring occasionally.

4. Meanwhile, grease interior of slow-cooker crock.

5. Place marinated steaks on broiler pan and broil at 400°F just until lightly browned. Place steaks in slow-cooker. Stagger the pieces so they don't directly overlap each other.

6. Mix soy sauce, olive oil, ginger, dry mustard, and remaining ½ teaspoon garlic powder. Pour over meat, making sure to spoon sauce on any steaks on the bottom layer.

7. Cook on Low 2–4 hours.

8. Serve with rice.

FRUITY FLANK STEAK

RUTH A. FEISTER, NARVON, PA

Makes: 6 servings
PREP. TIME: 10 MINUTES
COOKING TIME: 5–7 HOURS
IDEAL SLOW-COOKER SIZE: 4- OR 5-QUART

1½–2 lb. flank steak
    salt to taste
    pepper to taste
14½ oz. can mixed fruit, or your choice of canned fruit
  1 Tbsp. oil
  1 Tbsp. lemon juice
  ¼ cup teriyaki sauce
  1 tsp. cider vinegar
  1 garlic clove, minced

1. Grease interior of slow-cooker crock.
2. Sprinkle steak with salt and pepper. Place in slow-cooker.
3. Drain fruit, saving ¼ cup syrup. Set fruit aside.
4. In a small bowl, combine ¼ cup reserved syrup with remaining ingredients. Pour over steak.
5. Cover. Cook on Low 5–7 hours, or until instant-read meat thermometer reaches 145°F when stuck into the center of the steak.
6. Add drained fruit during last 15 minutes of cooking time.
7. Lift meat from cooker onto platter. Use a sharp knife to slice across the grain, making thin slices. Spoon fruit over meat.

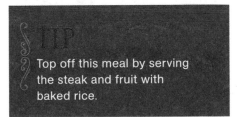

TIP
Top off this meal by serving the steak and fruit with baked rice.

STUFFED FLANK STEAK

RENEE BAUM, CHAMBERSBURG, PA

Makes: 6 servings
PREP. TIME: 30 MINUTES
COOKING TIME: 5–7 HOURS
IDEAL SLOW-COOKER SIZE: 5- OR 6-QUART

8 oz. pkg. crushed cornbread stuffing
1 cup chopped onion
1 cup chopped celery
¼ cup minced fresh parsley
2 eggs
1¼ cups beef broth
5⅓ Tbsp. (⅓ cup) butter, melted
½ tsp. seasoned salt, optional
½ tsp. pepper
1½ lb. flank steak

1. Grease interior of slow-cooker crock.

2. Combine stuffing, onion, celery, and parsley in large bowl.

3. In a small bowl, beat eggs. Stir in broth and butter. Pour over stuffing mixture. Sprinkle with seasoned salt if you wish, and pepper. Stir well.

4. Pound steak to ¼-inch thickness.

5. Spread 1½ cups stuffing mixture over steak. Roll up, starting with short side. Tie with string.

6. Place steak in slow-cooker.

7. Wrap remaining stuffing tightly in foil and place on top of rolled steak.

8. Cover. Cook on Low 5–7 hours, or until instant-read meat thermometer reaches 145°F when stuck into the center of the rolled steak.

9. Remove string before slicing.

TIP

If you have a helpful butcher, ask him/her to pound the steak for you.

THREE-PEPPER STEAK

RENEE HANKINS, NARVON, PA

Makes: 10 servings
PREP. TIME: 30 MINUTES
COOKING TIME: 4–5 HOURS
IDEAL SLOW-COOKER SIZE: 4- OR 5-QUART

3 bell peppers (one red, one orange, and one yellow pepper—or any combination of colors), cut into ¼-inch-thick slices

2 garlic cloves, sliced

1 large onion, sliced

1 tsp. ground cumin

½ tsp. dried oregano

1 bay leaf

3½ lb. beef flank steak, cut across the grain in ¼–½-inch-thick slices

salt to taste

14½ oz. can diced tomatoes in juice

jalapeño chilies, sliced, optional

1. Grease interior of slow-cooker crock.

2. Place sliced peppers, garlic, onion, cumin, oregano, and bay leaf in slow-cooker. Stir gently to mix.

3. Put steak slices on top of vegetable mixture. Season with salt.

4. Spoon tomatoes with juice over top. Sprinkle with jalapeño pepper slices if you wish. Do not stir.

5. Cover. Cook on Low 4–5 hours, depending on your slow-cooker. Check after 3½ hours to see if meat is tender. If not, continue cooking until tender but not dry.

TIP

This steak is great served over noodles, rice, or torn tortillas.

ROUND STEAK ROLL-UPS

LINDA SLUITER, SCHERERVILLE, IN

Makes: 4–6 servings
PREP. TIME: 15 MINUTES
COOKING TIME: 5–6 HOURS
IDEAL SLOW-COOKER SIZE: 4-QUART

1 lb. bacon

2–3 lb. round steak, about 1-inch thick, cut into strips

1 cup ketchup

¾ cup brown sugar

1 cup water

half a yellow onion, chopped

1. Grease interior of slow-cooker crock.

2. Lay a bacon strip down, then a strip of beef on top of the bacon slice. Roll up and secure with toothpick. Place in slow-cooker. Repeat with remaining bacon and steak.

3. Combine remaining ingredients in a bowl. Pour over meat roll-ups.

4. Cover. Cook on Low 5–6 hours, or until instant-read meat thermometer reaches 145°F when stuck into the center of a piece of steak.

FRUITY BEEF TAGINE

NAOMI E. FAST, HESSTON, KS

Makes: 6 servings
PREP. TIME: 20 MINUTES
COOKING TIME: 4–5 HOURS
IDEAL SLOW-COOKER SIZE: 5 QUART

    2 lbs. boneless beef chuck roast, cut into 1½-inch cubes
    4 cups sliced onions
    2 tsp. ground coriander
 1½ tsp. ground cinnamon
   ¾ tsp. ground ginger
14½ oz. can beef broth, plus enough water to equal 2 cups
   16 oz. pitted dried plums
       salt to taste
       fresh ground pepper to taste
       juice of one lemon

1. Grease interior of slow-cooker crock.
2. Place all ingredients except lemon juice into cooker.
3. Cook on Low 4–5 hours, or until meat is tender.
4. Stir in lemon juice during the last 10 minutes.

TIPS

Mix in a few very thin slices of lemon rind 10 minutes before end of cooking time to add flavor and eye appeal.

You can substitute lamb cubes for the beef.

HEARTY NEW ENGLAND DINNER

JOETTE DROZ, KALONA, IA

Makes: 6–8 servings
PREP. TIME: 10 MINUTES
COOKING TIME: 7–9 HOURS
IDEAL SLOW-COOKER SIZE: 5-QUART

2 medium carrots, sliced

1 medium onion, sliced

1 celery rib, sliced

3 lb. boneless beef chuck roast

1 tsp. salt, divided

¼ tsp. pepper

1 envelope dry onion soup mix

2 cups water

1 Tbsp. vinegar

1 bay leaf

half a small head of cabbage, cut in wedges

3 Tbsp. butter

2 Tbsp. flour

1 Tbsp. dried, minced onion

2 Tbsp. prepared horseradish

1. Grease interior of slow-cooker crock.

2. Place carrots, onion, and celery in slow-cooker. Place roast on top.

3. In a bowl, mix together ½ tsp. salt, pepper, dry onion soup mix, water, vinegar, and bay leaf.

4. Pour over roast and vegetables.

5. Cover. Cook on Low 6–8 hours, or until instant-read meat thermometer registers 145°F when stuck into center of roast.

6. Remove beef and keep warm.

7. Discard bay leaf. Add cabbage to juice in slow-cooker.

8. Cover. Cook on High 1 hour, or until cabbage is tender.

9. Melt butter in saucepan. Stir in flour and onion.

10. Add 1½ cups liquid from slow-cooker, stirring until smooth. Stir in horseradish and ½ tsp. salt.

11. Bring to boil. Stirring continually, cook over low heat until thick and smooth, about 2 minutes. Return to cooker and blend with remaining sauce in cooker.

12. Slice beef. Top with vegetables and gravy. Pass any extra gravy in a separate bowl.

BEEF RIBS WITH SAUERKRAUT

ROSARIA STRACHAN, FAIRFIELD, CT

Makes: 8–10 servings
PREP. TIME: 10 MINUTES
COOKING TIME: 3–8 HOURS
IDEAL SLOW-COOKER SIZE: 6-QUART

3–4 lbs. beef short ribs

32 oz. bag or 27-oz. can sauerkraut, drained

2 Tbsp. caraway seeds

¼ cup water

1. Put ribs in 6-quart slow cooker.

2. Place sauerkraut and caraway seeds on top of ribs.

3. Pour in water.

4. Cover. Cook on High 3–4 hours, or on Low 7–8 hours.

5. Serve with mashed potatoes.

VARIATION

If you really enjoy sauerkraut, double the amount of sauerkraut, and divide the recipe between two 4–5-quart cookers

ZINGY SHORT RIBS

JOAN TERWILLIGER, LEBANON, PA
Photo appears in color section.

Makes: 4–6 servings
PREP. TIME: 30 MINUTES
COOKING TIME: 9–10 HOURS
IDEAL SLOW-COOKER SIZE: 6-QUART

8 bone-in beef short ribs

15 oz. can crushed tomatoes

3 Tbsp. tomato paste

2–3 Tbsp. hot pepper jam or horseradish jam

6 cloves garlic, peeled

¾ tsp. dried rosemary, crushed

1 Tbsp. dried minced onions

½ tsp. ground ginger

¼ cup dry red wine

1. Grease interior of slow-cooker crock.

2. Broil ribs 6 inches from heat until browned, 5–10 minutes per side.

3. Stack ribs into slow-cooker. Stagger them so the top layer doesn't directly overlap the bottom layer.

4. Combine remaining ingredients in mixing bowl. Pour over ribs. (Lift the top layer and spoon sauce over bottom layer.)

5. Cover. Cook on Low 9–10 hours, or until meat is tender but not dry.

6. Spoon off fat. Then top ribs with sauce. Pass any remaining sauce in a bowl for individuals to add to their plates.

CONVENIENT SLOW COOKER LASAGNA

RACHEL YODER, MIDDLEBURY, IN

Makes: 6–8 servings
PREP. TIME: 20 MINUTES
COOKING TIME: 4 HOURS
IDEAL SLOW-COOKER SIZE: 6-QUART

1 lb. ground beef
2 29-oz. cans tomato sauce
8 oz. pkg. lasagna noodles, uncooked
4 cups shredded mozzarella cheese
1½ cups cottage cheese

1. Spray the interior of the cooker with nonstick cooking spray.
2. Brown the ground beef in a large nonstick skillet. Drain off drippings.
3. Stir in tomato sauce. Mix well.
4. Spread one-fourth of the meat sauce on the bottom of the slow cooker.
5. Arrange one-third of the uncooked noodles over the sauce. (I usually break them up so they fit better.)
6. Combine the cheeses in a bowl. Spoon one-third of the cheeses over the noodles.
7. Repeat these layers twice.
8. Top with remaining sauce.
9. Cover and cook on Low 4 hours.

VARIATIONS

❧ Add 1 chopped onion to the ground beef in Step 2.

❧ Add 1 tsp. salt to the tomato sauce and beef in Step 3.

❧ Add ½ cup grated Parmesan cheese to the mozzarella and cottage cheeses in Step 6.

❧ Add ½ cup additional shredded mozzarella cheese to the top of the lasagna 5 minutes before serving.

LASAGNA MEXICANA

BARBARA WALKER, STURGIS, SD

Makes: 6 servings
PREP. TIME: 20 MINUTES
COOKING TIME: 3–4 HOURS
STANDING TIME: 10–15 MINUTES
IDEAL SLOW-COOKER SIZE: 5-QUART

1 lb. ground beef

16 oz. can refried beans

2 tsp. dried oregano

1 tsp. ground cumin

¾ tsp. garlic powder

9 uncooked lasagna noodles, divided

1 cup salsa, as hot or as mild as you like

1 cup water

2 cups sour cream

2¼ oz. can sliced ripe olives, drained

1 cup Mexican-blend cheese, shredded

½ cup sliced green onions

1. Grease interior of slow-cooker crock.

2. If you have time, brown beef in a skillet. Using a slotted spoon, lift beef out of drippings and place in good-sized bowl. If you don't have time, place beef in bowl and use a sturdy spoon to break it up into small clumps.

3. Stir in beans and seasonings.

4. Place three uncooked noodles in bottom of crock, breaking and overlapping to fit.

5. Cover with half of meat/vegetable mixture.

6. Repeat layers of noodles and meat/vegetables.

7. Top with remaining noodles.

8. Combine salsa and water in a bowl. Pour over noodles.

9. Cover. Cook on Low 3–4 hours, or until noodles are tender but lasagna is not drying out around edges.

10. Spread lasagna with sour cream.

11. Sprinkle with olives, cheese, and green onions.

12. Let stand 10–15 minutes before serving to allow noodles and cheese to firm up.

NOTE This is a fun variation on traditional lasagna. It's always a hit as soon as people get past their surprise.

NACHOS DINNER

ARLENE MILLER, HUTCHINSON, KS
Photo appears in color section.

Makes: 8 servings
PREP. TIME: 15 MINUTES
COOKING TIME: 1 HOUR
IDEAL SLOW-COOKER SIZE: 4-QUART

1	lb. ground beef
¼	cup diced onions
¼	cup diced green peppers
1	pint taco sauce
1	can refried beans
10¾	oz. can cream of mushroom soup
1	envelope dry taco seasoning
	salt to taste
2	cups Velveeta or cheddar cheese
	tortilla chips
	lettuce
	chopped tomatoes
	sour cream

1. Brown ground beef, onions, and green peppers in saucepan. Drain.

2. Combine all ingredients except tortilla chips, lettuce, tomatoes, and sour cream in slow cooker.

3. Cover. Cook on High 1 hour, stirring occasionally until cheese is fully melted.

4. Pour into serving bowl and serve immediately with chips, lettuce, tomatoes, and sour cream, or turn to Low to keep warm and serve from cooker.

TIP
Keep a clean work area—as clean as possible. Clutter can cause confusion, which can lead to mistakes.

TEMPTING TORTILLA CASSEROLE

PHYLLIS GOOD, LANCASTER, PA
Photo appears in color section.

Makes: 4 servings
PREP. TIME: 20 MINUTES
COOKING TIME: 3–4 HOURS
IDEAL SLOW-COOKER SIZE: 3-QUART

1 lb. ground beef

1 envelope dry taco seasoning

1½ cups (6 oz.) grated cheese of your choice, divided

16 oz. can fat-free refried beans

bag of tortilla chips (for topping the casserole)

1. Brown the ground beef.

2. Add the browned ground beef and the taco seasoning to your slow cooker and mix well.

3. Sprinkle 1 cup of cheese over top of the meat.

4. Use a rubber spatula to scrape the refried beans on top of the cheese. Spread the beans out in an even layer. Be careful not to disturb the grated cheese while you do it.

5. Sprinkle the remaining cheese on top of the beans.

6. Cover your slow cooker. Cook on Low for 3–4 hours.

7. Top the casserole with tortilla chips just before serving.

ENCHILADA STACK-UP

SALLY HOLZEM, SCHOFIELD, WI
Photo appears in color section.

Makes: 8 servings
PREP. TIME: 30 MINUTES
COOKING TIME: 4 HOURS
STANDING TIME: 10–15 MINUTES
IDEAL SLOW-COOKER SIZE: 5-QUART

1	lb. ground beef
1	cup chopped onion
½	cup chopped red, yellow, or orange bell peppers, or a mixture
1	tsp. olive oil
15	oz. can kidney beans, rinsed and drained
15	oz. can black beans, rinsed and drained
14½	oz. can diced tomatoes and green chilies
1½	tsp. cumin
¼	tsp. black pepper
6	8-inch tortillas
2	cups shredded cheddar cheese

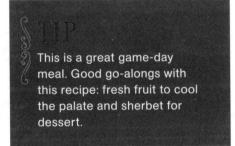

TIP

This is a great game-day meal. Good go-alongs with this recipe: fresh fruit to cool the palate and sherbet for dessert.

1. Grease interior of slow-cooker crock.

2. Create a tin foil sling for your crock before making the Enchilada Stack-Up. (See directions on page 173, Steps 2 and 3 in instructions for making Turkey Loaf.)

3. If you have time, brown ground beef, onions, and bell peppers in olive oil in skillet. Drain off drippings and discard. If you don't have time, place ground beef in good-sized bowl and break it up with a wooden spoon. Then stir in onions and bell peppers.

4. Stir kidney beans, black beans, tomatoes, cumin, and black pepper into beef-veggie mixture in bowl.

5. Lay 1 tortilla in bottom of crock (and over top of the foil strips). Spoon ¾ cup beef and veggie mixture over top. Sprinkle with ⅓ of cheese.

6. Repeat layers 5 times.

7. Cover and cook on Low 4 hours, until very hot in the middle.

8. Use foil strips as handles to remove stack from slow cooker to platter.

9. Gently ease foil strips out from underneath stack, or bend them over so they're out of the way.

10. Cover stack to keep warm. Allow to stand 10–15 minutes to firm up. Then cut into wedges and serve.

STUFFED GREEN PEPPERS WITH CORN

JEAN BUTZER, BATAVIA, NY

Makes: 6 servings
PREP. TIME: 20 MINUTES
COOKING TIME: 5–6 HOURS
IDEAL SLOW-COOKER SIZE: 5-QUART

  6 green bell peppers
½ lb. extra-lean ground beef
¼ cup finely chopped onions
  1 Tbsp. chopped pimento
¾ tsp. salt
¼ tsp. black pepper
12 oz. can low-sodium whole-kernel corn, drained
  1 Tbsp. Worcestershire sauce
  1 tsp. prepared mustard
10¾ oz. can condensed low-sodium cream of tomato soup

1. Cut a slice off the top of each pepper. Remove core, seeds, and white membrane.

2. In a small bowl, combine beef, onions, pimento, salt, black pepper, and corn.

3. Spoon into peppers. Stand peppers up in slow cooker.

4. Combine Worcestershire sauce, mustard, and tomato soup. Pour over peppers.

5. Cover. Cook on Low 5–6 hours.

STUFFED ACORN SQUASH

PHYLLIS GOOD, LANCASTER, PA

Makes: 6–8 servings
PREP. TIME: 45 MINUTES
COOKING TIME: 4–7 HOURS
IDEAL SLOW-COOKER SIZE: 6-QUART

2	acorn squash
1	lb. leftover ground beef
1	small onion, chopped
5	cups chopped, unpeeled apples, divided
4	tsp. curry powder
½	tsp. cardamom
½	tsp. ginger
	scant ½ tsp. black pepper
½	lb. sharp cheddar cheese, cubed
6	Tbsp. apricot preserves
1–1¼	tsp. salt
2	Tbsp. butter
	scant ½ tsp. ground cinnamon
	scant ½ tsp. ground nutmeg

1. Wash the squash, and then cut in half from top to bottom. Scrape out the seeds and stringy stuff. (A grapefruit spoon works well because of its teeth. But a regular spoon with some pressure behind it works, too.) Cut each half in half again.

2. Put four quarters into the bottom of the slow cooker side by side, cut side up. Set the other four quarters on top, but staggered so they're not sitting inside the four pieces on the bottom. Add about 2 Tbsp. water to the cooker. Cover. Turn the cooker to Low and let it go for 3–6 hours, or until you can stick a fork into the skin of the squash halves with very little resistance.

3. Sometime during those 3–6 hours, warm the leftover 1 lb. ground beef and the onions in a skillet over medium heat, and stir 2 cups chopped apples into beef and onions.

4. Mix in curry powder, cardamom, ginger, and black pepper.

5. Then add the cubed cheese, apricot preserves, and salt. Stir together gently. Set aside until squash is done softening up.

6. When squash is tender, divide the meat mixture among the 8 quarters evenly.

7. Put the filled quarters back into the cooker in staggered layers.

8. Cover. Cook on High for 45–60 minutes, or until the stuffing is heated through and the cheese is melted.

9. Sauté the remaining 3 cups apple slices in butter just until they're tender. Season lightly with cinnamon and nutmeg.

10. Remove the filled squash from cooker. Place a quarter on each serving plate. Top each with sautéed apples.

CREAMY STROGANOFF

EVELYN PAGE, RAPID CITY, SD

Makes: 10 servings
PREP. TIME: 10 MINUTES
COOKING TIME: 6–7 HOURS
IDEAL SLOW-COOKER SIZE: 5- TO 6-QUART

1½ lb. round steak, trimmed of fat

¼ cup flour

½ tsp. black pepper

½ tsp. salt

1 tsp. garlic, minced

1 small onion, chopped

1 Tbsp. low-sodium soy sauce

1 beef bouillon cube

10¾ oz. can 98% fat-free cream of mushroom soup

1 cup water

8 oz. pkg. fat-free cream cheese, cubed

1. Cut steak into strips 1 inch long and ½ inch wide.

2. Mix with flour, pepper, salt, and garlic.

3. Combine with onion, soy sauce, bouillon, soup, and water in slow cooker.

4. Cook on Low 6–7 hours, stirring occasionally.

5. Add cream cheese cubes for last 30 minutes of cooking.

6. Serve over cooked wide noodles.

BEEF-VEGETABLE CASSEROLE

EDWINA STOLTZFUS, NARVON, PA

Makes: 8 servings
PREP. TIME: 20 MINUTES
COOKING TIME: 4–5 HOURS
IDEAL SLOW-COOKER SIZE: 5-QUART

1 lb. extra-lean ground beef or turkey
1 medium onion, chopped
½ cup chopped celery
4 cups chopped cabbage
2½ cups canned stewed tomatoes, slightly mashed
1 Tbsp. flour
1 tsp. salt
1 Tbsp. sugar
¼–½ tsp. black pepper, according to your taste preference

1. Sauté meat, onion, and celery in nonstick skillet until meat is browned.
2. Pour into slow cooker.
3. Top with layers of cabbage, tomatoes, flour, salt, sugar, and pepper.
4. Cover. Cook on High 4–5 hours.

NOTE Assemble all of your measured ingredients first. Then add as the recipe calls for them.

HEARTY RICE CASSEROLE

DALE PETERSON, RAPID CITY, SD

Makes: 12–16 servings
PREP. TIME: 25 MINUTES
COOKING TIME: 6–7 HOURS
IDEAL SLOW-COOKER SIZE: 4-QUART

10¾ oz. can cream of mushroom soup
10¾ oz. can cream of onion soup
10¾ oz. can cream of chicken soup
1 cup water
1 lb. ground beef, browned
1 lb. pork sausage, browned
1 large onion, chopped
1 large green pepper, chopped
1½ cups long-grain rice
shredded cheese, optional

1. Combine all ingredients except cheese in slow cooker. Mix well.

2. Cover. Cook on Low 6–7 hours, sprinkling with cheese during last hour, if you wish.

BEEF AND NOODLE CASSEROLE

DELORES SCHEEL, WEST FARGO, ND

Makes: 10 servings
PREP. TIME: 20 MINUTES
COOKING TIME: 4 HOURS
IDEAL SLOW-COOKER SIZE: 4-QUART

  1 lb. extra-lean ground beef

  1 medium onion, chopped

  1 medium green bell pepper, chopped

17 oz. can whole-kernel corn, drained

  4 oz. can mushroom stems and pieces, drained

  1 tsp. salt

¼ tsp. black pepper

11 oz. jar salsa

  5 cups dry medium egg noodles, cooked

28 oz. can low-sodium diced tomatoes, undrained

  1 cup low-fat shredded cheddar cheese

1. Brown ground beef and onion in nonstick skillet over medium heat. Transfer to slow cooker.

2. Top with remaining ingredients in order listed.

3. Cover. Cook on Low 4 hours.

CASSEROLE VERDE

JULIA FISHER, NEW CARLISLE, OH

Makes: 6 servings
PREP. TIME: 35 MINUTES
COOKING TIME: 4 HOURS
IDEAL SLOW-COOKER SIZE: 4-QUART

1 lb. ground beef
1 small onion, chopped
⅛ tsp. garlic powder
8 oz. can tomato sauce
⅓ cup chopped black olives
4 oz. can sliced mushrooms, drained
8 oz. container sour cream
8 oz. container cottage cheese
4¼ oz. can chopped green chilies
12 oz. pkg. tortilla chips
8 oz. Monterey Jack cheese, shredded

1. Brown ground beef, onions, and garlic in skillet. Drain. Add tomato sauce, olives, and mushrooms.

2. In a separate bowl, combine sour cream, cottage cheese, and green chilies.

3. In slow cooker, layer a third of the chips, and half the ground beef mixture, half the sour cream mixture, and half the shredded cheese. Repeat all layers, except reserve last third of the chips to add just before serving.

4. Cover. Cook on Low 4 hours.

5. Ten minutes before serving time, scatter reserved chips over top and continue cooking, uncovered.

CHEESE MEAT LOAF

MARY SOMMERFELD, LANCASTER, PA

Makes: 8 servings
PREP. TIME: 15 MINUTES
COOKING TIME: 6–8 HOURS
IDEAL SLOW-COOKER SIZE: 4-QUART

2 lbs. ground chuck or ground beef

2 cups shredded sharp cheddar or American cheese

1 tsp. salt

1 tsp. dry mustard

¼ tsp. pepper

½ cup chili sauce

2 cups crushed cornflakes

2 eggs

½ cup milk

1. Combine all ingredients. Shape into loaf. Place in greased slow cooker.

2. Cover. Cook on Low 6–8 hours.

3. Slice and serve with your favorite tomato sauce or ketchup.

VARIATION

Before baking, surround meat loaf with quartered potatoes, tossed lightly in oil

CREAMY SPAGHETTI WITH BEEF AND VEGGIES

DALE PETERSON, RAPID CITY, SD

Makes: 6 servings
PREP. TIME: 25 MINUTES
COOKING TIME: 4–6 HOURS
IDEAL SLOW-COOKER SIZE: 5-QUART

1	cup chopped onions
1	cup chopped green peppers
1	Tbsp. butter
28	oz. can tomatoes with juice
4	oz. can mushrooms, chopped and drained
2¼	oz. can sliced ripe olives, drained
2	tsp. dried oregano
1	lb. ground beef, browned and drained
12	oz. spaghetti, cooked and drained
10¾	oz. can cream of mushroom soup
½	cup water
2	cups (8 oz.) shredded cheddar cheese
¼	cup grated Parmesan cheese

1. Sauté onions and green peppers in butter in skillet until tender. Add tomatoes, mushrooms, olives, oregano, and beef. Simmer for 10 minutes. Transfer to slow cooker.
2. Add spaghetti. Mix well.
3. Combine soup and water in a small bowl. Pour over casserole. Sprinkle with cheeses.
4. Cover. Cook on Low 4–6 hours.

NOTE Add 3 Tbsp. oil to water before cooking pasta. It keeps it from sticking together.

MEATBALLS AND SPAGHETTI SAUCE

CAROL SOMMERS, MILLERSBURG, OH

Makes: 6–8 servings
PREP. TIME: 35 MINUTES
COOKING TIME: 6–8 HOURS
IDEAL SLOW-COOKER SIZE: 4-QUART

Meatballs

1½ lbs. ground beef

2 eggs

1 cup bread crumbs

oil

Sauce

28 oz. can tomato puree

6 oz. can tomato paste

10¾ oz. can tomato soup

¼–½ cup grated Romano or Parmesan cheese

1 tsp. oil

1 garlic clove, minced

sliced mushrooms (either canned or fresh), optional

1. Combine ground beef, eggs, and bread crumbs. Form into 16 meatballs. Brown in oil in skillet.

2. Combine all sauce ingredients, except mushrooms, in slow cooker. Add meatballs. Stir together gently.

3. Cover. Cook on Low 6–8 hours. Add mushrooms 1–2 hours before sauce is finished.

4. Serve over cooked spaghetti.

FESTIVE MEATBALLS

JEAN BUTZER, BATAVIA, NY

Makes: 5–7 servings
PREP. TIME: 20 MINUTES
COOKING TIME: 3¼–4¼ HOURS
IDEAL SLOW-COOKER SIZE: 4-QUART

1½ lbs. ground beef
4¼ oz. can deviled ham
⅔ cup evaporated milk
2 eggs, beaten slightly
1 Tbsp. grated onion
2 cups soft bread crumbs
1 tsp. salt
¼ tsp. allspice
¼ tsp. pepper
¼ cup flour
¼ cup water
1 Tbsp. ketchup
2 tsp. dill weed
1 cup sour cream

1. Grease interior of slow-cooker crock.

2. Combine beef, ham, milk, eggs, onion, bread crumbs, salt, allspice, and pepper in large bowl. Shape into 2-inch meatballs. As you finish making a ball, place it in the slow cooker.

3. Cover. Cook on Low 3–4 hours. Turn to High.

4. In a bowl, dissolve flour in water until smooth. Stir in ketchup and dill weed. Add to meatballs, stirring gently.

5. Cook on High 15–20 minutes, or until slightly thickened.

6. Turn off heat. Stir in sour cream.

TIP
Serve over rice or pasta.

SLOW-COOKED STEAK FAJITAS

VIRGINIA GRAYBILL, HERSHEY, PA

Makes: 12 servings
PREP. TIME: 25 MINUTES
COOKING TIME: 8½–9½ HOURS
IDEAL SLOW-COOKER SIZE: 4-QUART

1½ lbs. beef flank steak

15 oz. can low-sodium diced tomatoes with garlic and onion, undrained

1 jalapeño pepper, seeded and chopped*

2 garlic cloves, minced

1 tsp. ground coriander

1 tsp. ground cumin

1 tsp. chili powder

½ tsp. salt

2 medium onions, sliced

2 medium green bell peppers, julienned

2 medium sweet red bell peppers, julienned

1 Tbsp. minced fresh parsley

2 tsp. cornstarch

1 Tbsp. water

12 6-inch flour tortillas, warmed

¾ cup fat-free sour cream

¾ cup low-sodium salsa

1. Slice steak thinly into strips across grain. Place in slow cooker.

2. Add tomatoes, jalapeño, garlic, coriander, cumin, chili powder, and salt.

3. Cover. Cook on Low 7 hours.

4. Add onions, peppers, and parsley.

5. Cover. Cook 1–2 hours longer, or until meat is tender.

6. Combine cornstarch and water until smooth. Gradually stir into slow cooker.

7. Cover. Cook on High 30 minutes, or until slightly thickened.

8. Using a slotted spoon, spoon about ½ cup of meat mixture down the center of each tortilla.

9. Add 1 Tbsp. sour cream and 1 Tbsp. salsa to each.

10. Fold bottom of tortilla over filling and roll up.

*When cutting jalapeño peppers, use rubber or plastic gloves to protect your hands. Avoid touching your face.

TIJUANA TACOS

HELEN KENAGY, CARLSBAD, NM

Makes: 6 servings
PREP. TIME: 20 MINUTES
COOKING TIME: 2 HOURS
IDEAL SLOW-COOKER SIZE: 3½-QUART

3 cups cooked chopped beef
1 lb. can refried beans
½ cup chopped onions
½ cup chopped green peppers
½ cup chopped ripe olives
8 oz. can tomato sauce
3 tsp. chili powder
1 Tbsp. Worcestershire sauce
½ tsp. garlic powder
¼ tsp. pepper
¼ tsp. paprika
⅛ tsp. celery salt
⅛ tsp. ground nutmeg
¾ cup water
1 tsp. salt
1 cup crushed corn chips
6 taco shells
shredded lettuce
chopped tomatoes
shredded cheddar cheese

1. Combine first 15 ingredients in slow cooker.
2. Cover. Cook on High 2 hours.
3. Just before serving, fold in corn chips.
4. Spoon mixture into taco shells. Top with lettuce, tomatoes, and cheese.

BEEF PITAS

DEDE PETERSON, RAPID CITY, SD

Makes: 2 sandwiches
PREP. TIME: 15 MINUTES
COOKING TIME: 3–4 HOURS
IDEAL SLOW-COOKER SIZE: 2-QUART

½ lb. beef or pork, cut into small cubes

½ tsp. dried oregano

dash of black pepper

1 cup chopped fresh tomatoes

2 Tbsp. diced fresh green bell peppers

¼ cup nonfat sour cream

1 tsp. red wine vinegar

1 tsp. vegetable oil

2 large pita breads, heated and cut in half

1. Place meat in slow cooker. Sprinkle with oregano and black pepper.

2. Cook on Low 3–4 hours.

3. In a separate bowl, combine tomatoes, green peppers, sour cream, vinegar, and oil.

4. Fill pitas with meat. Top with vegetable and sour cream mixture.

NEW MEXICO CHEESEBURGERS

COLLEEN KONETZNI, RIO RANCHO, NM

Makes: 8 servings
PREP. TIME: 30 MINUTES
COOKING TIME: 7–9 HOURS
IDEAL SLOW-COOKER SIZE: 4-QUART

1 lb. ground beef, browned
6 potatoes, peeled and sliced
½ cup chopped green chilies
1 onion, chopped
10¾ oz. can cream of mushroom soup
2 cups cubed Velveeta cheese
8 hamburger buns

1. Layer beef, potatoes, green chilies, and onions in slow cooker.

2. Spread soup over top.

3. Top with cheese.

4. Cover. Cook on High 1 hour. Reduce heat to Low and cook 6–8 hours.

5. Serve on hamburger buns.

BARBECUE SAUCE AND HAMBURGERS

DOLORES KRATZ, SOUDERTON, PA

Makes: 6 sandwiches
PREP. TIME: 25 MINUTES
COOKING TIME: 5–6 HOURS
IDEAL SLOW-COOKER SIZE: 4-QUART

14¾ oz. can beef gravy
½ cup ketchup
½ cup chili sauce
1 Tbsp. Worcestershire sauce
1 Tbsp. prepared mustard
6 grilled hamburger patties
6 slices cheese, optional
6 hamburger buns

1. Combine all ingredients except hamburger patties and cheese slices in slow cooker.
2. Add hamburger patties.
3. Cover. Cook on Low 5–6 hours.
4. Serve in buns, each topped with a slice of cheese if you like.

Freeze leftover sauce for future use.

This is both a practical and a tasty recipe for serving a crowd (picnics, potlucks, etc.). You can grill the patties early in the day, rather than at the last minute when your guests are arriving.

Date all containers that you put in the freezer so you're sure to use the oldest food first.

PIZZABURGERS

DEBORAH SWARTZ, GROTTOES, VA

Makes: 4–6 sandwiches
PREP. TIME: 20 MINUTES
COOKING TIME: 1–2 HOURS
IDEAL SLOW-COOKER SIZE: 4-QUART

1 lb. ground beef
½ cup chopped onions
¼ tsp. salt
⅛ tsp. pepper
8 oz. pizza sauce
10¾ oz. can cream of mushroom soup
2 cups shredded cheddar cheese
4–6 hamburger buns

1. Brown ground beef and onion in skillet. Drain.

2. Add remaining ingredients. Mix well. Pour into slow cooker.

3. Cover. Cook on Low 1–2 hours.

4. Serve on hamburger buns.

PITA BURGERS

PHYLLIS GOOD, LANCASTER, PA

Makes: 12 servings
PREP. TIME: 15–20 MINUTES
COOKING TIME: 4–6 HOURS
IDEAL SLOW-COOKER SIZE: 4-QUART

2 lbs. lean ground chuck

1 cup dry oatmeal

1 egg

1 medium onion, finely chopped

15 oz. can tomato sauce

2 Tbsp. brown sugar

½ tsp. salt

2 Tbsp. apple cider vinegar

1 Tbsp. Worcestershire sauce

1 Tbsp. soy sauce

12 slice pkg. pita bread

1. Combine the ground chuck, dry oatmeal, egg, and chopped onion in a mixing bowl. Shape the mixture into 12 burgers.

2. In a medium-sized bowl, combine the tomato sauce, brown sugar, salt, vinegar, Worcestershire sauce, and soy sauce.

3. Dip each burger in the sauce, and then stack them into your slow cooker. Pour any remaining sauce over the burgers in the cooker.

4. Cover. Cook on Low 4–6 hours, or until the burgers are as cooked as you like them.

5. Invite everyone who's eating to lift a burger out of the cooker with tongs and put it into a pita pocket with some dribbles of sauce.

BIG JUICY BURGERS

PHYLLIS GOOD, LANCASTER, PA
Photo appears in color section.

Makes: 8 servings
PREP. TIME: 15 MINUTES
COOKING TIME: 7–9 HOURS
IDEAL SLOW-COOKER SIZE: 4- OR 5-QUART

1 cup chopped onions
¼ cup chopped celery
2 lbs. ground beef
1 tsp. salt, divided
½ tsp. pepper
2 cups tomato juice
2 tsp. minced garlic
1 Tbsp. ketchup
1 tsp. Italian seasoning
8 hamburger buns

1. Place the chopped onions and celery in your slow cooker.

2. Place the beef, ½ tsp. salt, and pepper into a large mixing bowl. Use your hands to mix the salt and pepper into the beef. Divide the mixture in half. Wrap up half tightly and place in the refrigerator to use later this week. Divide the remaining dough into 8 balls, each the same size.

3. Flatten the 8 balls of beef so they look like hamburger patties. Place the patties in the slow cooker on top of the onions and celery. Try not to stack them. If you have to, stagger them so they don't lie exactly on top of each other. Wash your hands well.

4. In a medium-sized mixing bowl stir together the tomato juice, minced garlic, ketchup, Italian seasoning, and ½ tsp. salt. Pour this sauce over the patties in your slow cooker.

5. Cover your slow cooker. Cook the burgers on Low for 7–9 hours.

6. Serve each Big Juicy Burger on a hamburger bun.

SLOPPY JOES

NADINE MARTINITZ, SALINA, KS

Makes: 8–12 servings
PREP. TIME: 10–15 MINUTES
COOKING TIME: 2–6 HOURS
IDEAL SLOW-COOKER SIZE: 4- TO 5-QUART

2 lbs. ground beef

1 large onion, chopped

½ cup chopped green bell pepper

2 14½-oz. cans diced tomatoes

⅓ cup brown sugar

4 tsp. Worcestershire sauce

1 Tbsp. ground cumin

2 tsp. chili powder

1 tsp. salt

8–12 hamburger buns

1. Brown beef in skillet, stirring to break into small pieces.

2. Add onion and pepper to meat in skillet, cooking a few more minutes. Drain off drippings.

3. Transfer meat mixture to slow cooker.

4. Stir in tomatoes, brown sugar, Worcestershire sauce, and seasonings.

5. Cover and cook until flavors are well blended, 2 hours on High or 6 hours on Low.

6. Serve on hamburger buns.

NOTE To serve, fill each of 8–12 hamburger buns with ½ cup beef mixture.

HEARTY ITALIAN SANDWICHES

RHONDA LEE SCHMIDT, SCRANTON, PA
ROBIN SCHROCK, MILLERSBURG, OH

Makes: 8 sandwiches
PREP. TIME: 15 MINUTES
COOKING TIME: 6 HOURS
IDEAL SLOW-COOKER SIZE: 4-QUART

1½ lbs. ground beef
1½ lbs. bulk Italian sausage
2 large onions, chopped
2 large green peppers, chopped
2 large sweet red peppers, chopped
1 tsp. salt
1 tsp. pepper
   shredded Monterey Jack cheese
8 hoagie or hero rolls

1. In skillet brown beef and sausage. Drain.

2. Place one-third onions and peppers in slow cooker. Top with half of meat mixture. Repeat layers. Sprinkle with salt and pepper.

3. Cover. Cook on Low 6 hours, or until vegetables are tender.

4. With a slotted spoon, serve about 1 cup mixture on each roll. Top with cheese.

NOTE "High" on most slow cookers is approximately 300°F. "Low" is approximately 200°F.

TIP
For some extra flavor, add a spoonful of salsa to each roll before topping with cheese.

MIDDLE EAST SANDWICHES (FOR A CROWD)

ESTHER MAST, EAST PETERSBURG, PA

Makes: 10–16 sandwiches
PREP. TIME: 50 MINUTES
COOKING TIME: 4¼–5¼ HOURS
IDEAL SLOW-COOKER SIZE: 5- OR 6-QUART

    4 lbs. boneless beef chuck roast, or venison roast, cut in ½-inch cubes
    4 Tbsp. cooking oil
    2 cups chopped onions
    2 garlic cloves, minced
    1 cup dry red wine
    6 oz. can tomato paste
    1 tsp. dried oregano
    1 tsp. dried basil
    ½ tsp. dried rosemary
    2 tsp. salt
       dash of pepper
    ¼ cup cornstarch
    ¼ cup cold water
 10–16 pita breads
    2 cups shredded lettuce
    1 large tomato, seeded and diced
    1 large cucumber, seeded and diced
    8 oz. plain yogurt

> All you need to top this off is salad or applesauce.

1. Grease interior of slow-cooker crock.

2. If you have time, brown meat, 1 lb. at a time, in skillet in 1 Tbsp. oil. As you finish one batch, place browned beef in slow cooker. Reserve drippings. If you don't have time, place meat cubes into crock.

3. Sauté onions and garlic in drippings until tender. Then add to meat in crock. Or stir into crock with meat without sautéing.

4. Stir in wine, tomato paste, oregano, basil, rosemary, salt, and pepper.

5. Cover. Cook on Low 4–5 hours, or until meat and onions are tender but not dry.

6. Turn cooker to High. Combine cornstarch and water in small bowl until smooth. Stir into meat mixture. Cook just until bubbly and thickened, stirring frequently.

7. Split pita breads to make pockets. Fill each with meat mixture, topped with lettuce, tomato, cucumber, and yogurt.

LEG OF LAMB WITH ROSEMARY AND GARLIC

HOPE COMERFORD, CLINTON TOWNSHIP, MI

Makes: 6–8 servings
PREP. TIME: 5 MINUTES
COOKING TIME: 7–8 HOURS
IDEAL SLOW-COOKER SIZE: 7-QUART

1 tsp. olive oil

4–5 lb. leg of lamb

6 cloves garlic, crushed

3 Tbsp. Dijon mustard

1 Tbsp. fresh chopped rosemary

1 tsp. salt

1 tsp. black pepper

½ cup white wine

1. Coat the bottom of your crock with olive oil.

2. Pat the leg of lamb dry with a paper towel.

3. Mix together the garlic, Dijon mustard, rosemary, salt, and pepper. Rub this mixture all over the leg of lamb. Place the leg of lamb in the slow cooker.

4. Pour the wine into the crock around the leg of lamb.

5. Cover and cook on Low 7–8 hours.

SAVORY SLOW COOKER PORK TENDERLOIN

KATHY HERTZLER, LANCASTER, PA
Photo appears in color section.

Makes: 6 servings
PREP. TIME: 5–15 MINUTES
COOKING TIME: 3–4 HOURS
IDEAL SLOW-COOKER SIZE: 4-QUART

2 lb. pork loin roast, wide and short (not skinny and long)

1 cup water

¾ cup red wine

3 Tbsp. light soy sauce

1 1-oz. envelope dry onion soup mix

6 cloves garlic, peeled and chopped

freshly ground pepper

1. Grease interior of slow-cooker crock.

2. Place pork loin in slow cooker. Pour water, wine, and soy sauce over pork.

3. Turn pork over in liquid several times to completely moisten.

4. Sprinkle with dry onion soup mix. Top with chopped garlic and pepper.

5. Cover. Cook on Low 3–4 hours, or until instant-read meat thermometer registers 145°F when stuck into center of loin.

Here's a good go-along: mix ½ cup uncooked long grain white rice and ½ cup uncooked brown rice in a microwavable bowl. Stir in 2½ cups water and ¾ tsp. salt. Cover. Microwave 5 minutes on High, and then 20 minutes on 50%. Place finished pork on a large platter and the finished rice alongside, topped with the juice from the meat. A green salad goes well with this to make a meal.

PORK AND APRICOTS WITH MASHED SWEET POTATOES

CAROLYN BAER, CONRATH, WI

Makes: 8 servings
PREP. TIME: 35–40 MINUTES
COOKING TIME: 4–8 HOURS
IDEAL SLOW-COOKER SIZE: 6-QUART

2½ lbs. sweet potatoes, peeled and cut into 1-inch-thick chunks

3½–4 lb. boneless pork picnic shoulder roast

1 tsp. dried tarragon, crushed

1½ tsp. fennel seed, crushed

3 cloves garlic, minced

1½ tsp. salt

1 tsp. pepper

2 Tbsp. cooking oil

12–16 oz. kielbasa, or other smoked sausage links, cut in half lengthwise, then in 2-inch pieces

14 oz. can chicken broth

¾ cup apricot nectar, divided

½ cup dried apricots

4 tsp. cornstarch

1. Grease interior of slow-cooker crock.

2. Place sweet potato chunks in bottom of slow cooker.

3. Trim fat from pork roast.

4. Combine tarragon, fennel seed, minced garlic, salt, and pepper in small bowl.

5. Rub spice mix all over pork roast.

6. If you have time, brown roast on all sides in hot oil in large skillet. (Or eliminate oil and skip to Step 8.)

7. Drain off drippings.

8. Place roast on top of sweet potatoes.

9. Place sausage pieces around roast in cooker.

10. Pour broth and ½ cup apricot nectar over all.

11. Cover and cook for 3½ hours on High, or 7½ hours on Low, or until instant-read meat thermometer registers 145°F–150°F when stuck into center of roast.

12. Add dried apricots to cooker. Cover and continue cooking on High 30 more minutes.

13. With slotted spoon, transfer pork, sausage, and apricots to serving platter. Cover and keep warm.

14. Transfer sweet potatoes to a large bowl.

15. Mash with potato masher.

16. Strain cooking liquid from cooker into a glass measuring cup.

17. Skim and discard fat.

18. Reserve 2 cups liquid, adding chicken broth if necessary to make 2 cups.

19. In a small bowl, whisk together ¼ cup apricot nectar and cornstarch until smooth.

20. In a medium saucepan, combine cooking liquid and cornstarch mixture.

21. Cook and stir over medium heat until thick and bubbly. Cook 2 minutes longer.

22. Cut pork into chunks. Mix with sausage pieces and apricots. Place around edges of platter. Pile mashed sweet potatoes into center of platter. Spoon sauce over top. Place remaining sauce in bowl and pass with platter.

SPICY PORK CHOPS

CYNTHIA MORRIS, GROTTOES, VA

Makes: 4 servings
PREP. TIME: 5 MINUTES
COOKING TIME: 4–5 HOURS
IDEAL SLOW-COOKER SIZE: 5-QUART

4 bone-in, ¾-inch-thick, blade-cut pork chops
1 cup Italian salad dressing
½ cup brown sugar
⅓ cup prepared spicy mustard

1. Grease interior of slow-cooker crock.

2. Place pork chops in slow cooker.

3. Mix remaining 3 ingredients together in a bowl. Pour over chops.

4. Cover and cook on Low 4–5 hours, or until instant-read meat thermometer registers 145°F when stuck into center of chops (but not against bone).

VARIATION

You can substitute chicken thighs for pork chops.

TIP

Check the meat after cooking for 3 hours to make sure the meat is not overcooking.

OXFORD CANAL CHOPS DELUXE

WILLARD E. ROTH, ELKHART, IN

Makes: 6 servings
PREP. TIME: 25 MINUTES
COOKING TIME: 4–6 HOURS
IDEAL SLOW-COOKER SIZE: 5-QUART

6 6-oz. boneless pork chops
¼ cup flour
1 tsp. powdered garlic
1 tsp. sea salt
1 tsp. black pepper
1 tsp. dried basil and/or dried oregano
2 medium onions, sliced
2 Tbsp. oil
1 cup burgundy wine
14½ oz. can beef broth
1 soup can water
6 oz. can tomato sauce
8 oz. dried apricots
½ lb. fresh mushroom caps

1. Shake chops in bag with flour and seasonings.

2. Glaze onions in oil in medium hot skillet. Add chops and brown.

3. Pour extra flour over chops in skillet. In large bowl mix together wine, broth, water, and tomato sauce, then pour over meat. Bring to boil.

4. Remove chops from skillet and place in cooker. Layer in apricots and mushrooms. Pour broth over top.

5. Cover. Cook on High 4 hours, or on Low 6 hours.

6. Serve with the Celtic specialty Bubble and Squeak—Irish potatoes mashed with green cabbage or brussels sprouts.

NOTE 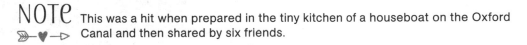 This was a hit when prepared in the tiny kitchen of a houseboat on the Oxford Canal and then shared by six friends.

APPLES, SAUERKRAUT, AND CHOPS

CAROL SHERWOOD, BATAVIA, NY

Makes: 4 servings
PREP. TIME: 25 MINUTES
COOKING TIME: 4–5 HOURS
IDEAL SLOW-COOKER SIZE: 5-QUART

- 1   onion, sliced and separated into rings, divided
- ⅛   tsp. garlic flakes or garlic powder, divided
- 3   cups sauerkraut, drained, divided
- 1   cup unpeeled apple slices, divided
- 1½ tsp. caraway seeds, divided
- ¼   tsp. salt, divided
- ¼   tsp. dried thyme, divided
- ¼   tsp. pepper, divided
- 4   bone-in, ¾-inch-thick, blade-cut pork chops
- ¾   cup apple juice

1. Grease interior of slow-cooker crock.

2. Place half of onion rings, garlic flakes, sauerkraut, apple slices, and caraway seeds in slow cooker.

3. Season with half the salt, thyme, and pepper.

4. Place pork chops on top of ingredients in slow cooker.

5. Layer remaining ingredients in order given.

6. Pour apple juice over all.

7. Cover. Cook on Low 4–5 hours, or until instant-read meat thermometer registers 145°F when stuck into center of chops (but not against bone).

8. Serve chops topped with onion-sauerkraut-apple mixture.

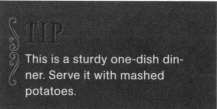

TIP

This is a sturdy one-dish dinner. Serve it with mashed potatoes.

PULLED PORK WITH DR PEPPER

CHRISTINA GERBER, APPLE CREEK, OH
Photo appears in color section.

Makes: 6–8 sandwiches
PREP. TIME: 20–25 MINUTES
COOKING TIME: 4–8 HOURS
IDEAL SLOW-COOKER SIZE: 6-QUART

- 1 medium onion, cut in eighths
- 2½–3 lb. pork butt roast
- 2 12-oz. cans Dr Pepper
- 1 garlic clove, minced
- 1½ tsp. dry mustard
- ¼–½ tsp. cayenne pepper, according to taste
- 1 tsp. salt
- 1 tsp. ground black pepper
- ¼ cup apple cider vinegar
- 3 Tbsp. Worcestershire sauce
- your favorite barbecue sauce
- your favorite rolls or buns

> **TIP**
> Serve this recipe with cole-slaw and oven fries.

1. Grease interior of slow-cooker crock.

2. Place cut-up onions on bottom of crock.

3. Place pork roast on top of onions.

4. Pour Dr Pepper over top.

5. In a bowl, mix together garlic, dry mustard, cayenne pepper, salt, black pepper, vinegar, and Worcestershire sauce.

6. Spoon sauce over roast, patting it on with your hands to help it stick.

7. Cover. Cook on Low 6–7 hours, or on High 3–4 hours, or until instant-read meat thermometer registers 145°F when stuck into center of roast.

8. Using 2 sturdy metal spatulas, remove meat from crock and place on large cutting board. Using 2 forks, shred pork.

9. Place shredded pork back into crock. Mix well with sauce.

10. Cover. Cook 1 more hour on Low.

11. Using a slotted spoon, lift shredded meat and onions out of crock and into large bowl.

12. Stir barbecue sauce into meat and onions, ¼ cup at a time, until you get the sauciness you like.

13. Serve in rolls or buns.

BALSAMIC-GLAZED PORK RIBS

PHYLLIS GOOD, LANCASTER, PA

Makes: 6–8 servings
PREP. TIME: 30 MINUTES
COOKING TIME: 4–6 HOURS
STANDING TIME: 2–12 HOURS
IDEAL SLOW-COOKER SIZE: 6-QUART

2 Tbsp. olive oil

½ tsp. dried rosemary

1 Tbsp. kosher salt

1 Tbsp. fennel seeds

1 tsp. freshly ground pepper

½ tsp. dried sage

¼ tsp. dried thyme

1 tsp. paprika

pinch–1 tsp. crushed red pepper, depending on the heat you like

½ tsp. ground coriander

¼ tsp. ground allspice

3 lbs. pork ribs

3 Tbsp. balsamic vinegar

1. In a small bowl, combine olive oil, rosemary, salt, fennel seeds, pepper, sage, thyme, paprika, red pepper, coriander, and allspice.

2. Rub spice paste all over ribs and let stand at room temperature for 2 hours, or refrigerate overnight.

3. Place ribs in slow cooker, cutting if needed to fit.

4. Cook on Low for 4–6 hours, until tender.

5. Remove ribs from slow cooker and place on rimmed baking sheet. Preheat broiler. Brush meaty side of ribs with balsamic vinegar and broil 6 inches from heat until browned, about 2 minutes.

6. Let stand for 5 minutes, then cut between ribs, or serve in slabs.

GIVE-ME-MORE BARBECUED RIBS

VIRGINIA BENDER, DOVER, DE
Photo appears in color section.

Makes: 6 servings
PREP. TIME: 10 MINUTES
COOKING TIME: 8–10 HOURS
IDEAL SLOW-COOKER SIZE: 6-QUART

 4 lbs. pork ribs
 ½ cup brown sugar
12 oz. jar chili sauce
 ¼ cup balsamic vinegar
 2 Tbsp. Worcestershire sauce
 2 Tbsp. Dijon mustard
 1 tsp. hot sauce

1. Place ribs in slow cooker.
2. Combine remaining ingredients. Pour half of sauce over ribs.
3. Cover. Cook on Low 8–10 hours.
4. Serve with remaining sauce.

SLURPING GOOD SAUSAGES

PHYLLIS GOOD, LANCASTER, PA
Photo appears in color section.

Makes: 10–12 servings
PREP. TIME: 20 MINUTES
COOKING TIME: 6 HOURS
IDEAL SLOW-COOKER SIZE: 4-QUART

4 lbs. sweet Italian sausage, cut into 5-inch lengths

24 oz. jar of your favorite pasta sauce

6 oz. can tomato paste

1 large green, yellow, or red bell pepper, chopped

1 large onion, sliced thin

1 Tbsp. grated Parmesan cheese, plus a little more

1 cup water

2 Tbsp. chopped fresh parsley, or 2 tsp. dried parsley

1. Place sausage pieces in skillet. Add water to cover. Simmer 10 minutes. Drain. (This cooks off some of the fat from the sausage.)

2. Combine pasta sauce, tomato paste, chopped bell pepper, sliced onion, 1 Tbsp. grated cheese, and water in slow cooker. Stir in sausage pieces.

3. Cover. Cook on Low 6 hours.

4. Just before serving, stir in parsley.

NOTE Serve in buns, or cut sausage into bite-sized pieces and serve over cooked pasta. Sprinkle with more Parmesan cheese.

ITALIAN SAUSAGE, PEPPERS, AND POTATOES

MARYANN MARKANO, WILMINGTON, DE
Photo appears in color section.

Makes: 4 servings
PREP. TIME: 15–20 MINUTES
COOKING TIME: 2–6 HOURS
IDEAL SLOW-COOKER SIZE: 5-QUART

2 lbs. sweet or hot Italian sausage, cut on the diagonal in 1-inch lengths

1 lb. small red potatoes, each cut in half

1 large onion, cut into 12 wedges

2 red or yellow bell peppers, or 1 of each color, cut into strips

1. Grease interior of slow-cooker crock.

2. Put sausage, potatoes, and onion into crock. Stir together well.

3. Gently stir in bell pepper strips.

4. Cover. Cook on Low 4–6 hours, or on High 2–3 hours, or until sausage is cooked through and potatoes and onions are as tender as you like them.

SAUSAGE TORTELLINI

CHRISTIE DETAMORE-HUNSBERGER, HARRISONBURG, VA
Photo appears in color section.

Makes: 8 servings
PREP. TIME: 25–30 MINUTES
COOKING TIME: 1½–2½ HOURS
IDEAL SLOW-COOKER SIZE: 6-QUART

leftover sausage

1 cup chopped onions

2 cloves garlic, minced

5 cups beef or chicken broth

¾ cup water

¾ cup red wine

2 14¾-oz. cans diced tomatoes, undrained

1 cup thinly sliced carrots

¾ tsp. dried basil

¾ tsp. dried oregano

16 oz. can tomato sauce

¾ cup sliced zucchini, optional

16 oz. pkg. tortellini

3 Tbsp. chopped fresh parsley

1. Add leftover sausage, onions, garlic, broth, water, wine, tomatoes, carrots, basil, oregano, and tomato sauce to crock. Stir together well.

2. Add zucchini if you wish, and tortellini.

3. Cover. Cook on High 1½–2½ hours, or until pasta is as tender as you like it, but not mushy.

4. Stir in parsley and serve.

PASTA À LA CARBONARA

HOPE COMERFORD, CLINTON TOWNSHIP, MI
Photo appears in color section.

Makes: 8 servings
PREP. TIME: 10 MINUTES
COOKING TIME: 8 HOURS
IDEAL SLOW-COOKER SIZE: 4- TO 6-QUART

- 1 pkg thick-cut bacon, sliced into bite-sized pieces
- 1 chicken bouillon cube
- 2 tsp. garlic powder
- 1 tsp. (or less depending on the level of heat you prefer) crushed red pepper flakes
- 1 lb. rotini pasta
- 2 egg yolks
- ½ tsp. pepper
- ¼ cup grated Parmesan cheese
- ½ cup flat-leaf parsley, chopped

1. Place the cut-up bacon in the bottom of your crock. Try to separate it as much as you can so the pieces are not all completely stuck together. Cover and cook on Low for 7 hours.

2. The last 30–45 minutes of cooking, turn your slow cooker up to High and add your bouillon cube, garlic powder, and crushed red pepper flakes. Give it a stir.

3. Cook your pasta according to the package instructions. When your pasta is done, reserve ¼ cup of water.

4. In a bowl, mix together the egg yolks, pepper, and Parmesan cheese. Next, whisk in the ¼ cup pasta water to temper your egg yolks.

5. Pour your pasta into the slow cooker, pour the egg/Parmesan mixture over the top, and toss in the parsley. Mix all together.

RASPBERRY-GLAZED HAM

GLORIA FREY, LEBANON, PA

Makes: 16–20 servings
PREP. TIME: 10–15 MINUTES
COOKING TIME: 4 HOURS
IDEAL SLOW-COOKER SIZE: 6-QUART

8–10 lb. boneless ham, fully cooked
¼ cup apple juice
2 Tbsp. lemon juice
2 tsp. cornstarch
⅓ cup seedless raspberry jam, divided
1 Tbsp. butter

1. Place ham in slow cooker. Cover. Cook on Low 2 hours.

2. While ham is cooking, blend apple juice, lemon juice, and cornstarch together in saucepan.

3. Stir in about half of jam after liquid is well blended.

4. Cook and stir until hot and bubbly. Add butter. Stir in remaining jam.

5. Spoon glaze over ham after it has cooked 2 hours.

6. Cover. Cook 2 more hours on Low.

7. Slice ham and serve.

ORCHARD HAM

PHYLLIS GOOD, LANCASTER, PA
Photo appears in color section.

Makes: 6–8 servings
PREP. TIME: 20 MINUTES
COOKING TIME: 8½–10½ HOURS
STANDING TIME: 10–15 MINUTES
IDEAL SLOW-COOKER SIZE: 4- OR 5-QUART

5–6 lb. bone-in ham (or larger; whatever fits your slow cooker)
4 cups cider, or apple juice
1 cup brown sugar
2 tsp. dry mustard
1 tsp. ground cloves
1¼ cups golden seedless raisins

1. Place ham in slow cooker. Pour cider over meat.

2. Cover. Cook on Low 8–10 hours.

3. While the ham is cooking, make a paste by mixing brown sugar, dry mustard, cloves, and a few tablespoons of hot cider from the cooker in a bowl. Set aside.

4. At the end of the cooking time, remove ham from cider and place in a 9×13-inch baking pan, or one that's big enough to hold the ham.

5. Brush paste over ham. Then pour a cup of juice from the slow cooker into the baking pan. (Don't pour it over the ham; you don't want to wash off the paste.) Stir raisins into the cider in the baking pan.

6. Bake at 375°F for 20–30 minutes, or until the paste has turned into a glaze.

7. Let the ham stand for 10–15 minutes, and then slice and serve. Top the slices with the cider-raisin mixture.

HAM WITH SWEET POTATOES AND ORANGES

ESTHER BECKER, GORDONVILLE, PA

Makes: 4 servings
PREP. TIME: 15 MINUTES
COOKING TIME: 3–4 HOURS
IDEAL SLOW-COOKER SIZE: 5- OR 6-QUART

2–3	sweet potatoes, peeled and sliced ¼ inch thick
1½–2	lb. ham slice
3	seedless oranges, peeled and sliced
3	Tbsp. orange juice concentrate
3	Tbsp. honey
½	cup brown sugar
2	Tbsp. cornstarch

1. Grease interior of slow-cooker crock.

2. Place sweet potato slices in slow-cooker.

3. Arrange ham and orange slices on top of potatoes.

4. Combine remaining ingredients in a small bowl. Drizzle over ham and oranges.

5. Cover. Cook on Low 3–4 hours.

NOTE This is my go-to recipe for our monthly church potluck. I know exactly how long my slow cooker needs with this recipe (2 hours), and I always take home an empty crock!

TIP

Delicious served with a fruit salad.

HOMINY AND HAM

REITA YODER, CARLSBAD, NM

Makes: 12–14 servings
PREP. TIME: 10 MINUTES
COOKING TIME: 1½–3 HOURS
IDEAL SLOW-COOKER SIZE: 3- TO 4-QUART

3 29-oz. cans hominy, drained

10¾ oz. can cream of chicken soup

½ lb. cheddar cheese, shredded or cubed

1 lb. cubed cooked ham

2 2¼-oz. cans green chilies, undrained

1. Mix all ingredients together in slow cooker.

2. Cover and cook on High for 1½ hours, or on Low for 2–3 hours, or until bubbly and cheese is melted.

Serve with fresh salsa.

HAM-BROCCOLI CASSEROLE

REBECCA MEYERKORTH, WAMEGO, KS

Makes: 4 servings
PREP. TIME: 20 MINUTES
COOKING TIME: 4–5 HOURS
IDEAL SLOW-COOKER SIZE: 4- TO 5-QUART

16 oz. pkg. frozen broccoli cuts, thawed and drained

2–3 cups cubed, cooked ham

10¾ oz. can cream of mushroom soup

4 oz. of your favorite mild cheese, cubed

1 cup milk

1 cup instant rice, uncooked

1 rib celery, chopped

1 small onion, chopped

1. Combine broccoli and ham in slow cooker.

2. Combine soup, cheese, milk, rice, celery, and onion. Stir into broccoli and ham.

3. Cover. Cook on Low 4–5 hours.

DEEP-DISH PEPPERONI PIZZA

Photo appears in color section.

Makes: 4 servings

PREP. TIME: 30 MINUTES

COOKING TIME: 2½ HOURS

RISING TIME: ABOUT 1 HOUR

IDEAL SLOW-COOKER SIZE: 6-QUART

½ cup unbleached all-purpose flour

½ cup whole wheat bread flour

½ tsp. instant yeast

½ tsp. salt

2 Tbsp. olive oil, divided

⅓ cup warm water

½ cup thick pizza sauce

1 cup shredded mozzarella cheese

3 oz. sliced pepperoni, or to taste

½ tsp. dried basil

1. In a medium mixing bowl, combine flours, yeast, salt, 1 Tbsp. olive oil, and water. Stir to form a shaggy dough.

2. Knead for several minutes until a stiff dough forms. Knead into a ball.

3. Pour in remaining 1 Tbsp. olive oil and grease the ball and the bowl. Cover with a cloth and set aside in a warm place for approximately 1 hour.

4. After 1 hour, grease slow cooker.

5. Remove ball of dough to counter. Roll out with a rolling pin into a large oval that is larger by a few inches than slow cooker.

6. Lift the dough into the slow cooker and gently pull it and shape it so that the dough lines the crock and comes up 2–3" on the sides.

7. Cook for 1½ hours on High, uncovered. Dough should be firm and getting brown at edges.

8. Spread pizza sauce on the floor of the dough. Sprinkle with cheese. Layer on pepperoni. Sprinkle with basil.

9. Cook an additional hour on High, with lid on cooker and vented with a wooden spoon handle or chopstick at one end. Toppings should be hot through and the cheese melted.

TIP

Use a large spatula to coax the pizza out of the cooker onto a platter, then cut it into slices. Or use a plastic or silicone knife to slice the pizza directly in the slow cooker and lift out the slices one by one.

POLISH PIZZA

Makes: 4 servings
PREP. TIME: 30 MINUTES
COOKING TIME: 3 HOURS
IDEAL SLOW-COOKER SIZE: 6-QUART

1 Tbsp. butter

3 cups shredded, unpeeled potatoes

½ cup finely diced onion

3 Tbsp. spicy brown mustard

16 oz. bag sauerkraut, drained well

13 oz. ring kielbasa, sliced

¾ cup shredded Swiss cheese

1. Grease crock with butter and turn slow cooker on High to preheat.

2. Place potatoes and onion in a kitchen towel or cloth that can get stained. Squeeze firmly to press out as much liquid as possible from potatoes and onions. Discard liquid.

3. Sprinkle onion and potatoes into cooker. Cover, but vent the lid at one end with a wooden spoon handle or chopstick.

4. Cook on High for 1½ hours. The potatoes and onions should be getting browned at edges.

5. Gently spread mustard over potato crust. Sprinkle with sauerkraut and arrange kielbasa slices on top. Sprinkle cheese over all.

6. Cook on High for another 1½ hours, again with lid vented at one end.

NOTE This is a hearty "pizza" that is nice to make on cold, snowy days. It is a meal in itself.

VEAL HAWAIIAN

DOROTHY VANDEEST, MEMPHIS, TN

Makes: 4 servings
PREP. TIME: 20 MINUTES
COOKING TIME: 6 HOURS
IDEAL SLOW-COOKER SIZE: 4-QUART

1½ lbs. boneless veal shoulder, trimmed of all fat and cut into 1-inch cubes
1 cup water
¼ cup sherry
2 Tbsp. low-sodium soy sauce
1 tsp. ground ginger
1 tsp. artificial sweetener

1. Lightly brown veal in a nonstick skillet.
2. Combine remaining ingredients in slow cooker. Stir in veal.
3. Cover. Cook on Low 6 hours.

VARIATION

You may substitute pork shoulder for the veal. This is tasty served over rice.

Poultry AND Fish
MAIN DISHES

CHICKEN TORTILLA SOUP

BECKY HARDER, MONUMENT, CO
Photo appears in color section.

Makes: 4 servings
PREP. TIME: 15 MINUTES
COOKING TIME: 5–6 HOURS
IDEAL SLOW-COOKER SIZE: 3-QUART

15 oz. can no-salt-added black beans, undrained

15 oz. can Mexican stewed tomatoes

½ cup salsa of your choice

4 oz. can chopped green chilies

6 oz. can no-salt-added tomato sauce

leftover chicken

1 oz. (about 12 chips) tortilla chips

½ cup fat-free cheddar cheese

1. Combine all ingredients except chicken, chips, and cheese in large slow cooker.

2. Cover. Cook on Low 5–6 hours. Add leftover chicken the last hour of cooking.

3. To serve, put a handful of chips in each individual soup bowl. Ladle soup over chips. Top with cheese.

NOTE Garnish with avocado and lime wedge.

MARINATED CHINESE CHICKEN SALAD

LEE ANN HAZLETT, DELAVAN, WI

Makes: 8 servings
PREP. TIME: 25 MINUTES
COOKING TIME: 3–8 HOURS
IDEAL SLOW-COOKER SIZE: 5- TO 6-QUART

Marinade

3 cloves minced garlic

1 Tbsp. fresh ginger, grated

1 tsp. dried red pepper flakes

2 Tbsp. honey

3 Tbsp. low-sodium soy sauce

6 boneless, skinless chicken breast halves

Dressing

½ cup rice wine vinegar

1 clove garlic, minced

1 tsp. fresh grated ginger

1 Tbsp. honey

Salad

1 large head iceberg lettuce, shredded

2 carrots, julienned

½ cup chopped roasted peanuts

¼ cup chopped cilantro

½ package maifun noodles, fried in hot oil

1. Mix marinade ingredients in a small bowl.

2. Place chicken in slow cooker and pour marinade over chicken, coating each piece well.

3. Cover. Cook on Low 6–8 hours, or on High 3–4 hours.

4. Remove chicken from slow cooker and cool. Reserve juices. Shred chicken into bite-sized pieces.

5. In a small bowl, combine the dressing ingredients with ½ cup of the juice from the slow cooker.

6. In a large serving bowl toss together the shredded chicken, lettuce, carrots, peanuts, cilantro, and noodles.

7. Just before serving, drizzle with the salad dressing. Toss well and serve.

VARIATION

You may substitute chow mein noodles for the maifun noodles.

SUNNY CHICKEN

PHYLLIS GOOD, LANCASTER, PA

Makes: 6–8 servings
PREP. TIME: 20–30 MINUTES
COOKING TIME: 4–6 HOURS
STANDING TIME: 15 MINUTES
IDEAL SLOW-COOKER SIZE: 6-QUART

1 large onion, sliced into thin rings, divided

3 sweet, juicy oranges, each cut into thin slices, divided

3 lemons, thinly sliced, divided

3 limes, thinly sliced, divided

9 fresh rosemary sprigs, divided

2 Tbsp. minced garlic, divided

6 lb. whole chicken

salt and pepper, to taste

1. Layer ⅓ of the onion slices, 1 sliced orange, 1 sliced lemon, and 1 sliced lime into your slow cooker. Top with 3 rosemary sprigs and ⅓ of the minced garlic.

2. Stuff the chicken with half the remaining onion slices, 1 sliced orange, 1 sliced lemon, and 1 sliced lime, 3 rosemary sprigs, and half the remaining garlic. Place the stuffed chicken— upside down—in your slow cooker. (That helps to keep the breast meat from drying out.)

3. Sprinkle with plenty of salt and pepper. Spread the rest of the onion, orange, lemon, and lime slices, and the remaining rosemary sprigs and garlic around the chicken and on top of it.

4. Cover. Cook on Low 4–6 hours, or until meat is tender but not dry.

5. Remove chicken from cooker and place right-side up on rimmed baking sheet. Place under broiler until top is nicely browned, only a minute or so, watching closely.

6. Cover chicken with foil for 15 minutes. Then carve, put the pieces on a platter, and spoon the citrus and onion slices over top before serving.

BEER BRAISED CHICKEN

HOPE COMERFORD, CLINTON TOWNSHIP, MI
Photo appears in color section.

Makes: 6–8 servings
PREP. TIME: 8–10 MINUTES
COOKING TIME: 8–9 HOURS
IDEAL SLOW-COOKER SIZE: 6½- TO 7-QUART

6 lb. whole chicken

1 medium onion, quartered

½ stick butter, cut up

12 oz. beer

Rub

½ tsp. salt

⅛ tsp. pepper

1 tsp. dried basil

1 Tbsp. garlic powder

1. Take the giblets out of your chicken breast; rinse the chicken and dry it. Place the chicken breast side down in your slow cooker insert.

2. Stuff it with your onion pieces and place some butter under the skin and around the chicken.

3. Pour the beer over the top. Combine the rub ingredients and sprinkle over the top.

4. Cover and cook on Low for 8–9 hours.

STEWED ASIAN CHICKEN

STANLEY KROPF, ELKHART, IN

Makes: 4–6 servings
PREP. TIME: 15–20 MINUTES
COOKING TIME: 4 HOURS
IDEAL SLOW-COOKER SIZE: 4- TO 5-QUART

1 whole chicken, cut up

3 Tbsp. hot sweet mustard, or 2 Tbsp. hot mustard and 1 Tbsp. honey

2 Tbsp. soy sauce

1 tsp. ground ginger

1 tsp. cumin

1. Place chicken in slow cooker.

2. Mix the remaining ingredients in a bowl. Taste and adjust seasonings if you want. Pour over chicken.

3. Cover and cook on High for at least 4 hours, or until tender.

TIPS

This is a folk recipe, so the cook should experiment to taste. Experiment with a variety of optional ingredients, such as teriyaki sauce, oyster sauce, cardamom, sesame and olive oil, dry vermouth, and garlic, in whatever amount and combination seems right.

If you cook the dish longer than 4 hours, the chicken tends to fall apart. In any event, serve it in a bowl large enough to hold the chicken and broth.

Serve this with cooked plain or saffron rice.

CURRIED CHICKEN WITH FRUIT

MARLENE BOGARD, NEWTON, KS

Makes: 5 servings
PREP. TIME: 20 MINUTES
COOKING TIME: 4¼–5¼ HOURS
IDEAL SLOW-COOKER SIZE: 5-QUART

2½–3½ lb. fryer chicken, cut up
  salt to taste
  pepper to taste
1 Tbsp. curry powder
1 garlic clove, crushed or minced
1 Tbsp. melted butter
½ cup chicken broth, or 1 chicken bouillon cube dissolved in ½ cup water
2 Tbsp. onion, chopped fine
29 oz. can sliced peaches
½ cup pitted dried plums
3 Tbsp. cornstarch
3 Tbsp. cold water

TIP

Serve over rice. Offer peanuts, shredded coconut, and fresh pineapple chunks as condiments.

1. Grease interior of slow-cooker crock.

2. Sprinkle chicken with salt and pepper. Arrange in slow cooker.

3. Combine curry, garlic, butter, broth, and onions in bowl.

4. Drain peaches, reserving syrup. Add ½ cup syrup to curry mixture. Pour over chicken. Lift top layer of meat and spoon syrup over pieces on bottom layer.

5. Cover. Cook on Low 4–5 hours, or until instant-read meat thermometer inserted in thighs (but not against bone) registers 165°F.

6. Remove chicken pieces from cooker to platter. Keep warm.

7. Turn cooker on High. Stir in dried plums.

8. Dissolve cornstarch in cold water in small bowl. Stir into hot sauce in cooker.

9. Cover. Cook on High 10 minutes, or until thickened.

10. Stir in peaches.

11. To serve, place chicken on platter and spoon fruit and sauce over top.

TWENTY-CLOVE CHICKEN

NANCY SAVAGE, FACTORYVILLE, PA

Makes: 6 servings
PREP. TIME: 10 MINUTES
COOKING TIME: 5–6 HOURS
IDEAL SLOW-COOKER SIZE: 4-QUART

¼ cup dry white wine

2 Tbsp. chopped dried parsley

2 tsp. dried basil leaves

1 tsp. dried oregano

pinch of crushed red pepper flakes

20 cloves of garlic (about 1 head)

4 celery ribs, chopped

6 boneless, skinless chicken breast halves

1 lemon, juice and zest

fresh herbs, optional

> **TIP**
> To preserve garlic longer, separate garlic cloves from the bud. Place in plastic containers and freeze. Take out what you need when you need it.

1. Combine wine, dried parsley, dried basil, dried oregano, and dried red peppers in large bowl.

2. Add garlic cloves and celery. Coat well.

3. Transfer garlic and celery to slow cooker with slotted spoon.

4. Add chicken to herb mixture. Coat well. Place chicken on top of vegetables in slow cooker.

5. Sprinkle lemon juice and zest in slow cooker. Add any remaining herb mixture.

6. Cover. Cook on Low for 5–6 hours, or until instant-read meat thermometer registers 165°F and chicken is no longer pink in center.

7. Garnish with fresh herbs if desired.

VARIATION

For browned chicken, sauté uncooked breasts in large skillet in 1 Tbsp. olive oil over medium heat. Cook for 5 minutes on each side, or until golden brown. Then proceed with steps above.

CHICKEN CORDON BLEU BUNDLES

MELANIE THROWER, MCPHERSON, KS

Makes: 6 servings
PREP. TIME: 15 MINUTES
COOKING TIME: 4 HOURS
IDEAL SLOW-COOKER SIZE: 4-QUART

3 whole chicken breasts, split and deboned
6 pieces thinly sliced ham
6 slices Swiss cheese
  salt to taste
  pepper to taste
6 slices bacon
¼ cup water
1 tsp. chicken bouillon granules
½ cup white cooking wine
1 tsp. cornstarch
¼ cup cold water

1. Flatten chicken to ⅛–¼-inch thickness. Place a slice of ham and a slice of cheese on top of each flattened breast. Sprinkle with salt and pepper. Roll up and wrap with strip of bacon. Secure with toothpick. Place in slow cooker.

2. Combine ¼ cup water, granules, and wine. Pour into slow cooker.

3. Cover. Cook on High 4 hours.

4. Combine cornstarch and ¼ cup cold water. Add to slow cooker. Cook until sauce thickens.

SPICY SWEET CHICKEN

CAROLYN BAER, CONRATH, WI
Photo appears in color section.

Makes: 8 servings
PREP. TIME: 25 MINUTES
COOKING TIME: 4–7½ HOURS
IDEAL SLOW-COOKER SIZE: 6-QUART

- 6 lbs. chicken breasts, thighs, and/or legs, skinned
- 1 Tbsp. oil of your choice
- 16 oz. can whole berry cranberry sauce, divided
- ¼ cup spicy-sweet Catalina salad dressing
- 2 Tbsp. dry onion soup mix
- 1 Tbsp. cornstarch

1. Rinse chicken. Pat dry. Brown in hot oil in skillet. Arrange in slow cooker.

2. In a bowl, combine half of cranberry sauce and all of salad dressing and soup mix. Pour over chicken.

3. Cover. Cook on Low 7 hours or on High 3½ hours.

4. Stir cornstarch into remaining cranberry sauce in bowl. Stir into chicken mixture.

5. Turn slow cooker to High. Cover and cook 30–45 minutes more, or until thickened and bubbly.

TIP
Serve over cooked noodles
or rice.

BUTTER CHICKEN

PAT BISHOP, BEDMINSTER, PA

Makes: 8–12 servings
PREP. TIME: 20 MINUTES
COOKING TIME: 4¼ HOURS
IDEAL SLOW-COOKER SIZE: 5- OR 6-QUART

2	onions, diced
3	cloves garlic, minced
3	Tbsp. butter, softened to room temperature
2	Tbsp. grated fresh ginger
2	Tbsp. packed brown sugar
2	tsp. chili powder
¾	tsp. ground coriander
¾	tsp. turmeric
½	tsp. ground cinnamon
½	tsp. ground cumin
½	tsp. salt
¼	tsp. black pepper
28	oz. can diced tomatoes, undrained
1	cup chicken broth
¼	cup peanut butter, almond butter, or cashew butter
3	lbs. boneless, skinless chicken thighs
1	cup sour cream
2	Tbsp. chopped fresh cilantro

1. Grease interior of slow-cooker crock.

2. In crock combine onions, garlic, butter, fresh ginger, brown sugar, chili powder, coriander, turmeric, cinnamon, cumin, salt, pepper, and tomatoes.

3. In a bowl, whisk broth with nut butter. Pour into crock. Stir everything together until well blended.

4. Settle chicken thighs into sauce, submerging as much as possible.

5. Cover. Cook on Low for 4 hours, or until instant-read meat thermometer registers 165°F when stuck in center of thigh pieces.

6. Remove chicken with slotted spoon and place in bowl. Cover and keep warm.

7. With immersion blender, purée sauce until smooth. Add chicken back into sauce.

8. Cover. Cook another 15 minutes, or until heated through.

9. Stir in sour cream. Serve sprinkled with cilantro over basmati rice.

HERBY BARBECUED CHICKEN

LAUREN M. EBERHARD, SENECA, IL

Makes: 4–6 servings
PREP. TIME: 10 MINUTES
COOKING TIME: 4 HOURS
IDEAL SLOW-COOKER SIZE: 4- OR 5-QUART

1 whole chicken, cut up, or 8 boneless, skinless chicken thighs

1 onion, sliced thin

1 bottle your favorite barbecue sauce

1 tsp. dried oregano

1 tsp. dried basil

1. Grease interior of slow-cooker crock.

2. Place chicken in slow cooker.

3. Mix onion slices, sauce, oregano, and basil together in a bowl. Pour over chicken, covering as well as possible.

4. Cover and cook on Low 4 hours, or until instant-read meat thermometer registers 165°F when stuck in center of thighs.

VARIATION

Use cubed chicken and then add a can of beans to Step 3.

HONEY GARLIC CHICKEN

DONNA TRELOAR, MUNCIE, IN

Makes: 4 servings
PREP. TIME: 10 MINUTES
COOKING TIME: 4 HOURS
IDEAL SLOW-COOKER SIZE: 4-QUART

4 boneless, skinless chicken thighs
⅓ cup honey
1 cup ketchup
2 Tbsp. soy sauce
4 garlic cloves, minced

1. Grease interior of slow-cooker crock.

2. Place chicken thighs in crock.

3. In a bowl, mix together honey, ketchup, soy sauce, and minced garlic. Pour over chicken.

4. Cover. Cook on Low 4 hours or until instant-read meat thermometer registers 165°F when inserted into center of thighs.

5. Serve chicken and sauce together.

VARIATION

Add sliced onions to the bottom of the crock before putting chicken in.

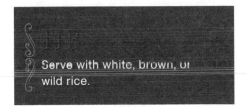

Serve with white, brown, or wild rice.

CHICKEN TIKKI MASALA

SUSAN KASTING, JENKS, OK

Makes: 6–8 servings
PREP. TIME: 20 MINUTES
COOKING TIME: 4¼ HOURS
IDEAL SLOW-COOKER SIZE: 6-QUART

4 lbs. boneless, skinless chicken thighs
1 medium onion, chopped
3 cloves garlic, minced
1½ Tbsp. grated ginger
29 oz. can pureed tomatoes
1 Tbsp. olive oil
1 Tbsp. garam masala
½ tsp. ground cumin
½ tsp. paprika
1 cinnamon stick
1 tsp. salt
1–1½ tsp. cayenne pepper, depending on how much heat you like
2 bay leaves
¾ cup plain Greek yogurt
½ cup cream
1½ tsp. cornstarch

TIP
Serve over rice.

1. Grease interior of slow-cooker crock.

2. Lay thighs in crock. If you need to make a second layer, stagger pieces so they don't directly overlap each other.

3. In a good-sized bowl, mix together onion, garlic, ginger, tomatoes, olive oil, garam masala, cumin, paprika, cinnamon stick, salt, cayenne pepper, and bay leaves. Pour over chicken.

4. Cover. Cook 4 hours on Low, or until instant-read meat thermometer registers 165°F when inserted in center of thigh.

5. Remove thighs and keep warm on platter or bowl.

6. Mix Greek yogurt into sauce in cooker.

7. In a small bowl, combine cream and cornstarch until smooth. Mix into sauce in cooker.

8. Return chicken to cooker.

9. Cover. Cook an additional 15–20 minutes, or until sauce has thickened. Discard bay leaves.

TANGY CHICKEN

MARILYN KURTZ, WILLOW STREET, PA

Makes: 6–8 servings
PREP. TIME: 15 MINUTES
COOKING TIME: 4–5 HOURS
IDEAL SLOW-COOKER SIZE: 5-QUART

16 oz. jar chunky salsa, as hot or mild as you like
     half an envelope dry taco seasoning mix
½   cup peach or apricot preserves
4   lbs. boneless, skinless chicken thighs

1. Grease interior of slow-cooker crock.

2. Pour salsa into cooker, and then stir in taco seasoning and preserves, mixing well.

3. Place chicken down into sauce, making sure all pieces are covered as much as possible.

4. Cover. Cook on Low 4–5 hours, or until instant-read meat thermometer registers 160°–165°F when stuck in center of thighs.

5. Serve over cooked rice.

Serve this with a side of steamed broccoli.

ASIAN-STYLE SESAME CHICKEN

ANNE TOWNSEND, ALBUQUERQUE, NM

Makes: 4 servings
PREP. TIME: 5 MINUTES
COOKING TIME: 4–8 HOURS
IDEAL SLOW-COOKER SIZE: 3-QUART

1 Tbsp. hot chili sesame oil

4 large chicken thighs

3 cloves garlic, sliced

½ cup brown sugar

3 Tbsp. soy sauce

1. Spread oil around the bottom of your slow cooker.

2. Rinse chicken well and remove excess fat. Pat dry. Place in your slow cooker.

3. Sprinkle garlic slices over top of the chicken. Crumble brown sugar over top. Drizzle with soy sauce.

4. Cover and cook on Low 4–8 hours, or until thighs are tender, but not dry.

5. Serve over rice, prepared with the juice from the cooked chicken instead of water.

GARLIC MUSHROOM CHICKEN THIGHS

ELAINE VIGODA, ROCHESTER, NY

Makes: 6 servings
PREP. TIME: 15 MINUTES
COOKING TIME: 4 HOURS
IDEAL SLOW-COOKER SIZE: 5-QUART

3	Tbsp. flour
6	boneless, skinless chicken thighs
8–10	garlic cloves, peeled and very lightly crushed
1	Tbsp. oil
¾	lb. fresh mushrooms, any combination of varieties, cut into bite-sized pieces or slices
⅓	cup balsamic vinegar
1¼	cups chicken broth
1–2	bay leaves
½	tsp. dried thyme, or 4 sprigs fresh thyme
2	tsp. apricot jam

1. Grease interior of slow-cooker crock.
2. Place flour in strong plastic bag without any holes. One by one, put each chicken thigh in bag, hold the bag shut, and shake it to flour the thighs fully.
3. Place thighs in crock. If you need to make a second layer, stagger the pieces so they don't directly overlap.
4. Sauté garlic in oil in skillet just until it begins to brown.
5. Sprinkle garlic over thighs, including those on the bottom layer.
6. Scatter cut-up mushrooms over thighs, too, remembering those on the bottom layer.
7. Mix remaining ingredients together in a bowl, stirring to break up the jam.
8. When well mixed, pour into the cooker along the edges so you don't wash the vegetables off the chicken pieces.
9. Cover. Cook on Low for 4 hours, or until an instant-read meat thermometer registers 165°F when stuck into thighs.
10. Serve meat topped with vegetables, with sauce spooned over, discarding bay leaves.

EASY CREAMY CHICKEN

COLLEEN HEATWOLE, BURTON, MI

Makes: 6 servings
PREP. TIME: 10 MINUTES
COOKING TIME: 4 HOURS
IDEAL SLOW-COOKER SIZE: 5-QUART

10 boneless, skinless chicken thighs

2 envelopes dry onion soup mix

1 cup reduced-fat sour cream

10¾ oz. can cream of chicken soup

1. Grease interior of slow-cooker crock.

2. Place chicken thighs in crock. If you need to make a second layer, stagger pieces so they don't directly overlap each other.

3. In a bowl combine dry soup mix, sour cream, and chicken soup until well mixed.

4. Pour over chicken, making sure to cover pieces on the bottom with sauce, too.

5. Cover. Cook on Low 4 hours, or until instant-read meat thermometer registers 165°F when stuck in center of thighs.

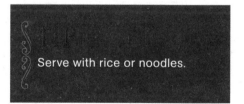

TIP
Serve with rice or noodles.

PASTA À LA CARBONARA ♥ page 119

ORCHARD HAM ♥ page 121

BEER BRAISED CHICKEN ♥ page 133

SPICY SWEET CHICKEN ♥ page 138

GARLIC MUSHROOM
CHICKEN THIGHS ♥ page 145

ITALIAN CHICKEN FAJITA WRAPS ♥ page 160

BUFFALO CHICKEN STROMBOLI ♥ page 164

SAUCY TURKEY BREAST ♥ page 168

TURKEY MEAT LOAF ♥ page 172

BBQ BALLS ♥ page 174

WHITE BEAN AND FENNEL SOUP ♥ page 190

LENTIL RICE SALAD BOWL ♥ page 191

CHERRY TOMATO SPAGHETTI SAUCE
page 192

PASTA BEAN POT
page 196

SUMMER SQUASH LASAGNA
page 198

VEGETARIAN LASAGNA
page 202

TOMATO GALETTE ♥ page 213

CHEESE-STUFFED PIZZA ♥ page 215

GOLDEN CARROTS
page 222

BEETS WITH CAPERS
page 228

HOMEMADE REFRIED BEANS ♥ page 246

BARBECUED CHICKEN WINGS

ROSEMARIE FITZGERALD, GIBSONIA, PA

Makes: 10 full-sized servings
PREP. TIME: 5 MINUTES
COOKING TIME: 3–4 HOURS
IDEAL SLOW-COOKER SIZE: 5-QUART

5 lbs. chicken wings, tips cut off

12 oz. bottle chili sauce

⅓ cup lemon juice

1 Tbsp. Worcestershire sauce

2 Tbsp. molasses

1 tsp. salt

2 tsp. chili powder

¼ tsp. hot pepper sauce

dash garlic powder

1. Grease interior of slow-cooker crock.

2. Use kitchen scissors or a sharp sturdy knife to cut through the 2 joints on each wing. Discard the wing tip.

3. Place the other 2 pieces of each wing into the crock. As you create layers, stagger the pieces so they don't directly overlap each other.

4. Combine remaining ingredients in a bowl. Spoon over chicken, lifting up pieces on top layers to sauce pieces on lower layers, too.

5. Cover. Cook on Low 3–4 hours, or until instant-read meat thermometer registers 160°–165° when stuck in meaty part of wings (but not against bone).

NOTE These wings are also a great appetizer, yielding about 15 appetizer-size servings.

TIP
Take any leftover chicken off the bone and combine with leftover sauce. Serve over cooked pasta for a second meal.

TASTY DRUMSTICKS

TRUDY KUTTER, CORFU, NY

Makes: 8 servings
PREP. TIME: 20 MINUTES
COOKING TIME: 6 HOURS
IDEAL SLOW-COOKER SIZE: 5-QUART

5–6 lbs. chicken drumsticks, skin removed

8 oz. can tomato sauce

½ cup soy sauce

½ cup brown sugar

2 tsp. minced garlic

3 Tbsp. cornstarch

¼ cup cold water

1. Place drumsticks in slow cooker.

2. Combine tomato sauce, soy sauce, brown sugar, and garlic in a bowl.

3. Pour over drumsticks, making sure that each drumstick is sauced.

4. Cover. Cook on Low 6 hours, or until chicken is tender.

5. Remove chicken with tongs to a platter and keep warm.

6. Strain juices into saucepan.

7. In a bowl combine cornstarch and water until smooth.

8. Add cornstarch mixture to saucepan.

9. Bring mixture to a boil, stirring continuously.

10. Stir for 2 minutes until thickened.

WILD RICE WITH CHICKEN

PHYLLIS GOOD, LANCASTER, PA

Makes: 4–5 servings
PREP. TIME: 20 MINUTES
COOKING TIME: 4–8 HOURS
IDEAL SLOW-COOKER SIZE: 4-QUART

1 cup wild rice, uncooked
¼ cup chopped onion
¼ cup chopped celery
  leftover chicken, chopped
3 cups chicken stock
¼–½ tsp. salt, depending how salty your stock is
⅛ tsp. pepper
¼ tsp. garlic powder
½ tsp. dried sage
¼ lb. fresh mushrooms, sliced
¼ cup slivered almonds
1 Tbsp. fresh parsley

1. Wash and drain rice.

2. Combine all ingredients, except mushrooms, almonds, and parsley, in greased slow cooker. Mix well.

3. Cover. Cook on Low 4–8 hours, or until rice is tender. Don't lift the lid to check on things until the rice has cooked at least 4 hours.

4. Ten minutes before the end of the cooking time, stir in the mushrooms. Cover and continue cooking.

5. Just before serving, stir in slivered almonds. Garnish with fresh parsley.

BASIL CHICKEN

SARAH NIESSEN, AKRON, PA

Makes: 4–6 servings
PREP. TIME: 15 MINUTES
COOKING TIME: 4–5 HOURS
IDEAL SLOW-COOKER SIZE: 5- OR 6-QUART

1 lb. baby carrots

2 medium onions, sliced

1–2 cups celery slices and leaves

3 lb. chicken, cut up

½ cup chicken broth, or white cooking wine

2 tsp. salt

½ tsp. black pepper

1 tsp. dried basil

1. Grease interior of slow-cooker crock.

2. Place carrots, onions, and celery in bottom of slow cooker.

3. Add chicken.

4. Pour broth over chicken.

5. Sprinkle with salt, pepper, and basil.

6. Cover. Cook on Low 4–5 hours, or until instant-read meat thermometer registers 165°F when stuck in center of thighs (but not against bone) and vegetables are as tender as you like them.

NOTE This is a favorite busy-day supper. All you have to do when you get home is cook some pasta or slice some French bread, and dinner is served!

COMFORTING CHICKEN AND STUFFING

ELVA ENGEL, GAP, PA
LAUREN BAILEY, DILLSBURG, PA

Makes: 10–12 servings
PREP. TIME: 20–25 MINUTES
COOKING TIME: 3–4 HOURS
IDEAL SLOW-COOKER SIZE: 7- TO 8-QUART

2½ cups chicken broth
2 sticks butter, melted
½ cup chopped onion
½ cup chopped celery
¼ cup dried parsley flakes
1½ tsp. rubbed sage
1 tsp. poultry seasoning
1 tsp. salt
1¼ tsp. coarsely ground black pepper
2 eggs
10¾ oz. can cream of chicken soup
12 cups day-old bread cubes, cut or torn into ½-inch pieces
leftover chicken, chopped, divided

1. Grease interior of slow-cooker crock.

2. In a bowl, combine chicken broth, melted butter, chopped onion, celery, parsley flakes, sage, poultry seasoning, salt, and pepper.

3. In another bowl, combine eggs and soup. Stir into broth mixture until smooth.

4. Put bread cubes in a large bowl. Pour broth-soup mixture over bread. Toss well until all bread cubes are dampened.

5. Layer ⅓ of bread mixture into crock.

6. Cover with half of cooked chicken.

7. Cover with half of remaining bread mixture.

8. Top with remaining chicken.

9. Cover with remaining bread mixture.

10. Cover. Cook on Low 3–4 hours. If you like a crusty finish on stuffing, take lid off during last 45 minutes of cooking.

OLD-FASHIONED STEWED CHICKEN

BONNIE GOERING, BRIDGEWATER, VA

Makes: 6–8 servings
PREP. TIME: 20 MINUTES
COOKING TIME: 3–4 HOURS
IDEAL SLOW-COOKER SIZE: 5-QUART

3–4 lb. chicken, cut up

1 small onion, cut into wedges

1 rib celery, sliced

1 carrot, sliced

1 Tbsp. chopped fresh parsley, or 1 tsp. dried parsley

1 Tbsp. chopped fresh thyme, or 1 tsp. dried thyme

1 Tbsp. chopped fresh rosemary, or 1 tsp. dried rosemary

3 tsp. salt

¼ tsp. pepper

3–4 cups hot water

⅓ cup flour

1. Grease interior of slow-cooker crock.

2. Place chicken in slow cooker. Scatter vegetables, herbs, and seasonings around it and over top. Pour water down along interior wall of cooker so as not to disturb the other ingredients.

3. Cover. Cook on Low 3–4 hours, or until instant-read thermometer registers 165°F when stuck in thighs, but not against bone.

4. Remove chicken from cooker. When cool enough to handle, debone. Set aside and keep warm.

5. In small bowl, stir ⅓ cup flour into 1 cup chicken broth from slow cooker.

6. When smooth, stir back into slow cooker. Continue cooking on Low until broth thickens, stirring occasionally to prevent lumps from forming.

7. When gravy is bubbly and thickened, stir in chicken pieces.

REUBEN CHICKEN CASSEROLE

MARYANN MARKANO, WILMINGTON, DE

Makes: 6 servings
PREP. TIME: 25–30 MINUTES
COOKING TIME: 4 HOURS
IDEAL SLOW-COOKER SIZE: 5-QUART

2 16-oz. cans sauerkraut, rinsed and drained, divided
1 cup Light Russian salad dressing, divided
6 boneless, skinless chicken breast halves, divided
1 Tbsp. prepared mustard, divided
6 slices Swiss cheese
    fresh parsley for garnish, optional

1. Place half the sauerkraut in the slow cooker. Drizzle with ⅓ cup dressing.

2. Top with 3 chicken breast halves. Spread half the mustard on top of the chicken.

3. Top with remaining sauerkraut and chicken breasts. Drizzle with another ⅓ cup dressing. (Save the remaining dressing until serving time.)

4. Cover and cook on Low for 4 hours, or until the chicken is tender, but not dry or mushy.

5. To serve, place a breast half on each of 6 plates. Divide the sauerkraut over the chicken. Top each with a slice of cheese and a drizzle of the remaining dressing. Garnish with parsley if you wish, just before serving.

> TIP
> Be sure to read a recipe the whole way through before beginning to cook, so you are certain you have all the ingredients you need.

CHICKEN CACCIATORE WITH SPAGHETTI

PHYLLIS GOOD, LANCASTER, PA

Makes: 4–5 servings
PREP. TIME: 15 MINUTES
COOKING TIME: 6–6½ HOURS
IDEAL SLOW-COOKER SIZE: 4-QUART

2 onions, sliced

2½–3 lbs. chicken legs

2 garlic cloves, minced

16 oz. can stewed tomatoes

8 oz. can tomato sauce

1 tsp. salt

¼ tsp. pepper

1–2 tsp. dried oregano

½ tsp. dried basil

1 bay leaf

¼ cup white wine

1. Place onions in bottom of slow cooker.

2. Lay chicken legs over onions.

3. Combine remaining ingredients. Pour over chicken.

4. Cover. Cook on Low 6–6½ hours.

5. Remove bay leaf. Serve over hot buttered spaghetti, linguini, or fettuccine.

CHICKEN PASTA

EVELYN L. WARD, GREELEY, CO

Makes: 4 servings
PREP. TIME: 25–30 MINUTES
COOKING TIME: 4¼ HOURS
IDEAL SLOW-COOKER SIZE: 4-QUART

    leftover chicken, diced
1   large zucchini, diced
1   envelope chicken gravy mix
2   Tbsp. water
2   Tbsp. evaporated milk, or cream
1   large tomato, chopped
4   cups cooked macaroni
8   oz. smoked Gouda cheese, grated

1. Place the chicken, zucchini, gravy mix, and water into the slow cooker and stir together.

2. Cover. Cook on Low 4 hours.

3. Add milk and tomato. Cook an additional 20 minutes.

4. Stir in pasta. Top with cheese. Serve immediately.

CHEESY BUFFALO CHICKEN PASTA

CHRISTINA GERBER, APPLE CREEK, OH

Makes: 6–8 servings
PREP. TIME: 15 MINUTES
COOKING TIME: 4½–5 HOURS
IDEAL SLOW-COOKER SIZE: 6-QUART

  3 cups chicken broth
  ½ cup buffalo wing sauce, divided
  1 Tbsp. dry ranch dressing mix
  ¾ tsp. garlic powder
  ½ tsp. salt
  ⅛ tsp. black pepper
  1½ lbs. boneless, skinless chicken thighs
  8 oz. pkg. cream cheese, cubed
  1 cup shredded sharp cheddar cheese
  1 Tbsp. cornstarch
  1 Tbsp. water
  1 lb. linguini
     chopped cilantro, optional

1. Grease interior of slow-cooker crock.

2. Mix broth, ¼ cup buffalo sauce, ranch dressing mix, and seasonings in crock.

3. Submerge chicken in sauce.

4. Scatter cubed cream cheese and shredded cheese over chicken.

5. Cover. Cook on Low 4 hours, or until instant-read thermometer registers 160°–165°F when stuck in thighs.

6. When chicken is fully cooked, remove to bowl and shred with 2 forks. (Cover crock to keep sauce warm.)

7. Add remaining ¼ cup buffalo sauce to shredded chicken and toss to coat. Set aside but keep warm.

8. In a small bowl, stir cornstarch and water together until smooth. Stir into warm sauce in crock until sauce smooths out and thickens.

9. Break linguini in half and place in crock.

10. Top with shredded chicken and cover.

11. Cook on High 30–60 minutes, or just until linguini is fully cooked. Stir 3–4 times during cooking.

12. If you need more liquid for noodles to cook, add water ¼ cup at a time.

13. Garnish with cilantro if you wish, and serve immediately.

NOTE This is a great one-pot meal. No extra pan needed to cook the pasta!

CHICKEN TETRAZZINI

JOYCE SLAYMAKER, STRASBURG, PA

Makes: 4 servings
PREP. TIME: 10 MINUTES
COOKING TIME: 6–8 HOURS
IDEAL SLOW-COOKER SIZE: 3- TO 4-QUART

2–3 cups diced cooked chicken
2 cups chicken broth
1 small onion, chopped
¼ cup sauterne, white wine, or milk
½ cup slivered almonds
2 4-oz. cans sliced mushrooms, drained
10¾ oz. can cream of mushroom soup
1 lb. spaghetti, cooked
grated Parmesan cheese

1. Combine all ingredients except spaghetti and cheese in slow cooker.

2. Cover. Cook on Low 6–8 hours.

3. Serve over buttered spaghetti. Sprinkle with Parmesan cheese.

VARIATIONS

❧ Place spaghetti in large baking dish. Pour sauce in center. Sprinkle with Parmesan cheese. Broil until lightly browned.

❧ Add 10-oz. pkg. frozen peas to Step 1.

TIP
Keep cooked, deboned chicken in the freezer for times when recipes call for prepped chicken. It cuts down on meal prepping time.

CHICKEN ALFREDO

HOPE COMERFORD, CLINTON TOWNSHIP, MI

Makes: 8–12 servings
PREP. TIME: 5 MINUTES
COOKING TIME: 4–6 HOURS
IDEAL SLOW-COOKER SIZE: 2- TO 3-QUART

3½ cups chicken broth
2 cups heavy cream
1 stick butter, unsalted
6 cloves garlic, minced
½ cup flour or cornstarch
1 cup grated Parmesan cheese or Parmesan/Romano blend
leftover chicken, chopped into bite-sized pieces
cooked pasta
fresh chopped parsley, optional

1. Spray the inside of your crock with nonstick spray, then add the chicken broth, cream, butter, and garlic.

2. Cook on Low for 4–6 hours.

3. Briskly whisk in the flour or cornstarch a very little at a time until it is thickened.

4. Add the cheese and chicken and cook for an additional 30–40 minutes, or until the chicken is warmed through.

5. Serve over cooked pasta. Garnish with fresh parsley if you wish.

TIP

Freeze the rest of this sauce to use another time.

ITALIAN CHICKEN FAJITA WRAPS

PHYLLIS GOOD, LANCASTER, PA
Photo appears in color section.

Makes: 6–8 servings
PREP. TIME: 20 MINUTES
COOKING TIME: 2–4 HOURS
CHILLING TIME: 4–8 HOURS OR OVERNIGHT
IDEAL SLOW-COOKER SIZE: 3-QUART

3 lbs. boneless, skinless chicken breasts

4 cloves garlic, sliced thinly

4 Tbsp. dried oregano

2 Tbsp. dried parsley

2 tsp. dried basil

1 tsp. dried thyme

½ tsp. celery seed

2 Tbsp. sugar

1 tsp. salt

1 tsp. freshly ground pepper

2 16-oz. bottles Italian salad dressing

2 cups salsa

2 green bell peppers, sliced in ribs

2 red bell peppers, sliced in ribs

1 large onion, sliced in rings

10 10-inch flour tortillas

Toppings (choose all or some)
freshly grated Parmesan cheese
fresh mozzarella cheese slices
hot sauce, or pickled Italian hot peppers
chopped olives
lemon wedges
shredded lettuce
chopped tomatoes
chopped fresh basil

1. Cut chicken into thin strips. Place in large mixing bowl.

2. Add garlic, herbs, sugar, salt, pepper, salad dressing, and salsa. Mix well. Cover and marinate 4–8 hours or overnight in the fridge.

3. Pour chicken and marinade into slow cooker. Cook on Low for 2–4 hours, until chicken is white through the middle and tender.

4. Spoon the chicken with its sauce into an ovenproof serving dish or rimmed baking sheet. Add the vegetables. Slide it under the broiler for a few minutes until browned spots appear on the chicken and vegetables.

5. Serve with tortillas and toppings and lots of napkins.

CHICKEN SOFT TACOS

KRISTEN ALLEN, HOUSTON, TX

Makes: 6 servings
PREP. TIME: 5 MINUTES
COOKING TIME: 6–8 HOURS
IDEAL SLOW-COOKER SIZE: 5- TO 6-QUART

1–1½ lbs. frozen, boneless, skinless chicken breasts

14½ oz. can low-sodium diced tomatoes with green chilies

1 envelope low-sodium taco seasoning

1. Place chicken breasts in slow cooker.

2. Mix tomatoes and taco seasoning. Pour over chicken.

3. Cover. Cook on Low 6–8 hours.

4. Serve in soft tortillas. Top with salsa, low-fat shredded cheddar cheese, guacamole if your diet allows, and fresh tomatoes.

BARBECUED CHICKEN SANDWICHES

BRITTANY MILLER, MILLERSBURG, OH

Makes: 10 servings
PREP. TIME: 25–30 MINUTES
COOKING TIME: 5 HOURS
IDEAL SLOW-COOKER SIZE: 5- OR 6-QUART

3 lbs. boneless, skinless chicken thighs
1 cup ketchup
1 small onion, chopped
¼ cup water
¼ cup cider vinegar
2 Tbsp. Worcestershire sauce
1 Tbsp. brown sugar
1 garlic clove, minced
1 bay leaf
2 tsp. paprika
1 tsp. dried oregano
1 tsp. chili powder
½ tsp. salt
½ tsp. pepper

TIP

This is enough chicken and sauce to fill up to 10 sandwich rolls.

1. Grease interior of slow-cooker crock.

2. Place chicken in slow cooker.

3. In a medium-sized mixing bowl, combine ketchup, onion, water, vinegar, Worcestershire sauce, brown sugar, garlic, bay leaf, and seasonings. Pour over chicken.

4. Cover. Cook on Low 4 hours, or until instant-read meat thermometer registers 160°–165°F when stuck in center of thighs.

5. Discard bay leaf.

6. Remove chicken to large bowl. Shred meat with 2 forks. Return chicken to slow cooker.

7. Stir shredded chicken and sauce together thoroughly.

8. Cover. Cook on Low 30 minutes.

9. Remove lid. Continue cooking 30 more minutes, allowing sauce to cook off and thicken.

BUFFALO CHICKEN STROMBOLI

Photo appears in color section.

Makes: 4–6 servings
PREP. TIME: 30 MINUTES
COOKING TIME: 2–3 HOURS
STANDING TIME: 5 HOURS OR OVERNIGHT
IDEAL SLOW-COOKER SIZE: 6-QUART

1   ball frozen pizza dough, about 15 oz.

2   cups cooked, shredded chicken

2   green onions, sliced

1   cup shredded mozzarella cheese

⅓   cup shredded sharp cheddar cheese

½   cup ranch dressing

3   Tbsp. Frank's RedHot® Sauce

      few drops liquid smoke, optional

1. Thaw pizza dough per package directions, usually about 5 hours at room temperature or overnight in the fridge.

2. Grease bottom of slow cooker crock. Turn on High and set aside to preheat while you assemble the stromboli.

3. On a lightly floured surface, roll dough out into rectangle, approximately 8" x 12".

4. Sprinkle and spread chicken, onions, and both cheeses evenly over the dough, leaving a 1" border on all sides.

5. In a small bowl, mix ranch dressing, RedHot® Sauce, and optional liquid smoke.

6. Drizzle evenly over layers on dough.

7. Gently tug one short side of the dough over to meet the other short side, nudging the stromboli onto its side as needed, encasing the filling. Pinch seam well to seal.

8. Ease the stromboli into the middle of a large square of parchment paper with the seam side down.

9. Pick up the parchment like a sling with the stromboli in the middle and place it in the hot slow cooker.

10. Cover and cook on High for 2–3 hours, until dough is firm and browned at edges, and filling is oozy and hot.

11. Lift stromboli out, using parchment as a sling. Slice and serve, or else place stromboli on baking sheet and run it under the broiler for a few minutes (watch closely!) to get brown and bubbly on top.

VARIATION

If you don't have Frank's RedHot® Sauce, use a tablespoon or two of the hot sauce you do have, adding white vinegar and a bit of minced garlic to make up 3 tablespoons.

> **TIP**
>
> If you keep the same proportions (2 cups filling, ½–⅔ cup sauce, 1⅓ cups cheese), you can play around with different flavor combinations. Change it up according to what you have on hand and what your family likes.

BARBECUED CHICKEN PIZZA

SUSAN ROTH, SALEM, OR

Makes: 4 to 6 servings
PREP. TIME: 20–25 MINUTES
COOKING TIME: 3 HOURS
STANDING TIME: 2 HOURS BEFORE
YOU BEGIN
IDEAL SLOW-COOKER SIZE: 6-QUART

8   or 12-oz. pkg. prepared pizza dough, depending how thick you like your pizza crust

1   cup barbecue sauce, teriyaki-flavored, or your choice of flavor

2   cups cooked, chopped chicken (your own leftovers, rotisserie chicken, or canned chicken)

20 oz. can pineapple tidbits, drained, optional

½   cup green bell pepper, chopped, optional

¼   cup red onion, diced or sliced, optional

2   cups shredded mozzarella cheese

1. If the dough's been refrigerated, allow it to stand at room temperature for 2 hours.

2. Grease interior of slow-cooker crock.

3. Stretch the dough into a large circle so that it fits into the crock, covering the bottom and reaching up the sides by an inch or so the whole way around. (If the dough is larger than the bottom of the cooker, fold it in half and stretch it to fit the bottom and an inch up the sides. This will make a thicker crust.)

4. Bake crust, uncovered, on High 1 hour.

5. Spread barbecue sauce over hot crust.

6. Drop chopped chicken evenly over sauce.

7. If you wish, spoon pineapple, chopped peppers, and onion over chicken.

8. Sprinkle evenly with cheese.

9. Cover. Cook on High for about 2 hours, or until the crust begins to brown around the edges.

10. Uncover, being careful not to let the condensation on the lid drip onto the pizza.

11. Let stand for 10 minutes. Cut into wedges and serve.

NOTE To make your own cooked chicken, see Old-Fashioned Stewed Chicken recipe on page 152.

HERB-ROASTED TURKEY BREAST

KRISTI SEE, WESKAN, KS

Makes: 6 servings
PREP. TIME: 15 MINUTES
COOKING TIME: 5–7 HOURS
IDEAL SLOW-COOKER SIZE: 6- OR 7-QUART OVAL

5 tsp. lemon juice
1 Tbsp. olive oil
1–2 tsp. pepper
1 tsp. dried rosemary, crushed
1 tsp. dried thyme
1 tsp. garlic salt
6–7 lb. bone-in turkey breast
1 medium onion, cut into wedges
1 celery rib, cut into 2-inch-thick pieces
½ cup white wine or chicken broth

1. Grease interior of slow-cooker crock.

2. In a small bowl, combine lemon juice and olive oil. In another bowl, combine pepper, rosemary, thyme, and garlic salt.

3. With your fingers, carefully loosen skin from both sides of breast. Brush oil mixture under skin. Rub herb-seasoning mixture under and on top of skin.

4. Arrange onion and celery in slow cooker. Place turkey breast, skin-side up, on top of vegetables.

5. Pour wine around breast.

6. Cover. Cook on Low 5–7 hours, or until instant-read meat thermometer registers 165°F when stuck in meaty part of breast (but not against bone).

VARIATION

❧ Add carrot chunks to Step 4 to add more flavor to the turkey broth.

Reserve broth for soups, or thicken with flour-water paste and serve as gravy over sliced turkey.

Freeze broth in pint-sized containers for future use.

Debone turkey and freeze in pint-sized containers for future use. Or freeze any leftover turkey.

SAUCY TURKEY BREAST

KELLY BAILEY, MECHANICSBURG, PA
MICHELE RUVOLA, SELDEN, NY
RUTH FISHER, LEICESTER, NY
Photo appears in color section.

Makes: 6–8 servings
PREP. TIME: 5 MINUTES
COOKING TIME: 1–5 HOURS
IDEAL SLOW-COOKER SIZE: 4- TO 6-QUART

salt and pepper to taste
1 envelope dry onion soup mix
3–5 lb. turkey breast, bone-in or boneless
16 oz. can cranberry sauce, jellied or whole-berry
2 Tbsp. cornstarch
2 Tbsp. cold water

1. Sprinkle salt and pepper and soup mix on the top and bottom of turkey breast. Place turkey in slow cooker.

2. Add cranberry sauce to top of turkey breast.

3. Cover and cook on Low 4–5 hours, or on High 1–3 hours, or until tender but not dry and mushy. (A meat thermometer should read 180°F.)

4. Remove turkey from cooker and allow to rest for 10 minutes. (Keep sauce in cooker.)

5. Meanwhile, cover cooker and turn to High. In a small bowl, mix together cornstarch and cold water until smooth. When sauce is boiling, stir in cornstarch paste. Continue to simmer until sauce thickens.

6. Slice turkey and serve topped with sauce from cooker.

NOTE Try out a recipe you've never had before. It is fun to see the family react to it.

LEMONY TURKEY BREAST

JOYCE SHACKELFORD, GREEN BAY, WI
CAROLYN BAER, CONRATH, WI

Makes: 12 servings
PREP. TIME: 15 MINUTES
COOKING TIME: 7–8 HOURS
STANDING TIME: 15 MINUTES
IDEAL SLOW-COOKER SIZE: 6-QUART

6 lb. bone-in turkey breast, cut in half and skin removed

1 medium lemon, halved

1 tsp. lemon pepper

1 tsp. garlic salt

4 tsp. cornstarch

½ cup fat-free, reduced-sodium chicken broth

1. Place turkey, meaty side up, in slow cooker sprayed with nonfat cooking spray.

2. Squeeze half of lemon over turkey. Sprinkle with lemon pepper and garlic salt.

3. Place lemon halves under turkey.

4. Cover. Cook on Low 7–8 hours or just until turkey is tender.

5. Remove turkey. Discard lemons.

6. Allow turkey to rest 15 minutes before slicing.

7. Combine cornstarch and chicken broth until smooth. Stir into liquid in slow cooker. Cook on High for 10 minutes or until thickened.

CRANBERRY-ORANGE TURKEY BREAST

LEE ANN HAZLETT, DELAVAN, WI

Makes: 9 servings
PREP. TIME: 20 MINUTES
COOKING TIME: 3½–8 HOURS
STANDING TIME: 15 MINUTES
IDEAL SLOW-COOKER SIZE: 6-QUART

½ cup orange marmalade
14 oz. can whole berry cranberry sauce
2 tsp. orange zest, grated
3–4 lb. turkey breast

1. Combine marmalade, cranberry sauce, and zest in a bowl.
2. Place turkey breast in slow cooker and pour half the cranberry-orange mixture over turkey.
3. Cover. Cook on Low 7–8 hours or on High 3½–4 hours, until turkey juices run clear.
4. Add remaining half of cranberry-orange mixture for last half hour of cooking.
5. Remove turkey to warm platter and allow to rest for 15 minutes before slicing.
6. Serve with orange-cranberry sauce.

TURKEY WITH SWEET POTATOES AND DRIED FRUIT

JEAN M. BUTZER, BATAVIA, NY

Makes: 4 servings
PREP. TIME: 30–40 MINUTES
COOKING TIME: 4–5 HOURS
IDEAL SLOW-COOKER SIZE: 5-QUART

2   medium (2 cups) yams or sweet potatoes, cut crosswise into ½-inch-thick slices

2–3   lbs. (3–4) boneless, skinless turkey thighs, cut in half lengthwise

1   cup mixed chopped dried fruit

1   tsp. chopped garlic

½   tsp. salt

¼   tsp. pepper

¾   cup orange juice

¼   cup chopped fresh parsley

1. Grease interior of slow-cooker crock.

2. Place yam slices in slow cooker. Top with turkey thighs.

3. Sprinkle with dried fruit, garlic, salt, and pepper.

4. Gently pour orange juice into cooker down along the sides, being careful not to disturb fruit and seasonings.

5. Cover. Cook on Low 4–5 hours, or until instant-read meat thermometer registers 165°F when stuck in center of thigh.

6. Slice. Spoon juice and dried fruit over top. Then sprinkle with parsley just before serving.

TURKEY MEAT LOAF

MARTHA ANN AUKER, LANDISBURG, PA
Photo appears in color section.

Makes: 8 servings
PREP. TIME: 15 MINUTES
COOKING TIME: 6–8 HOURS
IDEAL SLOW COOKER SIZE: 4-QUART

1½ lbs. lean ground turkey

2 egg whites

⅓ cup ketchup

1 Tbsp. Worcestershire sauce

1 tsp. dried basil

½ tsp. salt

½ tsp. black pepper

2 small onions, chopped

2 potatoes, finely shredded

2 small red bell peppers, finely chopped

1. Combine all ingredients in a large bowl.

2. Shape into a loaf to fit in your slow cooker. Place in slow cooker.

3. Cover. Cook on Low 6–8 hours.

TURKEY LOAF

DOTTIE SCHMIDT, KANSAS CITY, MO

Makes: 10–12 servings
PREP. TIME: 15 MINUTES
COOKING TIME: 3–4 HOURS
IDEAL SLOW-COOKER SIZE: 4- OR 5-QUART

2 lbs. ground turkey

¾ cup dry bread crumbs

⅔ cup finely chopped celery

2 eggs, beaten

4 green onions, finely chopped

½ tsp. salt

¼ tsp. black pepper

2 Tbsp. Worcestershire sauce

2 Tbsp. ketchup

1–2 Tbsp. sesame seeds

1. Grease interior of slow-cooker crock.

2. Make a tinfoil sling for your slow cooker so you can lift the cooked Turkey Loaf out easily. Begin by folding a strip of tinfoil accordion-fashion so that it's about 1½–2 inches wide, and long enough to fit from the top edge of the crock, down inside, and up the other side, plus a 2-inch overhang on each side of the cooker. Make a second strip exactly like the first.

3. Place the one strip in the crock, running from end to end. Place the second strip in the crock, running from side to side. The two strips should form a cross in the bottom of the crock.

4. Combine all ingredients except ketchup and sesame seeds in bowl, mixing together gently but well. Once well mixed, set aside half of the mixture and refrigerate for turkey burgers later this week.

5. Form the remaining turkey mixture into a 6-inch-long loaf and place in crock, centering loaf where foil strips cross.

6. Spread ketchup over top of loaf. Sprinkle with sesame seeds.

7. Cover. Cook on Low for 3–4 hours, or until instant-read meat thermometer registers 165°F when stuck in center of loaf.

8. Using foil handles, lift loaf out of crock and onto cutting board. Cover and keep warm for 10 minutes. Then slice and serve.

NOTE This recipe makes enough ground turkey mixture for burgers later in the week. If you prefer to just make the loaf, halve the ingredients.

BBQ BALLS

JUDY MOORE, PENDLETON, IN
Photo appears in color section.

Makes: 10 servings
PREP. TIME: 40 MINUTES
COOKING TIME: 2 HOURS
IDEAL SLOW-COOKER SIZE: 4-QUART

2 lbs. 99% fat-free ground turkey
4 eggs
2 cups uncooked instant rice
2 medium onions, chopped
2 1-lb. cans cranberry sauce
2 14-oz. bottles ketchup
4 Tbsp. Worcestershire sauce
1 tsp. garlic powder
   cooked rice

1. Blend ground turkey, eggs, instant rice, and onion. Form into ¾-inch balls.
2. Bake at 400°F for 20 minutes or until brown. Drain.
3. Combine cranberry sauce, ketchup, Worcestershire sauce, and garlic powder in a small bowl.
4. Place meatballs in slow cooker. Pour sauce over top. Stir to coat.
5. Cover. Cook on Low 2 hours.
6. Serve over rice.

TURKEY AND SWEET POTATO CASSEROLE

MICHELE RUVOLA, SELDEN, NY

Makes: 4 servings
PREP. TIME: 15 MINUTES
COOKING TIME: 8–10 HOURS
IDEAL SLOW COOKER SIZE: 4-QUART

3	medium sweet potatoes, peeled and cut into 2-inch pieces
10	oz. pkg. frozen cut green beans
2	lbs. turkey cutlets
12	oz. jar home-style turkey gravy
2	Tbsp. flour
1	tsp. parsley flakes
¼–½	tsp. dried rosemary
⅛	tsp. pepper

1. Layer sweet potatoes, green beans, and turkey in slow cooker.

2. Combine remaining ingredients until smooth. Pour over mixture in slow cooker.

3. Cover. Cook on Low 8–10 hours.

4. Remove turkey and vegetables and keep warm. Stir sauce. Serve with sauce over meat and vegetables, or with sauce in a gravy boat.

5. Serve with biscuits and cranberry sauce.

ITALIAN TURKEY SANDWICHES

JOETTE DROZ, KALONA, IA
BARBARA WALKER, STURGIS, SD

Makes: 10 sandwiches
PREP. TIME: 20 MINUTES
COOKING TIME: 5–6 HOURS
IDEAL SLOW-COOKER SIZE: 6-QUART

- 1 bone-in turkey breast (5½ lbs.), skin removed
- ½ cup chopped green bell pepper
- 1 medium onion, chopped
- ¼ cup chili sauce
- 3 Tbsp. white vinegar
- 2 Tbsp. dried oregano or Italian seasoning
- 4 tsp. beef bouillon granules

1. Place turkey breast, green pepper, and onion in slow cooker.

2. Combine chili sauce, vinegar, oregano, and bouillon. Pour over turkey and vegetables.

3. Cover. Cook on Low 5–6 hours, or until instant-read meat thermometer registers 165°F and meat juices run clear and vegetables are tender.

4. Remove turkey, reserving cooking liquid. Shred the turkey with 2 forks.

5. Return to cooking juices.

6. For each serving, spoon approximately ½ cup onto a Kaiser or hard sandwich roll.

Slow cookers fit any season. When it's hot outside, they don't heat up your kitchen. So turn on your cooker before heading to the pool or the beach—or the garden.

CRAB SOUP

SUSAN ALEXANDER, BALTIMORE, MD

Makes: 10 servings
PREP. TIME: 20 MINUTES
COOKING TIME: 8–10 HOURS
IDEAL SLOW-COOKER SIZE: 5-QUART

1 lb. carrots, sliced

½ bunch celery, sliced

1 large onion, diced

2 10-oz. bags frozen mixed vegetables, or your choice of frozen vegetables

12 oz. can tomato juice

1 lb. ham, cubed

1 lb. beef, cubed

6 slices bacon, chopped

1 tsp. salt

¼ tsp. pepper

1 Tbsp. Old Bay seasoning

1 lb. claw crabmeat

1. Combine all ingredients except seasonings and crabmeat in large slow cooker. Pour in water until cooker is half-full.

2. Add spices. Stir in thoroughly. Put crab on top.

3. Cover. Cook on Low 8–10 hours.

4. Stir well and serve.

TIP

Some new slow cookers cook hotter and faster than older models. So get to know your slow cooker. You'll find a range of cooking times for many of the recipes since cookers vary. When you've found the right length of time for a recipe done in your cooker, note that in your cookbook.

CREAMY SALMON CHOWDER

DIANE SHETLER, HYDE PARK, MA

Makes: 5 servings
PREP. TIME: 10 MINUTES
COOKING TIME: 3½–10 HOURS
IDEAL SLOW-COOKER SIZE: 3½-QUART

  2 cups fat-free chicken broth
  2 cups water
 10 oz. pkg. frozen corn
  1 cup chopped celery
  ½ cup chopped onions
  ¾ cup wheat berries
  8 oz. pkg. fat-free cream cheese, cut into cubes
 16 oz. can salmon, drained, skin and bones removed, and coarsely flaked
  1 Tbsp. dill weed

1. Combine chicken broth, water, corn, celery, onions, and wheat berries in slow cooker.

2. Cover. Cook on Low 8–10 hours, or on High 3½–4 hours.

3. Turn cooker to High. Add cheese, stirring until melted.

4. Stir in salmon and dill.

5. Cover. Cook 10 minutes longer.

TERIYAKI SALMON

HOPE COMERFORD, CLINTON TOWNSHIP, MI

Makes: 4 servings
PREP. TIME: 10 MINUTES
COOKING TIME: 1–2 HOURS
IDEAL SLOW-COOKER SIZE: 3- TO 4-QUART

4 salmon fillets

4 Tbsp. teriyaki sauce

4 Tbsp. hoisin sauce

1 Tbsp. low-sodium soy sauce

1 Tbsp. brown sugar

2 tsp. ground ginger

⅛ tsp. pepper

1. Lay out 4 pieces of foil, big enough to wrap the salmon fillets in. Lay the salmon fillets on top of each of them.

2. Mix together all remaining ingredients. Divide this mixture evenly over each salmon fillet and spread to coat evenly.

3. Close the packets up tightly and place them in the crock.

4. Cover and cook on Low for 1–2 hours. The fish should flake easily when done.

HERBED FLOUNDER

DOROTHY VANDEEST, MEMPHIS, TX

Makes: 6 servings
PREP. TIME: 5 MINUTES
COOKING TIME: 3–4 HOURS
IDEAL SLOW-COOKER SIZE: 6-QUART OVAL

2 lbs. flounder fillets, fresh or frozen
½ tsp. salt
¾ cup chicken broth
2 Tbsp. lemon juice
2 Tbsp. dried chives
2 Tbsp. dried minced onion
½–1 tsp. leaf marjoram
4 Tbsp. chopped fresh parsley

1. Wipe fish as dry as possible. Cut fish into portions to fit slow cooker.

2. Sprinkle with salt.

3. Combine broth and lemon juice. Stir in remaining ingredients.

4. Place a meat rack in the slow cooker. Lay fish on rack. Pour liquid mixture over each portion.

5. Cover. Cook on High 3–4 hours.

ASIAN-STYLE TUNA

LIZZIE ANN YODER, HARTVILLE, OH

Makes: 3 servings
PREP. TIME: 15 MINUTES
COOKING TIME: 1 HOUR
IDEAL SLOW-COOKER SIZE: 2-QUART

half a green bell pepper, cut in ¼-inch strips
1 small onion, thinly sliced
2 tsp. olive oil
⅓ cup unsweetened pineapple juice
1½ tsp. cornstarch
⅔ cup canned unsweetened pineapple chunks, drained
1 Tbsp. sugar (scant)
1 Tbsp. vinegar
6 oz. can solid, water-packed tuna, drained and flaked
⅛ tsp. black pepper
dash of Tabasco sauce

1. Cook green pepper and onion with oil in a skillet over medium heat, leaving the vegetables slightly crisp.

2. Mix pineapple juice with cornstarch. Add to green pepper mixture.

3. Cook, stirring gently until thickened.

4. Add remaining ingredients. Pour into slow cooker.

5. Cover. Cook on Low 1 hour.

TIP
This is tasty served over brown rice.

HERBY FISH ON A BED OF VEGETABLES

PHYLLIS GOOD, LANCASTER, PA

Makes: 4–5 servings
PREP. TIME: 20–30 MINUTES
COOKING TIME: 4¼–5¼ HOURS
IDEAL SLOW-COOKER SIZE: 4- OR 5-QUART

8–12 little new potatoes, peeled or not
4 Tbsp. olive oil, divided
salt, to taste
pepper, to taste
2–3 leeks
8–12 plum tomatoes, sliced in half, or 15½-oz. can diced tomatoes, undrained
¼–½ cup diced red or white onion
2 tsp. dried dill
2 tsp. dried basil
46 4–6-oz. white fish fillets (flounder, cod, or haddock work well)

1. Grease the interior of the crock.

2. Wash the potatoes well. Slice them thin. (Bring out your mandoline if you have one. If you don't, get one. You'll make this dish more often.)

3. Layer the slices into the slow cooker. Drizzle each layer with oil, using about 2 Tbsp. total. Salt and pepper each layer as you go.

4. Cut the dark green tops off each leek. Split each leak from top to bottom into quarters. Hold each quarter under running water to wash out any sand and dirt.

5. Chop leeks into ½-inch-wide slices. Layer into slow cooker on top of the potatoes. Salt and pepper these layers, too.

6. Scatter tomatoes over top.

7. Cover. Cook on Low 4–5 hours, or until potatoes and leeks are as soft as you like them.

8. Meanwhile, put the diced onion in a microwave-safe bowl. Cover and cook on High 1 minute, or just until onions are softened.

9. Add the remaining 2 Tbsp. oil to onions. Stir in dill and basil, too.

10. When the veggies are as tender as you want, lay the fish fillets on top of the vegetables. Lay the thicker ends of the fillets around the outside of the crock first; that's where the heat source is. Put the thinner fillets in the middle.

11. Spread the red onion–herb mixture over the tops of the fish.

12. Cover. Turn cooker to High and cook for 15 minutes. Using a fork, test the thicker parts of the fillets to see if they're flaky. If not, cook 5 minutes more and test again.

13. When the fish is flaky, use a fish spatula to lift the fish onto a plate. Tent with foil to keep warm.

14. Using a slotted spoon, lift out the layers of vegetables and put them on a platter or serving dish with low sides. Lay the fish over top and serve.

TEX-MEX LUAU

DOROTHY VAN DEEST, MEMPHIS, TN

Makes: 6 servings
PREP. TIME: 20 MINUTES
COOKING TIME: 2–3 HOURS
IDEAL SLOW-COOKER SIZE: 3- OR 4-QUART

1½ lbs. frozen firm-textured fish fillets, thawed
2 medium onions, thinly sliced
2 lemons, divided
2 Tbsp. butter, melted
2 tsp. salt
1 bay leaf
4 whole peppercorns
1 cup water

1. Cut fillets into serving portions.
2. Combine onion slices and 1 sliced lemon in butter, along with salt, bay leaf, and peppercorns. Pour into slow cooker.
3. Place fillets on top of onion and lemon slices. Add water.
4. Cover. Cook on High 2–3 hours or until fish is flaky.
5. Before serving, carefully remove fish fillets with a slotted spoon. Place on heatproof plate.
6. Sprinkle with juice of half of the second lemon. Garnish with remaining lemon slices.
7. Serve hot or chill and serve cold.

SPAGHETTI SAUCE WITH CRAB

DAWN DAY, WESTMINSTER, CA

Makes: 4–6 servings
PREP. TIME: 15 MINUTES
COOKING TIME: 4–6 HOURS
IDEAL SLOW-COOKER SIZE: 2- TO 3-QUART

1 medium onion, chopped

½ lb. fresh mushrooms, sliced

2 12-oz. cans low-sodium tomato sauce, or 1 12-oz. can low-sodium tomato sauce and 1 12-oz. can low-sodium chopped tomatoes

6 oz. can tomato paste

½ tsp. garlic powder

½ tsp. dried basil

½ tsp. dried oregano

½ tsp. salt

1 lb. crabmeat

16 oz. angel-hair pasta, cooked

1. Sauté onions and mushrooms in nonstick skillet over low heat. When wilted, place in slow cooker.

2. Add tomato sauce, tomato paste, and seasonings. Stir in crab.

3. Cover. Cook on Low 4–6 hours.

4. Serve over angel-hair pasta.

TIP
Date all containers that you put in the freezer so you're sure to use the oldest food first.

SLOW COOKER SHRIMP MARINARA

JUDY MILES, CENTREVILLE, MD

Makes: 6 servings
PREP. TIME: 10–15 MINUTES
COOKING TIME: 3¼–4¼ HOURS
IDEAL SLOW-COOKER SIZE: 3½-QUART

- 16 oz. can low-sodium chopped tomatoes
- 2 Tbsp. minced fresh parsley
- 1 clove garlic, minced
- ½ tsp. dried basil
- ½ tsp. salt
- ¼ tsp. black pepper
- 1 tsp. dried oregano
- 6 oz. can tomato paste
- ½ tsp. seasoned salt
- 1 lb. shrimp, cooked and shelled
- 3 cups cooked spaghetti (about 6 oz. dry)
- grated Parmesan cheese, for garnish

1. Combine tomatoes, parsley, garlic, basil, salt, pepper, oregano, tomato paste, and seasoned salt in slow cooker.

2. Cover. Cook on Low 3–4 hours.

3. Stir shrimp into sauce.

4. Cover. Cook on High 10–15 minutes.

5. Serve over cooked spaghetti. Top with Parmesan cheese.

CHICKEN AND SHRIMP JAMBALAYA

DORIS M. COYLE-ZIPP, SOUTH OZONE PARK, NY

Makes: 5–6 servings
PREP. TIME: 15 MINUTES
COOKING TIME: 2¼–3¾ HOURS
IDEAL SLOW-COOKER SIZE: 4-QUART

3½–4	lb. roasting chicken, cut up
3	onions, diced
1	carrot, sliced
3–4	garlic cloves, minced
1	tsp. dried oregano
1	tsp. dried basil
1	tsp. salt
⅛	tsp. white pepper
14	oz. can crushed tomatoes
1	lb. shelled raw shrimp
2	cups rice, cooked

1. Combine all ingredients except shrimp and rice in slow cooker.

2. Cover. Cook on Low 2–3½ hours, or until chicken is tender.

3. Add shrimp and rice.

4. Cover. Cook on High 15–20 minutes, or until shrimp are done.

Meatless
MAIN DISHES

WHITE BEAN AND FENNEL SOUP

JANIE STEELE, MOORE, OK
Photo appears in color section.

Makes: 6 servings
PREP. TIME: 20–30 MINUTES
COOKING TIME: 1–3 HOURS
IDEAL SLOW-COOKER SIZE: 5-QUART

1	large onion, chopped
1	small fennel bulb, sliced thin
1	Tbsp. olive or canola oil
5	cups fat-free chicken broth
15	oz. can white kidney or cannellini beans, rinsed and drained
14½	oz. can diced tomatoes, undrained
1	tsp. dried thyme
¼	tsp. black pepper
1	bay leaf
3	cups chopped fresh spinach

1. Sauté onion and fennel in oil in skillet until brown.

2. Combine onion, fennel, broth, beans, tomatoes, thyme, pepper, and bay leaf.

3. Cook on Low 2–3 hours, or on High 1 hour, until fennel and onions are tender.

4. Remove bay leaf.

5. Add spinach about 10 minutes before serving.

LENTIL RICE SALAD BOWL

PHYLLIS GOOD, LANCASTER, PA
Photo appears in color section.

Makes: 4–6 servings
PREP. TIME: 20 MINUTES
COOKING TIME: 3–4 HOURS
IDEAL SLOW-COOKER SIZE: 5-QUART

1 cup brown lentils, rinsed

1 cup brown long-grain rice, uncooked

1 medium onion, chopped

3½ cups water, stock, or combination

1 tsp. salt, or less if you used salted stock

¼ tsp. freshly ground pepper

1 bay leaf

½ tsp. ground cumin

Salad Topping

2 Tbsp. fresh lemon juice

½ tsp. grated lemon peel

2 Tbsp. olive oil

½ tsp. salt

2 small cucumbers, diced

2 medium tomatoes, diced

3 spring onions, sliced

⅓ cup chopped fresh basil

½ cup crumbled feta cheese

1. Combine lentils, rice, onion, water/stock, salt, pepper, bay leaf, and cumin in slow cooker.

2. Cook on High for 3–4 hours, until lentils and rice are tender but not mushy.

3. Remove bay leaf. Keep rice mixture in slow cooker while you prepare the salad topping. The salad will wilt if it sits in its dressing too long.

4. In a medium bowl, combine lemon juice, peel, olive oil, and salt. Whisk well.

5. Place the rest of the topping ingredients in the bowl and mix gently.

6. To serve, place a scoop of the lentil rice mixture in a soup bowl. Top with a scoop of the salad.

CHERRY TOMATO SPAGHETTI SAUCE

BEVERLY HUMMEL, FLEETWOOD, PA
Photo appears in color section.

Makes: 8–10 servings
PREP. TIME: 20 MINUTES
COOKING TIME: 4–5 HOURS
IDEAL SLOW-COOKER SIZE: 6-QUART

4 quarts cherry tomatoes
1 medium onion, chopped
2 cloves garlic, minced
3 tsp. sugar
1 tsp. dried rosemary
2 tsp. dried thyme
1 tsp. dried oregano
1 tsp. dried basil
1 tsp. salt
½ tsp. coarsely ground black pepper
cooked spaghetti

1. Grease interior of slow-cooker crock.

2. Stem tomatoes and cut them in half. Place in slow cooker.

3. Add chopped onions and garlic to cooker.

4. Stir in sugar, herbs, and seasonings, mixing well.

5. Cover. Cook on Low 4–5 hours, or until the veggies are as tender as you like them.

6. For a thicker sauce, uncover the cooker for the last 30–60 minutes of cooking time.

7. Serve over just-cooked spaghetti.

VEGETABLES WITH PASTA

DONNA LANTGEN, RAPID CITY, SD

Makes: 6 servings
PREP. TIME: 20 MINUTES
COOKING TIME: 6 HOURS
IDEAL SLOW-COOKER SIZE: 3½- TO
4-QUART

2 cups chopped zucchini
½ cup cherry tomatoes, cut in half
   half green or red bell pepper, sliced
   half medium onion, sliced
½ cup sliced fresh mushrooms
4 cloves garlic, minced
1 Tbsp. olive oil
1 Tbsp. Italian seasoning
8 oz. can tomato sauce

1. Combine all ingredients in slow cooker.

2. Cook on Low 6 hours, or until vegetables are tender.

NOTE Be sure vegetables are thinly sliced or chopped because they cook slowly in a slow cooker.

TIP
Serve with your favorite cooked pasta and top with grated low-fat Parmesan or mozzarella cheese.

VEGGIE MAC AND CHEESE

DOROTHY LINGERFELT, STONYFORD, CA

Makes: 8–10 servings
PREP. TIME: 15 MINUTES
COOKING TIME: 4–4½ HOURS
IDEAL SLOW-COOKER SIZE: 6-QUART

- 8 oz. uncooked elbow macaroni
- 3½ cups milk
- 3 cups chopped broccoli, fresh or frozen (and thawed)
- 2 cups chopped cauliflower, fresh or frozen (and thawed)
- 3 carrots, sliced thinly
- 1 medium onion, chopped
- ¼ tsp. black pepper
- ¾ tsp. salt
- ¼ tsp. paprika
- 1 Tbsp. Dijon mustard
- 4 cups shredded cheddar cheese

1. Grease interior of slow-cooker crock.

2. Gently mix all ingredients together in crock, making sure that everything gets distributed well.

3. Cover. Cook on Low 4 hours, or until vegetables and macaroni are as tender as you like them.

4. If you find water around the edges of the dish at end of cooking time, cook on High, uncovered, for 20 minutes. That will also make the top slightly crusty and crunchy.

NOTE This really is a one-pot dinner. I love the convenience of such meals on the days when I'm at the office.

HORSERADISH MAC AND CHEESE

PHYLLIS GOOD, LANCASTER, PA

Makes: 4–6 servings
PREP. TIME: 10–15 MINUTES
COOKING TIME: 4–4½ HOURS
IDEAL SLOW-COOKER SIZE: 4- OR 5-QUART

- 8 oz. uncooked elbow macaroni
- 12 oz. can evaporated milk
- 1½ cups milk, your choice of whole, skim, or in between
- 1 Tbsp., plus 1 tsp., horseradish mustard
- ¾ tsp. salt
- ¼ tsp. black pepper
- 1½ cups shredded Swiss cheese
- 1½ cups shredded horseradish cheese or cheddar cheese, divided

1. Grease interior of slow-cooker crock.
2. Combine all ingredients in crock except ¾ cup shredded horseradish or cheddar cheese.
3. Sprinkle top with remaining ¾ cup grated cheese.
4. Cover. Cook on Low 4 hours, or until macaroni is tender but not overcooked.
5. If there's water around the edges at end of cooking time, turn cooker to High for 20 minutes and continue cooking, uncovered.

NOTE This is a family favorite, and we often eat it at home, but we also make it to take to potlucks, too. We always have an empty crock to bring home!

PASTA BEAN POT

DONNA CONTO, SAYLORSBURG, PA
Photo appears in color section.

Makes: 8 servings
PREP. TIME: 10–15 MINUTES
COOKING TIME: 4–5 HOURS
IDEAL SLOW-COOKER SIZE: 4-QUART

 1 Tbsp. olive oil
 1 medium onion, chopped
 1 garlic clove, minced
 ½ tsp. vinegar
 8 oz. uncooked elbow macaroni
28 oz. can stewed or diced tomatoes
15 oz. can cannellini beans, undrained
15 oz. can kidney beans, undrained
12 oz. can chicken broth
 1 tsp. dried oregano
 1 tsp. parsley
    dash red pepper

1. Grease interior of slow-cooker crock.
2. Put all ingredients in slow cooker. Mix well.
3. Cover. Cook on Low 4–5 hours, or until macaroni is tender but not mushy.

BAKED ZITI

PHYLLIS GOOD, LANCASTER, PA

Makes: 8–10 servings
PREP. TIME: 15–20 MINUTES
COOKING TIME: 4½ HOURS
STANDING TIME: 15 MINUTES
IDEAL SLOW-COOKER SIZE: 5-QUART

1 lb. cottage cheese
2 Tbsp. Parmesan cheese
1 egg
1 tsp. parsley flakes
⅛ tsp. pepper
⅛ tsp. salt
1 tsp. dried minced garlic
45 oz. jar of your favorite spaghetti sauce, divided
14 oz. jar of your favorite spaghetti sauce, divided
1 lb. ziti, uncooked
½ lb. mozzarella cheese, grated

1. Blend cottage cheese, Parmesan cheese, egg, parsley, pepper, salt, and garlic together.
2. Pour 2 cups spaghetti sauce into your greased slow cooker.
3. Drop ⅓ of the uncooked ziti over the spaghetti sauce.
4. Spoon ⅓ of the cottage cheese mixture over the ziti.
5. Repeat the layers 2 more times.
6. Pour the remaining tomato sauce over top.
7. Cover. Cook on Low 4 hours.
8. Thirty minutes before the end of the cooking time, sprinkle the top of the ziti mixture with mozzarella cheese. Do not cover. Continue cooking 30 more minutes.
9. Let stand 15 minutes before serving to let everything firm up.

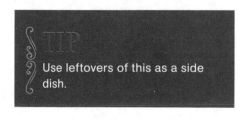

TIP
Use leftovers of this as a side dish.

SUMMER SQUASH LASAGNA

NATALIA SHOWALTER, MT. SOLON, VA
Photo appears in color section.

Makes: 12 servings
PREP. TIME: 30–45 MINUTES
COOKING TIME: 4–5 HOURS
STANDING TIME: 10–15 MINUTES
IDEAL SLOW-COOKER SIZE: 6- OR 7-QUART

2 medium zucchini squash, unpeeled and sliced thinly
2 medium yellow squash, unpeeled and sliced thinly
8 oz. portobello mushrooms, sliced
1 large onion, diced
1 red sweet bell pepper, chopped
4 cups fresh tomatoes, chopped
6 oz. can tomato paste
1 Tbsp. minced garlic
½ tsp. dried basil
1 Tbsp. brown sugar
½ tsp. salt
½ tsp. dried oregano
½ tsp. coarsely ground black pepper
15 oz. ricotta cheese or 12 oz. cottage cheese
8 oz. pkg. cream cheese, softened
2 large eggs, beaten
1 tsp. dried parsley
6–8 uncooked lasagna noodles, divided
2–4 cups shredded mozzarella cheese, divided
2 cups shredded Colby cheese, or Italian cheese blend, divided

1. Grease interior of slow-cooker crock.

2. Place green and yellow squash, mushrooms, onion, sweet pepper, tomatoes, tomato paste, garlic, basil, brown sugar, salt, oregano, and pepper into large bowl. Mix together gently but well.

3. In a separate bowl, combine ricotta, cream cheese, eggs, and parsley until well blended. Set aside.

4. Spread half of vegetable mixture in bottom of crock.

5. Top with 3 or 4 noodles, breaking them to fit and cover the vegetables.

6. Spread with half the ricotta mixture.

7. Sprinkle with half the mozzarella and Colby cheeses.

8. Repeat layers.

9. Cover. Cook on Low 4–5 hours, or until vegetables are as tender as you like them and noodles are fully cooked.

10. Let stand 10–15 minutes to allow lasagna to firm up before serving.

NOTE This is a favorite summer dish when the garden is in full swing. I love that I don't have to turn on the oven to make it!

CLASSIC SPINACH LASAGNA

BERNICE ESAU, NORTH NEWTON, KS

Makes: 10 servings
PREP. TIME: 30 MINUTES
COOKING TIME: 4–5 HOURS
STANDING TIME: 10–15 MINUTES
IDEAL SLOW-COOKER SIZE: 6- OR 7-QUART

1 small onion, chopped

1 medium garlic clove, minced

3 14½-oz. cans diced or stewed tomatoes, undrained

2 6-oz. cans tomato paste

¾ cup dry red wine

1 tsp. dried basil

½ tsp. salt

½ tsp. dried oregano

½ tsp. coarsely ground black pepper

2 16-oz. containers ricotta cheese

3 large eggs, divided

2 10-oz. pkgs. frozen chopped spinach, thawed and squeezed dry

8 oz. uncooked lasagna noodles, divided

16 oz. mozzarella cheese, sliced or shredded, divided

¼ cup grated Parmesan cheese

1. Grease interior of slow-cooker crock.

2. In a large bowl, gently mix together onion, garlic, tomatoes, tomato paste, red wine, basil, salt, oregano, and black pepper.

3. In a separate bowl, mix ricotta with 2 eggs.

4. In another bowl, mix spinach with 1 egg.

5. Spoon 2 cups tomato mixture into crock.

6. Arrange half the noodles over sauce, overlapping and breaking to fit.

7. Spoon half of ricotta mixture over noodles.

8. Top with half the mozzarella, half the spinach mixture, and half the remaining tomato sauce.

9. Repeat layers, ending with sauce.

10. Sprinkle with Parmesan cheese.

11. Cover. Cook on Low 4–5 hours, or until noodles are fully cooked.

12. Let stand 10–15 minutes so lasagna can firm up before serving.

MEAT-FREE LASAGNA

ROSEMARIE FITZGERALD, GIBSONIA, PA

Makes: 8 servings
PREP. TIME: 15 MINUTES
COOKING TIME: 5 HOURS
IDEAL SLOW-COOKER SIZE: 4- TO 5-QUART

4½ cups fat-free, low-sodium meatless spaghetti sauce

½ cup water

16 oz. container fat-free ricotta cheese

2 cups shredded part-skim mozzarella cheese, divided

¾ cup grated Parmesan cheese, divided

1 egg

2 tsp. minced garlic

1 tsp. Italian seasoning

8 oz. box no-cook lasagna noodles

1. Mix spaghetti sauce and ½ cup water in a bowl.

2. In a separate bowl, mix ricotta, 1½ cups mozzarella cheese, ½ cup Parmesan cheese, egg, garlic, and seasoning.

3. Spread ¼ of the sauce mixture in bottom of slow cooker. Top with ⅓ of the noodles, breaking if needed to fit.

4. Spread with ⅓ of the cheese mixture, making sure noodles are covered.

5. Repeat layers twice more.

6. Spread with remaining sauce.

7. Cover. Cook on Low 5 hours.

8. Sprinkle with remaining cheeses. Cover. Let stand 10 minutes to allow cheeses to melt.

VEGETARIAN LASAGNA

MARGARET W. HIGH, LANCASTER, PA
Photo appears in color section.

Makes: 8–10 servings
PREP. TIME: 25 MINUTES
COOKING TIME: 3–4 HOURS
STANDING TIME: 10–15 MINUTES
IDEAL SLOW-COOKER SIZE: 6-QUART OVAL

3 cups grated mozzarella

1½ cups ricotta cheese or cottage cheese

5 cups spaghetti sauce (the more herbs, the better), divided

½ lb. sliced fresh mushrooms, divided

12 lasagna noodles, uncooked, divided

½ lb. chopped fresh spinach, divided

6 oz. sliced black olives, divided, optional

¼ cup freshly grated Parmesan

¼ cup water (if your sauce is on the thin side, skip the water)

1. Grease interior of slow-cooker crock.

2. In a bowl, mix together grated mozzarella and ricotta cheeses. Set aside.

3. Put 1 cup spaghetti sauce in crock.

4. Scatter ⅓ of mushrooms over top.

5. Add ⅓ of noodles on top, breaking as necessary to fit them in, and covering the mushrooms as completely as possible.

6. Spread ⅓ of cheese mixture over noodles.

7. Top with half the spinach and half the black olives, then ⅓ of remaining sauce, half the remaining mushrooms, half the noodles, and half the cheese.

8. Make another whole set of layers, ending with a layer of sauce on top.

9. Sprinkle with Parmesan. Pour water down the side of crock if your sauce is really thick.

10. Cover. Cook on Low 3–4 hours, or until noodles are al dente.

11. Let stand 10–15 minutes before serving to allow cheeses to firm up.

VARIATION

Add other veggies if you wish, reducing the amount of spinach and mushrooms—broccoli, zucchini, Swiss chard. Cut-up artichokes instead of, or in addition to, black olives are also good.

NOTe This lasagna pairs nicely with a green salad and French bread dipped in olive oil with salt and pepper.

> TIP
>
> Use a metal serving spoon to cut out servings, but be careful not to scrape/scratch the ceramic crock. I never try to fuss with squares of lasagna with this recipe.

THREE-BEAN BURRITO BAKE

DARLA SATHRE, BAXTER, MN

Makes: 6 servings
PREP. TIME: 30 MINUTES
COOKING TIME: 8–10 HOURS
IDEAL SLOW-COOKER SIZE: 4-QUART

 1 onion, chopped
 1 green bell pepper, chopped
 2 garlic cloves, minced
 1 Tbsp. oil
16 oz. can pinto beans, drained
16 oz. can kidney beans, drained
15 oz. can black beans, drained
 4 oz. can sliced black olives, drained
 4 oz. can green chilies
 2 15-oz. cans diced tomatoes
 1 tsp. chili powder
 1 tsp. ground cumin
6–8 6-inch flour tortillas
 2 cups shredded Colby-Jack cheese
    sour cream

1. Sauté onions, green peppers, and garlic in large skillet in oil.

2. Add beans, olives, chilies, tomatoes, chili powder, and cumin.

3. In greased slow cooker, layer ¾ cup vegetables, a tortilla, ⅓ cup cheese. Repeat layers until all those ingredients are used, ending with sauce.

4. Cover. Cook on Low 8–10 hours.

5. Serve with dollops of sour cream on individual servings.

DOUBLE CORN TORTILLA BAKE

KATHY KEENER SHANTZ, LANCASTER, PA

Makes: 4 servings
PREP. TIME: 15 MINUTES
COOKING TIME: 2–3 HOURS
IDEAL SLOW-COOKER SIZE: 3- OR 4-QUART

8 corn tortillas, divided

1½ cups shredded Monterey Jack cheese, divided

1 cup corn, fresh, frozen, or canned (drained of juice), divided

4 green onions, sliced, about ½ cup, divided

2 eggs, beaten

1 cup buttermilk

4 oz. can diced green chilies

1. Grease interior of slow-cooker crock.

2. Tear 4 tortillas into bite-sized pieces. Scatter evenly over bottom of crock.

3. Top with half the cheese, half the corn, and half the green onions.

4. Repeat layers.

5. In a mixing bowl, stir together eggs, buttermilk, and chilies. Gently pour over tortilla mixture.

6. Cover. Cook on Low 2–3 hours, or until knife inserted in center comes out clean.

NOTE This is a potluck favorite because it's easy and uses common ingredients, but the flavor is amazing.

FLAVORFUL CHEESE SOUFFLÉ CASSEROLE

VICKI DINKEL, SHARON SPRING, KS

Makes: 4 servings
PREP. TIME: 15 MINUTES
COOKING TIME: 4–6 HOURS
IDEAL SLOW-COOKER SIZE: 5-QUART

14 slices fresh bread, crusts removed, divided

3 cups shredded sharp cheese, divided

2 Tbsp. butter, melted, divided

6 eggs

3 cups milk, scalded

2 tsp. Worcestershire sauce

½ tsp. salt

paprika

1. Tear bread into small pieces. Place half in well-greased slow cooker. Add half the shredded cheese and half the butter. Repeat layers.

2. Beat together eggs, milk, Worcestershire sauce, and salt. Pour over bread and cheese. Sprinkle top with paprika.

3. Cover. Cook on Low 4–6 hours.

TASTES-LIKE-CHILI-RELLENOS

ROSEANN WILSON, ALBUQUERQUE, NM

Makes: 6 servings
PREP. TIME: 10 MINUTES
COOKING TIME: 2–3 HOURS
IDEAL SLOW-COOKER SIZE: 3-QUART

2 tsp. butter

2 4-oz. cans whole green chilies

½ lb. grated cheddar cheese

½ lb. grated Monterey Jack cheese

14½ oz. can stewed tomatoes

4 eggs

2 Tbsp. flour

¾ cup evaporated milk

1. Grease sides and bottom of slow cooker with butter.

2. Cut chilies into strips. Layer chilies and cheeses in slow cooker. Pour in stewed tomatoes.

3. Combine eggs, flour, and milk. Pour into slow cooker.

4. Cover. Cook on High 2–3 hours.

NOTE My family always loved to order chilis rellenos at restaurants. They are peppers stuffed with cheese and dipped in batter and fried. I was thrilled to find this easy slow-cooker version that doesn't involve any frying.

FILLED ACORN SQUASH

TERESA MARTIN, NEW HOLLAND, PA

Makes: 4 servings
PREP. TIME: 20–30 MINUTES
COOKING TIME: 5–11 HOURS
IDEAL SLOW-COOKER SIZE: 7-QUART OVAL

2 medium acorn squash, about 1¼ lbs. each

2 Tbsp. water

15 oz. can black beans, rinsed and drained

½ cup pine nuts, raw, or toasted if you have time

1 large tomato, coarsely chopped

2 scallions, sliced thinly

1 tsp. ground cumin

½ tsp. coarsely ground black pepper, divided

2 tsp. olive oil

½–¾ cup shredded Monterey Jack cheese

TIPS

Serve this recipe in the fall when you can buy squash at your local farmers market or at roadside stands, where they are plentiful and inexpensive.

This dish is high in protein and fiber and low in fat.

1. Grease interior of slow-cooker crock.

2. Place washed whole squash in slow cooker.

3. Spoon in water.

4. Cover. Cook on High for 4–6 hours or on Low for 7–9 hours, or until squash are tender when you pierce them with a fork.

5. While squash are cooking, mix together beans, pine nuts, tomato, scallions, cumin, and ¼ tsp. black pepper. Set aside.

6. Use sturdy tongs, or wear oven mitts, to lift squash out of cooker. Let cool until you can cut them in half.

7. Scoop out seeds.

8. Brush cut sides and cavity of each squash half with olive oil.

9. Sprinkle all 4 cut sides with remaining black pepper.

10. Spoon heaping ½ cup of bean mixture into each halved squash, pressing down gently to fill cavity.

11. Return halves to slow cooker. Cover. Cook on High another hour, or on Low another hour or 2, until vegetables are as tender as you like them and thoroughly hot.

12. Uncover and sprinkle with cheese just before serving. When cheese has melted, put a filled half squash on each diner's plate.

ZUCCHINI TORTE

MARY CLAIR WENGER, KIMMSWICK, MO

Makes: 8 servings
PREP. TIME: 25 MINUTES
COOKING TIME: 4–5 HOURS
IDEAL SLOW-COOKER SIZE: 4-QUART

5 cups diced zucchini

1 cup grated carrots

1 small onion, diced finely

1½ cups biscuit baking mix

½ cup grated Parmesan cheese

4 eggs, beaten

¼ cup olive oil

2 tsp. dried marjoram

½ tsp. salt

pepper, to taste

1. Grease interior of slow-cooker crock.

2. Mix together all ingredients. Pour into greased slow cooker.

3. Cover and cook on Low for 4–5 hours, until set. Remove lid last 30 minutes to allow excess moisture to evaporate.

4. Serve hot or at room temperature.

MUSHROOMS, TOMATOES, AND ONION PIE

Makes: 6–8 servings
PREP. TIME: 15–20 MINUTES
COOKING TIME: 1½–2 HOURS
STANDING TIME: 20–30 MINUTES
IDEAL SLOW-COOKER SIZE: 5-QUART

pastry for 10" pie

4 spring onions, sliced thin

½ cup halved and de-seeded grape tomatoes

½ cup sliced fresh mushrooms

1 Tbsp. olive oil

6 oz. container plain, non-fat Greek yogurt

1⅓ cups egg substitute

1⅓ cups skim milk

salt and pepper to taste

½ cup shredded low-fat cheddar or Colby Jack cheese

1. Take rolled out pastry and fit it into slow cooker crock as you would line a pie plate, bringing it up the sides 1–2" and gently pushing it into the bottom.

2. Sauté onions, tomatoes, and mushrooms in olive oil in skillet for 5 minutes. Drain on paper towel.

3. In a mixing bowl, whisk together yogurt, egg substitute, milk, salt, and pepper.

4. Scatter drained onions, tomatoes, and mushrooms over bottom of pie crust.

5. Sprinkle cheese on top of veggie layer.

6. Pour egg mixture over top.

7. Cover. Bake on High 1½–2 hours, or until knife inserted into center of pie comes out clean.

8. Uncover swiftly, swooping the lid away from yourself, making sure that no water drips from the inside of the lid onto the pie. Remove crock from cooker and place on baking rack to cool.

9. Allow to stand 20–30 minutes to firm up, before slicing to serve.

NOTE This lets the fresh veggies sing. And don't miss how light it is, despite its creaminess.

FRESH TOMATO BASIL PIE

Makes: 6 servings
PREP. TIME: 30 MINUTES
COOKING TIME: 1½–2 HOURS
STANDING TIME: 30 MINUTES
IDEAL SLOW-COOKER SIZE: 5-QUART

pastry for 9" pie

1½ cups shredded mozzarella cheese, divided

5 plum or 4 medium-sized tomatoes

1 cup loosely packed fresh basil leaves, plus additional leaves for garnish

4 cloves garlic

½ cup mayonnaise

¼ cup grated Parmesan cheese

⅛ tsp. ground white pepper

1. Take rolled out pastry and fit it into slow cooker crock as you would line a pie plate, bringing it up the sides 1–2" and gently pushing it into the bottom.

2. Sprinkle ½ cup mozzarella cheese over bottom of pie crust.

3. Cut tomatoes into wedges. Drain in single layer on paper towels for 10 minutes.

4. Arrange tomato wedges on top of cheese in crust.

5. In a food processor, combine basil and garlic, processing until coarsely chopped. Sprinkle over tomatoes.

6. In a medium-sized bowl, combine remaining mozzarella, mayonnaise, Parmesan cheese, and pepper.

7. Spoon cheese mixture over basil mixture, spreading to cover evenly.

8. Cover. Bake on High 1½–2 hours, or until knife inserted into center of pie comes out clean.

9. Uncover quickly, swooping lid away from yourself so no water from inside of lid drips on the pie. Remove crock from cooker and place on baking rack to cool.

10. Let stand 20–30 minutes, or until firm, before slicing to serve.

11. Garnish individual servings with fresh basil leaves.

AMISH CORN PIE

Makes: 6–8 servings
PREP. TIME: 30 MINUTES
COOKING TIME: 1½–2 HOURS
STANDING TIME: 20 MINUTES
IDEAL SLOW-COOKER SIZE: 5-QUART

pastry for a double-crust 9" pie
3 cups fresh or frozen corn
2 Tbsp. chopped onion, optional
1½ cups diced potatoes, steamed or microwaved until just tender
3 hard-boiled eggs, diced
salt and pepper to taste
2 Tbsp. flour
milk

1. Take bottom part of rolled out pastry and fit it into slow cooker crock as you would line a pie plate, bringing it up the sides 1–2" and gently pushing it into the bottom. (Reserve top part of pastry for later.)

2. Combine corn, onions if you wish, potatoes, and eggs in a good sized bowl. Pour into crust in crock.

3. Sprinkle with salt, pepper, and 2 Tbsp. flour.

4. Slowly pour in milk, just enough to barely cover the vegetables.

5. Fit top pastry over filling. Cut several slits (or interesting shapes!) into top crust to allow steam to escape.

6. Cover with lid of cooker. Bake on High 1 hour.

7. Remove cover with a quick swoop (you don't want water to drip on the crust) to allow top crust to dry out and bake through. Continue baking 30–60 minutes, or until milk bubbles around the edges and top crust is dry.

8. Remove crock from cooker and place on wire baking rack to cool.

9. Allow to stand 20 minutes. Then slice and serve.

TOMATO GALETTE

Photo appears in color section.

Makes: 2 full-size or 6 appetizer-size servings
PREP. TIME: 15–20 MINUTES
COOKING TIME: 1½–2 HOURS
STANDING TIME: 15 MINUTES
IDEAL SLOW-COOKER SIZE: 5- OR 6-QUART ROUND

9" refrigerated pie crust, or a frozen one, or your favorite from-scratch one
½ cup ricotta cheese
¼ cup goat cheese, cubed or crumbled
2 tsp. pesto, your choice of flavors
¼ lb. sliced tomatoes
1 egg, slightly beaten

1. Grease interior of round slow cooker crock.
2. Roll out pie dough on a lightly floured surface.
3. In a small bowl, mix ricotta and goat cheeses together.
4. Spread over crust, leaving a 1½" border.
5. Spread pesto over cheeses.
6. Arrange tomato slices on top.
7. Fold edges of crust over filling, pleating as needed, and leaving center uncovered.
8. Brush egg over crust.
9. Using a wide spatula, lift galette up and into crock.
10. Cover. Bake on High for 1½–2 hours, or until pie crust browns well and firms up.
11. Uncover, swooping lid quickly away from yourself to prevent condensation from inside of lid dripping on the galette.
12. Allow to stand for 15 minutes. Then cut into wedges and serve.

Since this is so attractive before it's cut, get someone to help you lift it out of the cooker uncut—each of you armed with a broad and sturdy metal spatula. Have a platter ready and gently lay it down together! In case you're wondering, lots of kids like this dish!

ARTISAN PIZZA IN THE CROCK

Photo appears in color section.

Makes: 2–4 servings
PREP. TIME: 30 MINUTES
COOKING TIME: 2½ HOURS
RISING TIME: 6–8 HOURS
IDEAL SLOW-COOKER SIZE: 6-QUART

1 cup unbleached white bread flour
⅛ tsp. instant yeast
¼ tsp. salt
⅓ cup water
1–2 Tbsp. coarse cornmeal
⅓ cup thick pizza sauce
   handful spinach leaves
4 oz. sliced smoked Gouda
2 garlic cloves, chopped

1. In a bowl with a lid, mix flour, yeast, salt, and water. The dough should be shaggy and on the dry side. Cover bowl tightly and set aside in a warm place for 6–8 hours.

2. Lightly grease slow cooker. Sprinkle bottom of slow cooker with cornmeal to help prevent sticking.

3. Take ball of dough in hand and stretch it gently to form a rough oval, slightly larger than the floor of the slow cooker. The dough will be sticky and you can flour it lightly for easier handling.

4. Place stretched dough in crock so that it comes up the sides 1".

5. With the lid off, cook the crust on High for 1½ hours, until crust is firm and browning at edges.

6. Smooth the pizza sauce over the floor of the crust. Spread spinach leaves over the sauce in an even layer, topping with a layer of Gouda slices. Sprinkle with chopped garlic.

7. Place the lid on the cooker with a wooden spoon handle or chopstick venting it at one end.

8. Cook for an hour, until spinach leaves are wilted and cheese is melted.

9. Slip a wide spatula under the pizza and remove it to a cutting board to slice.

> **TIP**
>
> The long rise of this dough takes the place of kneading and the tiny bit of yeast makes it taste more like pizzeria dough. If you misjudged your time, simply pop the covered bowl of dough in the fridge after its long rise. It can keep for up to 3 days—just bring it to room temperature again before trying to stretch it into an oval.

CHEESE-STUFFED PIZZA

Photo appears in color section.

Makes: 6 servings
PREP. TIME: 30 MINUTES
COOKING TIME: 2 HOURS
IDEAL SLOW-COOKER SIZE: 5-QUART

11 or 13 oz. pkg. refrigerated pizza dough
1½ cups shredded mozzarella, divided
½ cup thick pizza sauce
1 cup or less favorite pizza toppings such as chopped veggies or cooked meat

1. Divide dough in half. Roll and/or stretch each piece of dough into an oval to match the size of the bottom of the crock.

2. Place 1 dough oval in greased slow cooker, pushing and stretching it out to the edges. Sprinkle with ½ cup mozzarella.

3. Place the other dough oval on top of the cheese, stretching it to the edges of the crock.

4. Cook, uncovered, for 1 hour on High. Dough should be puffy and getting brown at edges.

5. Spread pizza sauce on top. Sprinkle with remaining 1 cup cheese and any toppings you wish.

6. Place lid on cooker with chopstick or wooden spoon handle venting it at one end.

7. Cook on High for an additional hour, until toppings are heated through.

WHITE PIZZA IN THE CROCK

Makes: 4 servings
PREP. TIME: 30 MINUTES
RISING TIME: 1 HOUR
COOKING TIME: 3 HOURS
IDEAL SLOW-COOKER SIZE: 6-QUART

½ cup + 1 Tbsp. unbleached all-purpose flour, divided
½ cup whole wheat bread flour
½ tsp. instant yeast
½ tsp. salt
2 Tbsp. olive oil, divided
⅓ cup warm water
⅔ cup cottage cheese
1 garlic clove
2 Tbsp. grated Parmesan cheese
1 cup loose fresh spinach leaves
2 Tbsp. chopped olives of choice
1 tsp. dried basil

1. In a medium mixing bowl, combine ½ cup all-purpose flour, whole wheat flour, yeast, salt, 1 Tbsp. olive oil, and water. Stir to form a shaggy dough.

2. Knead for several minutes until a stiff dough forms. Knead into a ball.

3. Pour in remaining 1 Tbsp. olive oil and grease the ball and the bowl. Cover with a damp cloth and set aside in a warm place for approximately 1 hour.

4. Make the white sauce. Place cottage cheese, garlic clove, Parmesan, and 1 Tbsp. all-purpose flour in food processor or blender. Process until smooth. Set aside.

5. Place ball of dough on counter. Roll out with a rolling pin into a large oval that is larger by a few inches than slow cooker.

6. Lift the dough into greased slow cooker and gently pull it and shape it so that the dough lines the crock and comes up 2–3" on the sides.

7. Cook for 2 hours on High, uncovered. Dough should be firm and getting brown at edges.

8. Spread spinach leaves evenly over dough. Dollop and spread white sauce over spinach leaves. Sprinkle with chopped olives and basil.

9. Cover cooker with lid and vent lid at one end with a wooden spoon handle or chopstick.

10. Cook an additional hour on High, until spinach is wilted and toppings are heated through.

VARIATION

Slip some sundried tomato slices in with the filling, or top with thinly sliced fresh tomatoes.

CRAZY-CRUST PIZZA

Makes: 4 servings
PREP. TIME: 20 MINUTES
COOKING TIME: 2 HOURS
IDEAL SLOW-COOKER SIZE: 6-QUART

1⅓ cups all-purpose flour

½ tsp. salt

1 tsp. Italian herb seasoning

2 eggs

⅔ cup milk

½ cup thick pizza sauce

1 cup shredded mozzarella

½ cup favorite pizza toppings

1. Grease slow cooker. Turn on High to preheat while you mix up the batter.

2. In a mixing bowl, mix flour, salt, Italian herb seasoning, eggs, and milk until smooth.

3. Pour into heated, greased cooker. Put lid on, with one side vented with a wooden spoon handle or chopstick.

4. Cook on High for 1 hour, until crust is set and starting to brown at edges.

5. Spread pizza sauce over crust. Sprinkle with mozzarella and any toppings you wish.

6. Place lid on cooker, venting it again.

7. Cook an additional hour on High, until toppings are heated through.

VARIATION

Try using odds and ends from your fridge as pizza toppings. Use about 2 cups broccoli florets and ½ cup chopped red onion. Microwave them just a bit to take off the raw edge, then sprinkle them over the pizza sauce with some chopped cilantro. Then sprinkle the mozzarella over all. Delicious!

TIP
May substitute whole wheat flour for the all-purpose flour.

ZUCCHINI CRUST PIZZA

Makes: 6 servings
PREP. TIME: 20 MINUTES
COOKING TIME: 3½–5 HOURS
IDEAL SLOW-COOKER SIZE: 4-QUART

2½ cups packed, grated zucchini
2 eggs
⅓ cup all-purpose flour
1 cup shredded mozzarella, divided
¼ cup freshly grated Parmesan
¼ tsp. dried basil
¼ tsp. dried marjoram
    freshly ground pepper, to taste
½ cup thick pizza sauce
¼ cup chopped green olives
¼ cup chopped mushrooms
2 cloves garlic, chopped

1. In a mixing bowl, combine zucchini, eggs, flour, ½ cup mozzarella, Parmesan, basil, marjoram, and pepper.

2. Pour mixture into greased slow cooker. Smooth top.

3. Cover and cook on Low for 3–4 hours, until set.

4. Smooth pizza sauce on top of baked crust. Add olives, mushrooms, garlic, and ½ cup mozzarella.

5. With lid off, cook an additional 30–60 minutes on Low until toppings are hot and any moisture has evaporated at sides.

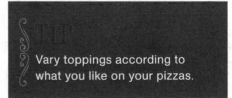

TIP
Vary toppings according to
what you like on your pizzas.

Grain *and* Vegetable SIDES

GOLDEN CARROTS

JAN MAST, LANCASTER, PA
Photo appears in color section.

Makes: 6 servings
PREP. TIME: 5 MINUTES
COOKING TIME: 3–4 HOURS
IDEAL SLOW-COOKER SIZE: 2-QUART

2 lb. pkg. baby carrots
½ cup golden raisins
1 stick (½ cup) butter, melted or softened
⅓ cup honey
2 Tbsp. lemon juice
½ tsp. ground ginger, optional

1. Combine all ingredients in slow cooker.
2. Cover and cook on Low 3–4 hours, or until carrots are tender-crisp.

VARIATION

To use whole carrots, cut into 1-inch-long chunks. If the carrots are thick, you may need to cook them 5–6 hours until they become tender-crisp.

TIP

To clear honey out of your measuring cup easily, first spray the measuring cup with cooking spray.

SAUCY MUSHROOMS

DONNA LANTGEN, ARVADA, CO

Makes: 4 servings
PREP. TIME: 15 MINUTES
COOKING TIME: 3¼–4¼ HOURS
IDEAL SLOW-COOKER SIZE: 3- OR 4-QUART

- 1 lb. small, whole, fresh mushrooms, cleaned
- 4 cloves garlic, minced
- ¼ cup chopped onion
- 1 Tbsp. olive oil
- ¾ cup red wine
- ½ tsp. salt
- ⅛ tsp. pepper
- ¼ tsp. dried thyme
- ¼ cup water
- 2 Tbsp. cornstarch

1. Grease interior of slow-cooker crock.

2. Combine mushrooms, garlic, onion, olive oil, red wine, salt, pepper, and thyme in slow cooker.

3. Cover. Cook on Low 3–4 hours, or until mushrooms are soft but still holding their shape.

4. In a small bowl, whisk together water and cornstarch. Turn cooker to High and stir in cornstarch mixture. Cook, stirring occasionally, until thickened, 10–15 minutes.

5. Serve as a sauce over pasta, or as a side dish with steak and baked potatoes.

NOTE No competition here from other strong flavors. The mushrooms step forward.

BROCCOLI DELIGHT

NANCY WAGNER GRAVES, MANHATTAN, KS

Makes: 4–6 servings
PREP. TIME: 15 MINUTES
COOKING TIME: 2–6 HOURS
IDEAL SLOW-COOKER SIZE: 3½- TO
4-QUART

1–2 lbs. broccoli, chopped

2 cups cauliflower, chopped

10¾ oz. can 98% fat-free cream of celery soup

½ tsp. salt

¼ tsp. black pepper

1 medium onion, diced

2–4 garlic cloves, crushed, according to your taste preference

½ cup vegetable broth

1. Combine all ingredients in slow cooker.
2. Cook on Low 4–6 hours, or on High 2–3 hours.

BRUSSELS SPROUTS WITH PIMENTOS

DONNA LANTGON, RAPID CITY, SD

Makes: 8 servings
PREP. TIME: 5 MINUTES
COOKING TIME: 6 HOURS
IDEAL SLOW-COOKER SIZE: 3½- TO
4-QUART

2   lbs. brussels sprouts
¼   tsp. dried oregano
½   tsp. dried basil
2   oz. jar pimentos, drained
¼   cup, or 1 small can, sliced black olives, drained
1   Tbsp. olive oil
½   cup water

1. Combine all ingredients in slow cooker.

2. Cook on Low 6 hours.

MEDITERRANEAN EGGPLANT

WILLARD E. ROTH, ELKHART, IN

Makes: 8 servings
PREP. TIME: 20 MINUTES
COOKING TIME: 5–6 HOURS
IDEAL SLOW-COOKER SIZE: 5-QUART

1 medium red onion, chopped

2 cloves garlic, crushed

1 cup fresh mushrooms, sliced

2 Tbsp. olive oil

1 eggplant, unpeeled, cubed

2 green bell peppers, coarsely chopped

28 oz. can crushed tomatoes

28 oz. can garbanzo beans, drained and rinsed

2 Tbsp. fresh rosemary

1 cup chopped fresh parsley

½ cup kalamata olives, pitted and sliced

1. Sauté onion, garlic, and mushrooms in olive oil in a skillet over medium heat. Transfer to slow cooker coated with non-fat cooking spray.

2. Add eggplant, peppers, tomatoes, garbanzo beans, rosemary, and parsley.

3. Cover. Cook on Low 5–6 hours.

4. Stir in olives just before serving.

5. Serve with couscous or polenta.

COUNTRY FRENCH VEGETABLES

PHYLLIS GOOD, LANCASTER, PA

Makes: 4–5 servings
PREP. TIME: 10 MINUTES
COOKING TIME: 3–6 HOURS
IDEAL SLOW-COOKER SIZE: 5-QUART

3 Tbsp. extra-virgin olive oil, divided

3 potatoes, unpeeled, cut in 1-inch pieces

2 carrots, unpeeled, cut in 1-inch pieces

1 parsnip, peeled, cut in 1-inch pieces

1 turnip or rutabaga, peeled, cut in 1-inch pieces

2 medium onions, cut in wedges

½ lb. fresh mushrooms, halved

1 Tbsp. minced fresh, or ½ tsp. dried, rosemary

1 Tbsp. minced fresh, or ½ tsp. dried, thyme

⅓ cup chopped fresh parsley

¾ tsp. salt

¼ tsp. freshly ground black pepper

1. Lightly grease slow cooker with 1 Tbsp. olive oil.

2. Combine all ingredients with remaining 2 Tbsp. olive oil in slow cooker.

3. Cover and cook on Low for 3–6 hours, depending how tender you want the vegetables or how long you want to be away from home.

BEETS WITH CAPERS

MARY CLAIR WENGER, KIMMSWICK, MO
Photo appears in color section.

Makes: 6 servings
PREP. TIME: 20 MINUTES
COOKING TIME: 3–4 HOURS
IDEAL SLOW-COOKER SIZE: 3-QUART

- 8 cups diced fresh, uncooked beets, peeled or not
- 3 Tbsp. olive oil
- 4 garlic cloves, chopped
- ¼ tsp. fresh ground pepper
- ½ tsp. salt
- 1 tsp. dried rosemary
- 1–2 Tbsp. capers with brine

1. Grease interior of slow-cooker crock.
2. In slow-cooker, mix together beets, olive oil, garlic, pepper, salt, and rosemary.
3. Cover and cook on High until beets are tender, 3–4 hours.
4. Stir in capers and brine. Taste for salt. Add more if needed.
5. Serve beets hot or at room temperature.

BAKED STUFFED TOMATOES

LESLIE SCOTT, TROY, NY

Makes: 6 servings
PREP. TIME: 30 MINUTES
COOKING TIME: 2–3 HOURS
IDEAL SLOW-COOKER SIZE: 5-QUART OVAL

6 medium-sized tomatoes

3 Tbsp. butter, melted

2 tsp. chopped fresh basil

2 tsp. chopped fresh oregano

2 tsp. chopped fresh parsley

2 garlic cloves, minced

1 cup grated Parmesan cheese

¾ cup fine bread crumbs

salt and pepper to taste

1. Grease interior of slow-cooker crock.

2. Remove cores from tomatoes, and cut away an additional inch or so underneath the core to make a cavity in each tomato.

3. Mix together butter, herbs, garlic, Parmesan, bread crumbs, and salt and pepper.

4. Gently stuff each tomato with mixture.

5. Set tomatoes in lightly greased slow cooker.

6. Cover and cook on Low 2–3 hours, until tomatoes are soft and heated through.

VARIATION

If you don't have fresh herbs, use ⅔ tsp. each of dried basil, oregano, and parsley instead.

YUMMY SPINACH

JEANETTE OBERHOLTZER, MANHEIM, PA

Makes: 8 servings
PREP. TIME: 10 MINUTES
COOKING TIME: 2½–3 HOURS
STANDING TIME: 15 MINUTES
IDEAL SLOW-COOKER SIZE: 4-QUART

3   10-oz. boxes frozen spinach, thawed and squeezed dry
2   cups cottage cheese
1½ cups grated cheddar cheese
3   eggs
¼   cup flour
1   tsp. salt
¼   cup (½ stick) butter, melted

1. Grease interior of slow-cooker crock.
2. Mix together all ingredients in the slow cooker.
3. Cover. Cook on Low 2½–3 hours, or until the dish sets up and is no longer jiggly in the center.
4. Let stand for 15 minutes so the cheeses can firm before cutting and serving.

NOTE This recipe is downright tasty and a perfect dish for anyone who's cautious about spinach. It's a finger food. It works for any time of the day.

GREEN BEANS CAESAR

CAROL SHIRK, LEOLA, PA

Makes: 6–8 servings
PREP. TIME: 15 MINUTES
COOKING TIME: 3½– 8½ HOURS
IDEAL SLOW-COOKER SIZE: 4-QUART

1½ lbs. fresh green beans, ends trimmed

2 Tbsp. olive oil

1 Tbsp. red wine vinegar

1 Tbsp. minced garlic

salt and pepper to taste

½ tsp. dried basil

½ tsp. dried oregano

¼ cup plain bread crumbs

¼ cup grated Parmesan cheese

1 Tbsp. butter, melted

1. Grease interior of slow-cooker crock.

2. In slow-cooker, combine green beans, olive oil, vinegar, garlic, salt and pepper, basil, and oregano.

3. Cover. Cook on High 3–4 hours or on Low 6–8 hours, or until green beans are as soft as you like them. Stir.

4. Combine bread crumbs, Parmesan, and butter in a bowl. Sprinkle over green beans and cook an additional 30 minutes on High with lid off.

NOTE In case you thought green beans were ho hum, this dressing and topping will change your mind. This is guest-worthy eating.

EASY FLAVOR-FILLED GREEN BEANS

PAULA SHOWALTER, WEYERS CAVE, VA

Makes: 10 servings
PREP. TIME: 5–10 MINUTES
COOKING TIME: 3–4 HOURS
IDEAL SLOW-COOKER SIZE: 3- TO
3½-QUART

2 quarts green beans, drained
⅓ cup chopped onions
4 oz. can mushrooms, drained
2 Tbsp. brown sugar
3 Tbsp. butter
   pepper to taste

1. Combine beans, onions, and mushrooms in slow cooker.

2. Sprinkle with brown sugar.

3. Dot with butter.

4. Sprinkle with pepper.

5. Cover. Cook on High 3–4 hours. Stir just before serving.

GREEN BEAN CASSEROLE

VICKI DINKEL, SHARON SPRINGS, KS

Makes: 9–11 servings
PREP. TIME: 10 MINUTES
COOKING TIME: 3–10 HOURS
IDEAL SLOW-COOKER SIZE: 3½- TO
4-QUART

3 10-oz. pkgs. frozen, cut green beans
2 10½-oz. cans cheddar cheese soup
½ cup water
¼ cup chopped green onions
4 oz. can sliced mushrooms, drained
8 oz. can water chestnuts, drained and sliced, optional
½ cup slivered almonds
1 tsp. salt
¼ tsp. pepper

1. Combine all ingredients in lightly greased slow cooker. Mix well.
2. Cover. Cook on Low 8–10 hours, or on High 3–4 hours.

DRESSED-UP ACORN SQUASH

DALE PETERSON, RAPID CITY, SD

Makes: 4 servings
PREP. TIME: 15 MINUTES
COOKING TIME: 6–8 HOURS
IDEAL SLOW-COOKER SIZE: 5- OR 6-QUART,
OR 2 4- OR 6-QUART, DEPENDING ON SIZE
OF SQUASH

2   acorn squash
⅔   cup cracker crumbs
½   cup coarsely chopped pecans
5⅓   Tbsp. (⅓ cup) butter, melted
4   Tbsp. brown sugar
½   tsp. salt
¼   tsp. ground nutmeg
2   Tbsp. orange juice

1. Grease interior of slow-cooker crock.

2. Cut squash in half through the middle. Remove seeds.

3. Combine remaining ingredients in a bowl. Spoon into squash halves.

4. Place squash halves in slow cooker side by side.

5. Cover. Cook on Low 6–8 hours, or until squash is tender.

TIP

Because squash is so mildly flavored, it accepts the citrus/butter/nutty additions well. Again, adapt this recipe to fit the taste preferences of the people around your table. Just follow Steps 1, 2, 4, and 5, and you'll have perfectly cooked squash. Do what you want with Step 3.

WILD RICE

RUTH S. WEAVER, REINHOLDS, PA

Makes: 5 servings
PREP. TIME: 10 MINUTES
COOKING TIME: 2½–3 HOURS
IDEAL SLOW-COOKER SIZE: 3-QUART

1 cup wild rice or wild rice mixture, uncooked
½ cup sliced fresh mushrooms
½ cup diced onions
½ cup diced green or red bell peppers
1 Tbsp. oil
½ tsp. salt
¼ tsp. black pepper
2½ cups fat-free, low-sodium chicken broth

1. Layer rice and vegetables in slow cooker. Pour oil, salt, and pepper over vegetables. Stir.

2. Heat chicken broth. Pour over ingredients in slow cooker.

3. Cover. Cook on High 2½–3 hours, or until rice is soft and liquid is absorbed.

PARTY WILD RICE

SUSAN KASTING, JENKS, OK

Makes: 4 servings
PREP. TIME: 10 MINUTES
COOKING TIME: 2½–3 HOURS
IDEAL SLOW-COOKER SIZE: 4-QUART

1½ cups wild rice, uncooked
3 cups chicken stock
3 Tbsp. orange zest
2 Tbsp. orange juice
½ cup raisins (I like golden raisins)
1½ tsp. curry powder
1 Tbsp. butter, softened
½ cup fresh parsley
½ cup chopped pecans
½ cup chopped green onion

1. Grease interior of slow-cooker crock.

2. Mix rice, chicken stock, orange zest, orange juice, raisins, curry powder, and butter in slow cooker.

3. Cover and cook on High 2½–3 hours, or until rice is tender and has absorbed most of the liquid, but is not dry.

4. Stir in parsley, pecans, and green onion just before serving.

SPINACH RICE BAKE

ESTHER PORTER, MINNEAPOLIS, MN

Makes: 4 servings
PREP. TIME: 10–15 MINUTES
COOKING TIME: 1¼–2¼ HOURS
IDEAL SLOW-COOKER SIZE: 3-QUART

10 oz. pkg. frozen chopped spinach
¾ cup grated cheese of your choice
½ tsp. garlic salt
1 Tbsp. diced onion
⅓ cup uncooked instant rice
1 egg, beaten
1 cup milk

1. Grease interior of slow-cooker crock.

2. Thaw spinach. Squeeze it as dry as you can. Place in crock.

3. Stir grated cheese, garlic salt, onion, and rice into spinach, mixing well.

4. Mix in egg and milk.

5. Cook on Low 1–2 hours, or until set in the middle. (Stick the blade of a knife into the center. If it comes out clean, the bake is done. If it doesn't, cover and continue cooking another 15 minutes.)

Serve this rice with baked sweet potatoes or baked squash.

FOIL-WRAPPED BAKED POTATOES

VALERIE HERTZLER, WEYERS CAVE, VA
CAROL PEACHEY, LANCASTER, PA
JANET L. ROGGIE, LOWVILLE, NY

PREP. TIME: 5 MINUTES
COOKING TIME: 3–10 HOURS
IDEAL SLOW-COOKER SIZE: DEPENDS ON
HOW MANY POTATOES YOU'RE DOING

uncooked potatoes

1. Prick potatoes with fork and wrap in foil.
2. Cover. Do not add water.
3. Cook on High 3–5 hours, or on Low 6–10 hours.

Bake extra potatoes to have ready for later in the week.

COTTAGE POTATOES

MARGARET W. HIGH, LANCASTER, PA

Makes: 6–8 servings
PREP. TIME: 15 MINUTES
COOKING TIME: 3 HOURS
IDEAL SLOW-COOKER SIZE: 5-QUART

5–6 large cooked potatoes, peeled or unpeeled, and diced
1 onion, diced
½ green bell pepper, diced, optional
2 cups diced bread, preferably dry and stale
2 cups diced sharp cheese
¾ tsp. salt
¼ tsp. pepper
1 tsp. dried rosemary
¼ cup (½ stick) butter, melted

1. In lightly greased slow cooker, combine all ingredients except melted butter. Stir gently.

2. Pour melted butter over all.

3. Cover and cook on High 2½ hours. Remove lid and cook uncovered an additional 30 minutes.

NOTE Make extra baked potatoes at one meal in order to have enough for this dish later in the week.

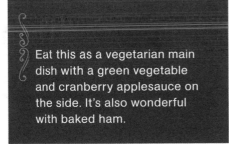

Eat this as a vegetarian main dish with a green vegetable and cranberry applesauce on the side. It's also wonderful with baked ham.

MAKE-AHEAD MIXED POTATOES FLORENTINE

BECKY FREY, LEBANON, PA

Makes: 8–10 servings
PREP. TIME: 45–60 MINUTES
COOKING TIME: 8–10 HOURS
IDEAL SLOW-COOKER SIZE: 5- OR 6-QUART

6 medium-sized white potatoes, uncooked
3 medium-sized sweet potatoes, uncooked
1 large onion, chopped
1–2 cloves garlic, pressed
2 Tbsp. (¼ stick) butter
2 Tbsp. olive oil
8 oz. low-fat or nonfat cream cheese, at room temperature
½ cup nonfat sour cream
½ cup nonfat plain yogurt
1 tsp. salt or to taste
1–1½ tsp. dill weed
¼ tsp. black pepper
10 oz. pkg. frozen, chopped spinach, thawed and squeezed dry

1. Grease interior of slow-cooker crock.

2. Peel and quarter both white and sweet potatoes. Place in slow cooker. Barely cover with water.

3. Cover. Cook on Low 6–8 hours, or until potatoes are falling-apart tender.

4. Meanwhile, in a saucepan, sauté onion and garlic in butter and olive oil on low heat, until soft and golden. Or place in a microwave-safe bowl and cook for 2 minutes on High, or until tender.

5. In an electric mixer bowl, combine sautéed onion and garlic with cream cheese, sour cream, yogurt, salt, dill weed, and pepper. Whip until well blended. Set aside.

6. Drain the potato cooking water in the slow cooker. Reserve 1 cup.

7. Mash potatoes in some of their cooking water until soft and creamy. Add more cooking water if you'd like them to be creamier.

8. Stir onion-cheese mixture into mashed potatoes.

9. Fold spinach into potato mixture.

10. Turn into greased slow cooker. Cover. Cook 2 hours on Low, or until heated through. Serve!

NOTE
≫─♥─▷
If you've made the recipe a day or so in advance of serving it, refrigerate it until the day you need it. Then, heat potatoes in slow cooker, covered, for 3–4 hours on Low, or until hot in the middle.

TIP

You can use 1 cup plain yogurt and omit the sour cream, or vice versa. The more yogurt, the greater the savory tang.

DO-AHEAD MASHED POTATOES

SHARI AND DALE MAST, HARRISONBURG, VA

Makes: 8 servings
PREP. TIME: 45 MINUTES
COOKING TIME: 3–4 HOURS
STANDING TIME: OVERNIGHT
IDEAL SLOW-COOKER SIZE: 6-QUART

12 medium potatoes, washed, peeled, and quartered

 1 small or medium onion, chopped

 4 oz. Neufchatel or fat-free cream cheese

 1 tsp. salt

 ¼ tsp. black pepper

 1 cup skim milk

1. In a saucepan, cover potatoes and onion with water. Bring to a boil, and then simmer over medium-low heat for 30 minutes or so, until fully softened. Drain.

2. Mash potatoes and onion with a potato masher to remove chunks.

3. In a large mixing bowl, combine partially mashed potatoes, cream cheese, salt, pepper, and milk. Whip together on High for 3 minutes.

4. Transfer potatoes into slow cooker. Cover and refrigerate overnight.

5. Cook on Low 3–4 hours.

VARIATION

If your diet allows, you may want to increase the salt to 1¼ or 1½ tsp. in Step 3.

POTATO-STUFFED CABBAGE

JEANETTE OBERHOLTZER, MANHEIM, PA

Makes: 10 servings
PREP. TIME: 20 MINUTES
COOKING TIME: 4–6 HOURS
IDEAL SLOW-COOKER SIZE: 6-QUART

half a large head cabbage, thinly sliced
2½ lbs. potatoes (6 or 7 medium), peeled and grated
1 onion, sliced
¼ cup rice, uncooked
1 apple, peeled and sliced
½–1 tsp. dried dill, according to your taste preference
¼–½ tsp. black pepper, according to your taste preference
¼ tsp. ground ginger
1 egg white
14¼ oz. can tomatoes

1. Spray inside of cooker with nonfat cooking spray. Then begin layering vegetables into cooker. Place one-third of the cabbage, one-third of the potatoes, one-third of the onion, one-third of the rice, one-third of the apple, and one-third of the spices and seasonings into the cooker.

2. Repeat twice.

3. Beat egg white until frothy. Fold into tomatoes. Spoon over top of vegetables.

4. Cover. Cook on Low 4–6 hours, or until vegetables are tender.

CORNBREAD-TOPPED FRIJOLES

ANDY WAGNER, QUARRYVILLE, PA

Makes: 8–10 servings
PREP. TIME: 20–30 MINUTES
COOKING TIME: 3 HOURS
IDEAL SLOW-COOKER SIZE: 5-QUART

  1 medium onion, chopped
  1 medium green bell pepper, chopped
  2 garlic cloves, minced
 16 oz. can kidney beans, rinsed and drained
 15 oz. can pinto beans, rinsed and drained
14½ oz. can diced tomatoes, undrained
  8 oz. can tomato sauce
  1 tsp. chili powder
  ½ tsp. coarsely ground black pepper
  ¼ tsp. hot pepper sauce

Cornbread Topping
  ½ cup flour
  ½ cup yellow cornmeal
  2 tsp. sugar
  1 tsp. baking powder
  ¼ tsp. salt
  1 egg, lightly beaten
  ¾ cup skim milk
  ½ cup cream-style corn
1½ Tbsp. canola oil

1. Grease interior of slow-cooker crock.

2. Stir onion, green pepper, garlic, both beans, tomatoes, tomato sauce, chili powder, black pepper, and hot sauce together in crock.

3. Cover. Cook on High 1 hour.

4. While frijoles are cooking, in a large bowl, mix together flour, cornmeal, sugar, baking powder, and salt.

5. In another bowl, combine egg, milk, corn, and oil.

6. Add wet ingredients to dry, mixing well.

7. Spoon evenly over frijoles in crock. Do not stir.

8. Cover. Cook on High 2 more hours, or until a toothpick inserted in center of cornbread comes out clean.

 NOTE "Frijoles" are just beans in Mexican cooking. Here, they get a tasty cornbread lid that soaks up some of the beans' juice as they bake. Serve this with a green tossed salad.

HOMEMADE REFRIED BEANS

EMILY FOX, BETHEL, PA
Photo appears in color section.

Makes: 15 servings
PREP. TIME: 15 MINUTES
COOKING TIME: 4–8 HOURS
IDEAL SLOW-COOKER SIZE: 6-QUART

1 onion, peeled and halved

3 cups dry pinto or black beans, rinsed

½ fresh or frozen jalapeño, chopped

2 cloves garlic

3–4 tsp. salt

1¾ tsp. black pepper

⅛ tsp. ground cumin

9 cups water

1. Grease interior of slow-cooker crock.

2. Place all ingredients in slow cooker and stir to combine.

3. Cook on Low 4–8 hours.

4. Drain off liquid, reserving it. Mash beans with potato masher, adding liquid as needed to reach the consistency you want.

TIP

These are much better than canned refried beans! Eat alone or with rice and tortillas, or use in other recipes.

BARBECUED BEANS

JANE STEINER, ORRVILLE, OH

Makes: 12–15 servings
PREP. TIME: 5–10 MINUTES
COOKING TIME: 4 HOURS
IDEAL SLOW-COOKER SIZE: 5-QUART

4 11-oz. cans pork and beans, undrained
¾ cup brown sugar
1 tsp. dry mustard
6 slices bacon, diced
½ cup ketchup

1. Grease interior of slow-cooker crock.

2. Pour 2 cans pork and beans into slow cooker.

3. In a small bowl, combine brown sugar and mustard. Sprinkle half of mixture over beans.

4. Cover with remaining cans of pork and beans. Sprinkle with rest of brown sugar and mustard.

5. Layer bacon over top. Spread ketchup over all.

6. Cut through bean mixture a bit before heating to lightly blend ingredients.

7. Cover. Cook on Low 4 hours.

NOTE This is deep rich flavor. And you don't have to pre-cook the bacon!

Cakes, Cupcakes, and Bars

DEEP AND DARK CHOCOLATE CAKE

Photo appears in color section.

Makes: 12 servings
PREP. TIME: 20 MINUTES
COOKING TIME: 3 HOURS
COOLING TIME: 30 MINUTES
IDEAL SLOW-COOKER SIZE: 5- OR 6-QUART

1 tsp. baking powder

2 tsp. baking soda

2 cups flour

pinch of salt, optional

2 cups sugar

¾ cup unsweetened cocoa powder

2 eggs

½ cup vegetable oil

1 cup hot strong coffee

1 cup milk

2 tsp. vanilla

Icing

2 cups confectioners sugar

1 Tbsp. butter, melted

1 cup peanut butter, smooth or chunky

1 tsp. vanilla

milk, enough to spread icing

TIP

When making this recipe, use a 2½-qt. baking insert that fits perfectly inside your 5-qt. slow cooker. When you bake this cake in it, it stands taller than a single layer cake, and you don't need to worry about balancing layers so they're straight and even.

1. In a large bowl, combine baking powder, baking soda, flour, and salt if you wish.

2. Stir in sugar and cocoa powder.

3. Beat in eggs. Add oil, coffee, milk, and vanilla. Mix together well. Batter will be thin and runny.

4. Grease and flour interior of baking insert or baking dish that fits in your slow cooker. Pour batter into insert or dish.

5. Cover with lid of insert or dish, or foil. Place in slow cooker crock. Cover slow cooker.

6. Cook on High 2–3 hours, or until tester inserted in middle of cake comes out clean.

7. When the cake is done, carefully lift the insert or dish out of the crock, set it on a wire rack, and let it cool for 20–30 minutes before cutting and serving.

8. If you wish, and after the cake has cooled, ice it with peanut butter icing: Cream together sugar, butter, and peanut butter.

9. Add vanilla and enough milk (begin with 1–2 Tbsp.) to make icing spread easily.

QUICK CHOCOLATE FUDGE CAKE

Makes: 10–12 servings
PREP. TIME: 15 MINUTES
COOKING TIME: 2½–3½ HOURS
IDEAL SLOW-COOKER SIZE: 5-QUART

2 layer chocolate fudge cake mix, or German chocolate cake mix
2 eggs
21 oz. can cherry pie filling
1 tsp. vanilla or almond extract, optional

1. Grease and flour interior of slow cooker crock.
2. In a good-sized bowl, mix together dry cake mix, eggs, pie filling, and extract if you wish. Batter will be pretty stiff.
3. Spoon into greased and floured crock.
4. Cover with slow cooker lid.
5. Bake on High 2½–3½ hours, or until tester inserted into center of cake comes out clean.
6. Remove crock from cooker and allow to cool, uncovered.
7. Serve from crock, either in wedges, or spoonfuls.

TIP

Drops of water will gather on the inside of the slow cooker lid while the cake bakes. To keep the water from dripping onto the finished cake, remove the lid by lifting it quickly and swooping it away from yourself.

HOT FUDGE CAKE

EVELYN L. WARD, GREELEY, CO

Makes: 8 servings
PREP. TIME: 10 MINUTES
COOKING TIME: 1½–1¾ HOURS
IDEAL SLOW COOKER SIZE: 3½-QUART

1¾ cups brown sugar, divided

1 cup flour

3 Tbsp., plus ¼ cup, unsweetened cocoa, divided

1½ tsp. baking powder

½ tsp. salt

½ cup skim milk

2 Tbsp. butter, melted

½ tsp. vanilla

1¾ cups boiling water

1. In a mixing bowl, mix together 1 cup brown sugar, flour, 3 Tbsp. cocoa, baking powder, and salt.

2. Stir in milk, butter, and vanilla.

3. Pour into slow cooker sprayed with non-fat cooking spray.

4. In a separate bowl, mix together ¾ cup brown sugar and ¼ cup cocoa. Sprinkle over batter in the slow cooker. Do not stir.

5. Pour boiling water over mixture. Do not stir.

6. Cover. Cook on High 1½–1¾ hours, or until toothpick inserted into cake comes out clean.

§ TIP

Serve with low-fat ice cream or fat-free whipped topping if you wish, and if diets allow.

SPICY CHOCOLATE PUMPKIN CAKE

Photo appears in color section.

Makes: 10–12 servings
PREP. TIME: 15–20 MINUTES
COOKING TIME: 3½–4 HOURS
IDEAL SLOW-COOKER SIZE: 5-QUART

2 layer spice cake mix
½ cup water
½ cup vegetable oil
3 large eggs
4 oz. cream cheese, softened
1 cup canned or cooked pumpkin
6 squares semisweet baking chocolate, coarsely chopped

1. Grease and flour interior of slow cooker crock.

2. Using an electric mixer, blend together cake mix, water, oil, and eggs.

3. Blend in cream cheese and pumpkin, beating on medium speed.

4. Stir in chopped chocolate.

5. Pour into prepared crock, smoothing it out evenly.

6. Cover. Bake on High 3½–4 hours, or until tester inserted into center of cake comes out clean.

7. Uncover, making sure condensation on inside of lid doesn't drip on finished cake.

8. Remove crock from cooker and allow cake to cool.

9. When cake is completely cool, frost with cream cheese frosting (recipe on page 267) if you wish.

CHOCOLATE APPLESAUCE CAKE

Makes: 12–15 servings
PREP. TIME: 20 MINUTES
COOKING TIME: 2½–3 HOURS
COOLING TIME: 30 MINUTES
IDEAL SLOW-COOKER SIZE: 5- OR 6-QUART

1½ cups sugar

½ cup oil

2 eggs

2 cups applesauce

2 cups flour

1½ tsp. baking soda

½ tsp. cinnamon

2 Tbsp. unsweetened cocoa powder

Topping

3 Tbsp. sugar

1 cup chocolate chips

½ cup chopped nuts, optional

1. In a medium-sized bowl, combine 1½ cups sugar, oil, eggs, and applesauce, mixing well.

2. Add flour, baking soda, cinnamon, and cocoa powder. Stir together thoroughly.

3. Grease and flour a baking insert or baking dish that fits in your slow cooker.

4. Pour batter into insert or baking dish.

5. In a small bowl, mix sugar and chocolate chips together, plus chopped nuts if you wish.

6. Sprinkle over batter.

7. Cover with insert or baking dish lid, or foil. Place in slow cooker crock. Cover with cooker lid.

8. Bake on High 2½–3 hours, or until tester inserted in center of cake comes out clean.

9. Carefully remove insert or baking dish from cooker. Place on wire baking rack and uncover. Allow to cool for 20–30 minutes before slicing to serve.

NOTE You get away with fewer calories in this cake because of the 2 cups of apple-sauce. But you don't suffer when you eat it. The chocolate chips—and pick your favorite variety of chocolate—melt beguilingly into the cake.

APPLE GERMAN CHOCOLATE CAKE

Photo appears in color section.

Makes: 10–12 servings
PREP. TIME: 15–20 MINUTES
COOKING TIME: 3½–4 HOURS
IDEAL SLOW-COOKER SIZE: 5 QUART

21 oz. can apple pie filling

2 layer German chocolate cake mix

3 eggs

¾ cup coarsely chopped walnuts

½ cup miniature semisweet chocolate chips

1. Grease and flour interior of slow cooker crock.

2. Place pie filling in blender or food processor. Cover and process until apples are in ¼" chunks.

3. If using food processor, add dry cake mix and eggs. Process until smooth. (If you used a blender for the apples, pour them into an electric mixer bowl, add dry cake mix and eggs, and beat on medium speed for 5 minutes.)

4. Pour into prepared slow cooker crock.

5. Sprinkle with walnuts and chocolate chips.

6. Cover. Bake on High 3½–4 hours, or until tester inserted into center of cake comes out clean.

7. Remove crock from cooker. Allow to cool completely before serving.

NOTE The apples here add a comforting tenderness, but they let the chocolate reign.

MOIST AND CREAMY COCONUT CAKE

Photo appears in color section.

Makes: 10–12 servings
PREP. TIME: 20 MINUTES
COOKING TIME: 2½–3½ HOURS
CHILLING TIME: OVERNIGHT
IDEAL SLOW-COOKER SIZE: 5-QUART

2 layer yellow cake mix

1¼ cups milk

½ cup sugar

2 cups flaked unsweetened coconut, divided

9 oz. container frozen whipped topping, thawed

1 tsp. vanilla

1. Grease and flour interior of slow cooker crock.

2. Prepare cake mix as directed on package.

3. Spoon into prepared crock, smoothing batter out evenly.

4. Bake on High 2½–3½ hours, or until tester inserted into center of cake comes out clean.

5. Uncover, making sure that condensation on inside of lid doesn't drip onto finished cake.

6. Remove crock from cooker and allow to cool for 15 minutes.

7. Meanwhile, combine milk, sugar, and ½ cup coconut in a saucepan. Bring to a boil, stirring frequently. Reduce heat and simmer 1 minute.

8. Spoon evenly over warm cake. Let cool completely.

9. Fold together ½ cup coconut, whipped topping, and vanilla. Spread over cooled cake.

10. Sprinkle remaining coconut evenly over top of cake.

11. Cover and chill overnight in fridge.

12. Slice, or spoon out of crock, to serve.

TIP

You've got three toppings going here—which is what makes this cake such a stand-out, especially for coconut lovers. Make sure you've got enough time to chill the finished cake for 8 hours before serving it.

BEST PINEAPPLE CAKE

PHYLLLIS GOOD, LANCASTER, PA
Photo appears in color section.

Makes: 10–12 servings
PREP. TIME: 20 MINUTES
COOKING TIME: 2½–3 HOURS
IDEAL SLOW-COOKER SIZE: 5- OR 6-QUART

2 cups flour

2 cups sugar

2 tsp. baking powder

2 eggs

1 tsp. vanilla

20 oz. can crushed pineapple, undrained

1 cup chopped nuts

Topping

3 oz. pkg. cream cheese, softened

4 Tbsp. (½ stick) butter, softened

¾ cup confectioners' sugar

¼ tsp. vanilla

¼ cup chopped nuts

1. Mix together flour, sugar, and baking powder in a big bowl.

2. Stir in eggs, vanilla, and undrained pineapple.

3. When well blended, stir in nuts.

4. Grease interior of baking insert or baking dish that fits in your slow cooker.

5. Pour in batter. Cover with lid or greased foil.

6. Place baking insert or dish in slow cooker. Cover with slow cooker lid.

7. Bake on High 2½–3 hours, or until tester inserted in center comes out clean.

8. When cake is fully baked, carefully remove insert or dish from cooker. Place on wire baking rack and let cool completely.

9. When cake is nearly cool, mix together cream cheese, butter, sugar, and vanilla. Spread over cooled cake. Sprinkle with chopped nuts.

10. Cut into wedges and serve.

NOTE Whenever I serve this, no one can believe how moist and wonderfully fruity this cake is. I made a batch for my daughter's Supper Club, and she said, "I've never heard guys use the word 'tender' to describe a cake before!"

SUMMER BREEZES CAKE

Photo appears in color section.

Makes: 10–12 servings
PREP. TIME: 20 MINUTES
COOKING TIME: 2½–3½ HOURS
IDEAL SLOW-COOKER SIZE: 5-QUART

2 layer yellow cake mix

11 oz. can mandarin oranges, undrained

4 eggs

½ cup cooking oil

Frosting

½ cup whipped topping, thawed

8 oz. can crushed pineapple, drained

3 oz. pkg. instant vanilla pudding

1. Grease and flour interior of slow cooker crock.

2. In a large mixing bowl, thoroughly combine dry cake mix, undrained oranges, eggs, and cooking oil.

3. Pour into prepared crock, spreading batter out evenly.

4. Cover. Bake on High 2½–3½ hours, or until tester inserted into center of cake comes out clean.

5. Uncover, making sure that condensation on inside of cooker lid doesn't drip on finished cake.

6. Remove crock from cooker and allow cake to cool completely.

7. When cake is cooled, prepare frosting by folding together whipped topping, drained crushed pineapple, and dry pudding mix.

8. Spread over cake. Refrigerate until ready to serve cake, sliced, or spooned out of crock.

CHERRY SWIRL CAKE

Makes: 12–14 servings
PREP TIME: 10–20 MINUTES
COOKING TIME: 3–4 HOURS
IDEAL SLOW-COOKER SIZE: 6- OR 7-QUART OVAL

¾ cup sugar

4 Tbsp. (half a stick) butter, softened

¼ cup shortening

¾ tsp. baking powder

½ tsp. vanilla

½ tsp. almond extract

2 eggs

1½ cups flour

half a 21-oz. can cherry pie filling

Glaze

½ cup confectioners' sugar

½–1 Tbsp. milk

1. Mix all cake ingredients together except pie filling. Stir just until mixed.

2. Grease a loaf pan. Spread ⅔ of batter into pan.

3. Spread pie filling over batter.

4. Drop remaining batter by tablespoonfuls onto pie filling. Spread batter over pie filling as well as you can, but it's okay if you can't cover it completely. With a knife, swirl the batter through the pie filling—but don't stir or you'll lose the swirl effect.

5. Cover loaf pan with greased foil. Place pan into slow cooker crock. Cover with cooker lid.

6. Bake on High for 3–4 hours, or until tester inserted in center comes out clean.

7. Carefully remove pan from crock. Place on wire baking rack, uncovered, and allow to cool.

8. When cake is just warm, stir glaze ingredients together and then drizzle over cake.

9. Slice and serve.

NOTE This is good for breakfast, good for lunch, good anytime! The bread is absolutely fabulous as a quick bread, sliced and toasted and spread with butter while warm.

BLUEBERRY SWIRL CAKE

Photo appears in color section.

Makes: 10–12 servings
PREP. TIME: 15–20 MINUTES
COOKING TIME: 3½–4 HOURS
IDEAL SLOW-COOKER SIZE: 5-QUART

3 oz. pkg. cream cheese, softened

2 layer white cake mix

3 eggs

3 Tbsp. water

21 oz. can blueberry pie filling

1. Grease and flour interior of slow cooker crock.

2. Beat cream cheese in a large mixing bowl until soft and creamy.

3. Stir in dry cake mix, eggs, and water. Blend well with cream cheese.

4. Pour batter into prepared crock, spreading it out evenly.

5. Pour blueberry pie filling over top of batter.

6. Swirl blueberries and batter by zigzagging a table knife through the batter.

7. Cover. Bake on High 3½–4 hours, or until a tester inserted into center of cake comes out clean.

8. Uncover, being careful to not let condensation from lid drop on finished cake.

9. Remove crock from cooker.

10. Serve cake warm or at room temperature.

TIP

Keep a box of the cake mix and a can of blueberry pie filling in your pantry, and a package of cream cheese in the fridge, and you're set up for spontaneous guests. Invite everyone back for dessert after a soccer game or a movie—and serve them this. Remember, it's been cooking while you've been out having fun!

LOTSA BLUEBERRIES CAKE

Photo appears in color section.

Makes: 8 servings
PREP. TIME: 15 MINUTES
COOKING TIME: 2–3 HOURS
IDEAL SLOW-COOKER SIZE: 5-QUART (OR
6- OR 7-QUART OVAL)

1 egg
1 cup sugar
3 Tbsp. butter, melted
½ cup milk
2 cups flour
1 tsp. baking powder
   pinch of salt
1 pint fresh blueberries

1. Cream together egg, sugar, and butter. Add milk and mix well. Stir in flour, baking powder, and salt. Mix again.

2. Fold blueberries into this stiff batter.

3. Grease interior of loaf pan, slow cooker baking insert, or baking dish that fits in your slow cooker.

4. Cover either with greased foil or lid of baking insert or baking dish.

5. Place baking container into slow cooker crock. Cover with cooker lid.

6. Bake on High 2–3 hours, or until tester inserted in center comes out clean.

7. When finished baking, carefully remove baking container from crock. Set on wire baking rack to cool.

8. When cool, slice and serve.

> **TIP**
> You can make this out of blueberry season by using frozen blueberries. Don't thaw them. Just toss the frozen berries with a tablespoon or two of flour in a bowl before stirring them into the batter (in Step 4). Continue with the recipe—and you'll love the outcome!

RHUBARB SOUR CREAM CAKE

Photo appears in color section.

Makes: 10 servings
PREP. TIME: 35 MINUTES
COOKING TIME: 3 HOURS
COOLING TIME: 30 MINUTES
IDEAL SLOW-COOKER SIZE: 6-QUART OVAL

4 Tbsp. (½ stick) butter, softened

¾ cup brown sugar, firmly packed

1 egg

1 Tbsp. vanilla

2 cups flour

1 tsp. baking soda

1 tsp. salt

1 cup sour cream

2 cups rhubarb, cut into ½"-thick pieces

½ cup sugar

½ tsp. cinnamon

dash of nutmeg

1. In a large bowl, cream butter and brown sugar together until fluffy.

2. Beat in egg and vanilla.

3. In a separate bowl, sift flour with baking soda and salt. Stir into creamed ingredients.

4. Fold in sour cream and rhubarb pieces.

5. Grease full-sized loaf pan.

6. Spoon batter into loaf pan.

7. Mix together ½ cup sugar, ½ tsp. cinnamon, and dash of nutmeg. Sprinkle over batter.

8. Cover loaf pan with foil. Place filled pan in oval slow cooker. Cover with cooker lid.

9. Bake on High 3 hours, or until tester inserted in center of cake comes out clean.

10. Remove pan carefully from slow cooker. Place on wire baking rack to cool 20–30 minutes. Serve warm or at room temperature.

NOTE If you love rhubarb and are always on the prowl for good recipes that include it, add this one to your list. There's something about the balance between sweet and tart here that's irresistible.

LIGHTLY WHITE PEAR CAKE

Photo appears in color section.

Makes: 10–12 servings
PREP. TIME: 15–20 MINUTES
COOKING TIME: 3½–4 HOURS
IDEAL SLOW-COOKER SIZE: 5-QUART

15¼ oz. can pears (you're going to chop them, so buy pear pieces if you can find them)

2 layer white cake mix

1 egg

2 egg whites

2 tsp. confectioners sugar

1. Grease and flour interior of slow cooker crock.

2. Fish pears out of syrup to chop them, but keep the syrup.

3. Place chopped pears and syrup into electric mixing bowl. Add dry cake mix, egg, and egg whites.

4. Beat with electric mixer on low speed for 30 seconds, and then on high speed for 4 minutes.

5. Spoon batter into prepared crock, spreading it out evenly.

6. Cover cooker. Bake on High 3½–4 hours, or until tester inserted in center of cake comes out clean.

7. Uncover without letting condensation drip on cake. Remove crock from cooker. Allow to cool completely.

8. Dust with confectioners sugar before slicing or spooning out to serve.

> **TIP**
>
> Don't add more chopped fruit than your cake recipe calls for. The moisture content will keep the cake or bread from rising and it will be gummy.

BANANA NUT CAKE

Photo appears in color section.

Makes: 12–14 servings
PREP. TIME: 20 MINUTES
COOKING TIME: 2½–3 HOURS
IDEAL SLOW-COOKER SIZE: 5-QUART (OR
6- OR 7-QUART OVAL)

2 cups flour

1 tsp. baking powder

1 tsp. baking soda

½ tsp. salt

1½ cups sugar

½ cup shortening

½ cup buttermilk*

1½ cups sliced bananas

2 eggs

1 tsp. vanilla

½ cup chopped nuts

Banana Frosting

4 Tbsp. (half a stick) butter, softened

½ tsp. vanilla

1¾ cups, or a bit more, confectioners' sugar

2 Tbsp. mashed bananas

½ tsp. lemon juice

1. Sift flour, baking powder, baking soda, and salt together in a good-sized mixing bowl.

2. Combine sugar, shortening, buttermilk, bananas, eggs, and vanilla in a food processor until smooth.

3. Pour wet ingredients into dry. Add nuts. Mix just until combined.

4. Grease and flour a baking insert, baking dish, or loaf pan that fits in your slow cooker.

5. Pour in batter.

6. Cover with lid of insert or dish, or with greased foil. Place container in slow cooker crock. Cover with cooker lid.

7. Bake on High for 2½–3 hours, or until tester inserted in center of cake comes out clean.

8. Carefully remove pan from cooker. Place on wire baking rack, uncovered, and allow to cool.

9. While cake is cooling, make frosting. Cream together butter and vanilla by hand or with an electric mixer until well mixed. Gradually beat in sugar. Stir in bananas and lemon juice. Spread over cooled cake.

* If you don't have buttermilk, put 1½ tsp. lemon juice or white vinegar in a ½-cup measure. Fill measuring cup with milk. Stir. Let stand 5–7 minutes. Then add to wet ingredients, including any curds that have formed.

> **TIP**
>
> You've got bananas two ways here—sliced and smashed. You'll be all right if you've got three medium-sized ones. Don't skip the frosting—just mix it up with no cooking required.

SOUR CREAM PEACH CAKE

Photo appears in color section.

Makes: 10–12 servings
PREP. TIME: 15 MINUTES
COOKING TIME: 3½–4 HOURS
IDEAL SLOW-COOKER SIZE: 5-QUART

2   layer orange-flavored cake mix
21   oz. can peach pie filling
½   cup sour cream
2   eggs
    confectioners sugar or whipped topping

1. Grease and flour interior of slow cooker crock.

2. Mix dry cake mix, pie filling, sour cream, and eggs together until thoroughly blended.

3. Pour batter into prepared crock, spreading it out evenly.

4. Cover. Bake on High 3½–4 hours, or until tester inserted into center of cake comes out clean.

5. Remove crock from cooker and allow to cool to room temperature.

6. Sprinkle cake with confectioners sugar, or spread with whipped topping just before serving.

UNBELIEVABLE CARROT CAKE

Photo appears in color section.

Makes: 12–14 servings
PREP. TIME: 15 MINUTES
COOKING TIME: 3½–4 HOURS
IDEAL SLOW-COOKER SIZE: 6- OR 7-QUART
OVAL

2 layer spice cake mix

2 cups (½ lb.) shredded carrots

1 cup crushed pineapple with juice

3 egg whites

½ cup All-Bran cereal

Cream Cheese Frosting

3 oz. pkg. cream cheese, softened

¼ cup (half a stick) butter, softened

2 cups confectioners sugar

1 tsp. vanilla

milk (start with 1 Tbsp. and increase gradually if you need more)

1. Combine the dry cake mix, shredded carrots, crushed pineapple with juice, egg whites, and All-Bran cereal thoroughly in a big bowl.

2. Grease and flour a loaf pan.

3. Pour batter into prepared pan.

4. Cover with greased foil and place in slow cooker.

5. Cover cooker with its lid.

6. Bake on High for 3½–4 hours, or until tester inserted in center of cake comes out clean.

7. Carefully remove pan from cooker. Place on wire baking rack to cool, uncovered.

8. As the cake cools, make the frosting by mixing together the softened cream cheese and butter, confectioners sugar, and vanilla. When well combined, stir in milk, starting with 1 Tbsp. and adding more if necessary, until the frosting becomes spreadable.

9. Frost cake when it's completely cooled.

10. Slice and serve.

TIP

No need to shred carrots yourself anymore if you're short on time. You can buy them shredded.

PUMPKIN CAKE

Photo appears in color section.

Makes: 12 servings
PREP. TIME: 20 MINUTES
COOKING TIME: 2½–3 HOURS
IDEAL SLOW-COOKER SIZE: 5- OR 6-QUART

2 eggs
1 cup sugar
¾ cup vegetable oil
1½ cups flour
1½ tsp. baking powder
1 tsp. cinnamon
1 tsp. baking soda
pinch of salt
¼ tsp. ground ginger
1 cup pumpkin
½ cup chopped walnuts

Cream Cheese Frosting
4 Tbsp. (half a stick) butter, softened
3 oz. pkg. cream cheese, softened
2 cups confectioners sugar
1 tsp. vanilla

1. Beat the eggs well in a large bowl. Stir in the sugar and blend well.
2. Beat in the oil.
3. In a separate bowl, stir together flour, baking powder, cinnamon, baking soda, salt, and ground ginger.
4. Add the dry ingredients alternately with the pumpkin to the wet.
5. When well mixed, stir in the walnuts.
6. Grease and flour a baking insert or baking dish that fits into your slow cooker.
7. Spoon batter into insert or dish. Cover with its lid or greased foil.
8. Place filled insert or dish into cooker. Cover with the cooker lid.
9. Bake on High 2½–3 hours, or until tester inserted in center comes out clean.
10. Carefully remove insert or dish from cooker and place on wire baking rack.

11. Allow to cool, uncovered.

12. Meanwhile, make the cream cheese frosting. Stir butter and cream cheese together until smooth.

13. Carefully fold in sugar. Stir in vanilla.

14. When cake is completely cooled, cover with frosting.

15. Cut in half, and then in wedges to serve.

SHOOFLY CAKE

Photo appears in color section.

Makes: 8–10 servings
PREP. TIME: 20–30 MINUTES
COOKING TIME: 2½–3 HOURS
IDEAL SLOW-COOKER SIZE: 6- OR 7-QUART
OVAL

2 cups flour
1 cup + 2 Tbsp. brown sugar
8 Tbsp. (1 stick) butter, softened
½ cup light molasses*
1 cup boiling water
1 tsp. baking soda

1. Combine flour, sugar, and butter in a good-sized bowl. Work into fine crumbs with your fingers.

2. Scoop out 1½ cups crumbs and reserve for topping the cake.

3. Add molasses, boiling water, and baking soda to crumbs left in the bowl. Mix together well.

4. Grease and flour a loaf pan. Pour thin batter into pan. Sprinkle with reserved 1½ cups crumbs.

5. Cover pan with greased foil, and then place in oval cooker. Cover with cooker lid.

6. Bake on High for 2½–3 hours, or until tester inserted in center comes out clean.

7. Carefully remove pan from slow cooker. Place on wire baking rack to cool.

8. Serve warm or at room temperature, as is, or topped with ice cream. (Some people like it in a cereal bowl with milk—for breakfast!)

* In eastern Pennsylvania, where Shoofly has its roots, King Syrup is preferred over light molasses. Use it if you can find it.

SUNNY SPICE CAKE

Photo appears in color section.

Makes: 10–12 servings
PREP. TIME: 15 MINUTES
COOKING TIME: 2½–3½ HOURS
IDEAL SLOW-COOKER SIZE: 5-QUART

2 layer spice cake mix

3⅝ oz. pkg. butterscotch instant pudding

2 cups milk

2 eggs

10–12 fresh or canned peach halves, drained if canned

frozen whipped topping, thawed

1. Grease and flour interior of slow cooker crock.

2. In a mixing bowl, blend together cake mix, pudding mix, milk, and eggs.

3. Pour into prepared crock, spreading batter out evenly.

4. Cover. Bake on High 2½–3½ hours, or until tester inserted into center of cake comes out clean.

5. Uncover, being careful not to let condensation from inside of lid drip on finished cake.

6. Remove crock from cooker and let cool.

7. When ready to serve, cut into serving-size pieces. Place a peach half on each serving of cake. Top each with a dollop of whipped topping.

NOTE A combination you might not have thought of putting together, but the peaches are a wonderful addition. Plus, you don't need to make frosting.

SPICE CAKE

Makes: 12 servings
PREP. TIME: 20 MINUTES
COOKING TIME: 2–3 HOURS
IDEAL SLOW-COOKER SIZE: 6- OR 7-QUART
OVAL

2 cups brown sugar

8 Tbsp. (1 stick) butter, softened

2 eggs

2½ cups sifted flour

1½ tsp. baking powder

1 tsp. cinnamon

1 tsp. nutmeg

1 tsp. baking soda

1 cup sour milk*

1 tsp. vanilla

Caramel Icing

4 Tbsp. (½ stick) butter

½ cup brown sugar

2 Tbsp. milk

¾–1 cup confectioners sugar

1. Cream sugar and butter together until fluffy.

2. Add eggs and beat until mixture is light.

3. In a separate bowl, sift together flour, baking powder, cinnamon, nutmeg, and baking soda. Mix together well.

4. Add dry ingredients alternately with the sour milk to the creamed ingredients. Beat well after each addition.

5. Stir in vanilla.

6. Grease and flour a loaf pan. Pour batter into pan. Cover with greased foil.

7. Place loaf pan into slow cooker crock. Cover with slow cooker lid.

8. Bake on High 2–3 hours, or until tester inserted in center comes out clean.

9. When finished baking, carefully remove pan from cooker. Set on wire baking rack to cool.

10. When cake is nearly cooled to room temperature, make icing. Melt butter in saucepan. Stir in brown sugar, stirring continually over heat for 2 minutes. Add milk. Continue stirring until mixture comes to a boil. Remove from heat and let cool. Sift ¾ cup confectioners sugar over caramel mixture. Stir in until smooth. Sift in more if needed until icing can be spread over the cooled cake.

11. When cake is completely cooled, spread with caramel icing.

To make sour milk, put 1 Tbsp. lemon juice or white vinegar in a 1-cup measure. Then fill the cup with milk. Stir. Let stand for 5–10 minutes. It will curdle slightly, as it's supposed to do. Use the whole works in the batter.

GINGERBREAD WITH LEMON SAUCE

Photo appears in color section.

Makes: 10 servings
PREP. TIME: 20–30 MINUTES
COOKING TIME: 2–3 HOURS
IDEAL SLOW-COOKER SIZE: 5-QUART (OR
6- OR 7-QUART OVAL)

2 cups flour

1 cup sugar

1 tsp. ground ginger

1 tsp. ground cinnamon

½ cup shortening

1 egg, beaten

2 Tbsp. strong molasses

½ tsp. salt

1 tsp. baking soda

1 cup buttermilk*

   whipped cream, optional

Lemon Sauce

2 cups water

4 Tbsp. cornstarch

1½ cups sugar

¼ tsp. salt

3 egg yolks

1½ Tbsp. butter

   juice of 2 lemons

   zest of 1 lemon

1. To make the gingerbread, sift flour, sugar, ginger, and cinnamon into large bowl. Mix together.

2. Cut shortening into flour mixture to make fine crumbs.

3. Take out ½ cup crumbs and set aside.

4. To crumbs remaining in mixing bowl, add egg, molasses, salt, baking soda, and buttermilk (or your substitute). Beat well.

5. Grease and flour either a baking insert, a baking dish, or a loaf pan that fits into your slow cooker.

6. Pour batter into baking container. Sprinkle with ½ cup reserved crumbs.

7. Place baking container into slow cooker crock. Cover with the container's lid or greased foil. Cover slow cooker with its lid.

8. Bake on High 2–3 hours, or until tester inserted in center of gingerbread comes out clean.

9. Carefully remove container from cooker. Place on wire baking rack and uncover to cool.

10. To make lemon sauce while gingerbread is baking, bring water to boil in saucepan.

11. Combine cornstarch, sugar, and salt in a bowl, mixing well.

12. Whisk dry ingredients into boiling water, stirring constantly. Cook about 5 minutes over low heat until mixture thickens.

13. Beat egg yolks in a bowl. Stir a small amount of hot sugar mixture into beaten yolks, whisking continually.

14. Return the whole mixture to the pan and cook 1 more minute, stirring constantly.

15. Remove from heat. Add butter, lemon juice, and lemon zest. Stir to combine.

16. Serve over warm slices of gingerbread. Top with whipped cream, if you wish.

If you don't have buttermilk, put 1 Tbsp. lemon juice or white vinegar in a 1-cup measure. Fill the cup with milk. Stir. Let stand for 5–10 minutes. Then pour into batter according to instructions, curds and all.

NOTE This sturdy, old-fashioned dessert gets a nice lift from the lemon sauce made with fresh lemons. The sauce isn't required, of course, but it adds a good zing.

PEACHY GINGERBREAD

Makes: 12–14 servings
PREP. TIME: 20–30 MINUTES
COOKING TIME: 2½–3½ HOURS
IDEAL SLOW-COOKER SIZE: 6- OR 7-QUART
OVAL

⅓ cup butter, softened

½ cup brown sugar

½ cup strong molasses

1 egg

1¾ cups flour

½ tsp. salt

1 tsp. baking powder

½ tsp. baking soda

1½ tsp. ground ginger

1 tsp. cinnamon

¾ cup sour milk or buttermilk*

2 cups canned sliced peaches,
   well-drained

TIP

Try Brer Rabbit Molasses's mild flavor for this recipe so the strength of the molasses doesn't overwhelm the peach flavor.

1. Cream butter and sugar together, beating until fluffy.

2. Add molasses and egg and beat until well mixed.

3. In a separate bowl, stir together flour, salt, baking powder, baking soda, ginger, and cinnamon.

4. Add dry ingredients to wet ingredients, alternately with sour milk. Beat well after each addition.

5. Grease interior of loaf pan. Cover bottom with well-drained sliced peaches.

6. Pour batter over peaches. Cover with greased foil.

7. Place pan into slow cooker crock. Cover with crock lid.

8. Bake on High for 2½–3½ hours, or until tester inserted in center of cake comes out clean.

9. Carefully remove pan from crock. Place on wire baking rack. Allow to cool. Serve warm or at room temperature, making sure to scoop out peaches from the bottom with each serving.

If you don't have sour milk or buttermilk, place 1 Tbsp. lemon juice or white vinegar in a 1 cup-measure. Pour in milk to the ¾-cup line. Stir. Let stand for 5–10 minutes. Then add to batter according to instructions above, including the curds if some have formed.

FRESH PLUM KUCHEN

Makes: 6–8 servings
PREP. TIME: 20 MINUTES
COOKING TIME: 2–3 HOURS
IDEAL SLOW-COOKER SIZE: 3- OR 4-QUART

4   Tbsp. (half a stick) butter, softened
¾   cup sugar
2   eggs
1   tsp. lemon zest
1   cup flour
1   tsp. baking powder
¼   cup milk
     sugar
4   fresh plums
1   Tbsp. cinnamon
½   cup brown sugar

1. In a mixing bowl, beat butter and sugar together until light and creamy.

2. Beat in the eggs and lemon zest.

3. In a separate bowl, combine flour and baking powder.

4. Add dry ingredients to wet. Add milk, mixing well.

5. Grease interior of slow cooker crock.

6. Sprinkle bottom and sides of crock lightly with sugar.

7. Spoon in batter, spreading it out evenly.

8. Slice plums and arrange on top of dough.

9. In dry ingredient bowl, stir cinnamon and brown sugar together. Sprinkle over plums.

10. Cover with slow cooker lid. Bake on High 2–3 hours, until middle is set and juice is bubbling.

11. Remove lid with a big swoop away from yourself to prevent condensation on inside of lid from dripping onto the kuchen.

12. Lift crock out of cooker and let kuchen cool until warm or room temperature before eating.

TIP

It's not a bad idea to keep a fresh lemon in your fridge all the time. Then you can add a teaspoon of zest to a dessert like this one. You'll start to see possibilities for using fresh lemon juice in salad dressings or grating zest over roasted pork and grilled beef. Or add slices of lemon to your drinking water any time.

ONE-POT SHORTCAKE

Photo appears in color section.

Makes: 10–12 servings
PREP. TIME: 15 MINUTES
COOKING TIME: 2½–3 HOURS
COOLING TIME: 30 MINUTES
IDEAL SLOW-COOKER SIZE: 6-QUART OVAL

2 Tbsp. (¼ stick) butter

1 cup sugar

2 eggs

2½ cups flour

½ tsp. salt

2 tsp. baking powder

1 cup milk

1 tsp. vanilla

1. Melt butter in good-sized, microwave-safe bowl.

2. Stir in sugar and eggs thoroughly.

3. Add flour, salt, and baking powder. Mix together until crumbly.

4. Stir in milk and vanilla until well mixed. (The batter won't be completely smooth, but that's okay.)

5. Grease loaf pan.

6. Pour batter into loaf pan. Cover with greased foil.

7. Set in oval slow cooker. Cover cooker.

8. Bake on High for 2½–3 hours, or until tester inserted in center comes out clean.

9. Allow to cool for 20–30 minutes before slicing and serving.

NOTE Don't you love a recipe that you can mix up in only one dish? And one that calls for ingredients you have on hand? Topped with sliced strawberries, this recipe lets the strawberries shine!

DEEP AND DARK CHOCOLATE CAKE ♥ page 250

SPICY CHOCOLATE PUMPKIN CAKE ♥ page 253

APPLE GERMAN CHOCOLATE CAKE ♥ page 255

MOIST AND CREAMY COCONUT CAKE ♥ page 256

BEST PINEAPPLE CAKE ♥ page 257

SUMMER BREEZES CAKE ♥ page 258

BLUEBERRY SWIRL CAKE ♥ page 260

LOTSA BLUEBERRIES CAKE ♥ page 261

RHUBARB SOUR CREAM CAKE
page 262

LIGHTLY WHITE PEAR CAKE
page 263

BANANA NUT CAKE
page 264

SOUR CREAM PEACH CAKE ♥ page 266

UNBELIEVABLE CARROT CAKE
page 267

PUMPKIN CAKE
page 268

SHOOFLY CAKE ♥ page 270

SUNNY SPICE CAKE
page 271

GINGERBREAD
WITH LEMON SAUCE
page 274

ONE-POT SHORTCAKE ♥ page 278

LIGHT AND FLUFFY CHOCOLATE CHIP CHEESECAKE ♥ page 279

FRESH PEACH CUPCAKES
page 282

BANANA GROVE CUPCAKES
page 284

CHOCOLATE CHIP PIZZA ♥ page 285

PHILLY CHIPPERS ♥ page 286

LIGHT AND FLUFFY CHOCOLATE CHIP CHEESECAKE

Photo appears in color section.

Makes: 30 1" square servings
PREP. TIME: 20–30 MINUTES
COOKING TIME: 1½–2 HOURS
CHILLING TIME: 3 HOURS
IDEAL SLOW-COOKER SIZE: 6-QUART OVAL

3	eggs
¾	cup sugar
3	8-oz. pkgs. cream cheese, softened
1	tsp. vanilla
1½	16-oz. rolls refrigerated chocolate chip cookie dough*
	whipped cream, optional
	chocolate topping, optional

1. Place all ingredients except cookie dough in large mixer or food processor bowl.

2. Blend together just until creamy, about 20–30 seconds. Do not overmix. Set aside.

3. Slice cookie dough into ¼"-thick slices. Set aside 9 slices.

4. Lightly grease interior of slow cooker crock. Lay remaining slices over bottom of cooker. Pat them together to form a solid crust.

5. Spoon in cream cheese mixture. Spread over cookie crust.

6. Arrange the reserved 9 cookie slices on top of cream-cheese mixture.

7. Cover cooker. Bake on High 1½–2 hours, or until cookies are baked but not burned and cream cheese sets up.

8. Uncover and allow to cool to room temperature.

9. Then refrigerate for 3 hours or more. When firm, cut into 1" squares.

10. If you wish, top with whipped cream and/or chocolate topping to serve.

> * Keep the dough refrigerated until you're ready to use it. It's easiest to work with when it's stiff. You'll have half a roll left over to make cookies.

TIP

Have your nose on alert while you're baking this cheesecake. If your slow cooker cooks hot, flip it off the minute you smell that the cookie crust might be getting dark. Leave the cheesecake in the crock for another hour so that the creamy filling sets up, without the crust burning.

GRAHAM CRACKER CUPCAKES

Makes: 4 large cupcakes
PREP. TIME: 15–20 MINUTES
COOKING TIME: 2 HOURS
STANDING TIME: 1 DAY
IDEAL SLOW-COOKER SIZE: 6- OR 7-QUART OVAL

1   Tbsp. shortening

¼   cup sugar

1   small egg

8   graham crackers, crushed

½   tsp. baking powder

¼   cup chopped nuts of your choice, optional

¼   tsp. vanilla

¼   cup milk

¼   cup unsweetened crushed pineapple

¼   cup sugar

1. Beat shortening and sugar together until creamy.

2. Beat in egg, crushed graham crackers, baking powder, nuts if you wish, vanilla, and milk. Mix well.

3. Grease interior of four 3-oz. ramekins. Divide batter among them.

4. Place filled ramekins into slow cooker crock. Cover with slow cooker lid.

5. Bake on High 2 hours, or until tester inserted in center of ramekins comes out clean.

6. While cupcakes are baking, cook unsweetened pineapple and sugar together for a few minutes, until sugar melts.

7. Spoon mixture over tops of baked cupcakes. Allow to stand, covered, for at least a day before serving.

NOTE If you still feel warm about graham crackers from when you were a kid, here's a tasty twist on them, kept moist by the pineapple surprise.

PUMPKIN COCONUT CUPCAKES

Makes: 4 large cupcakes
PREP. TIME: 20 MINUTES
COOKING TIME: 2 HOURS
IDEAL SLOW-COOKER SIZE: 6- OR 7-QUART OVAL

½ cup sugar

½ cup cooked or canned pumpkin

⅓ cup cooking oil

1 egg

½ cup flour

¼ tsp. salt

½ tsp. baking powder

½ tsp. baking soda

½ tsp. cinnamon

dash of nutmeg

2 Tbsp. unsweetened grated coconut

cinnamon and sugar

1. Mix together ½ cup sugar, pumpkin, oil, and egg.

2. In a separate bowl, mix together flour, salt, baking powder, baking soda, cinnamon, and nutmeg. Pour into wet ingredients and mix well.

3. Fold in coconut.

4. Grease interior of four ramekins.

5. Divide batter among them. Place in slow cooker crock.

6. Sprinkle each filled ramekin with a light dusting of cinnamon and sugar.

7. Cover crock with slow cooker lid.

8. Bake on High 2 hours, or until tester inserted in center of ramekins comes out clean.

9. Pull on oven mitts to lift ramekins out of crock, or use a sturdy set of tongs. Place ramekins on wire baking rack to cool.

TIP

If you open a can of pumpkin to make these, put what's left in a freezable container, and mark the amount that remains on top. Then you can make another batch of Pumpkin Coconut Cupcakes whenever you get the inspiration. Grated coconut freezes well, too.

FRESH PEACH CUPCAKES

Makes: 4 large cupcakes
PREP. TIME: 20 MINUTES
COOKING TIME: 2 HOURS
IDEAL SLOW-COOKER SIZE: 6- OR 7-QUART
OVAL

5⅓ Tbsp. (⅓ stick) butter, softened

⅔ cup sugar

1 large egg

⅔ cup flour

⅔ tsp. baking powder

1 Tbsp. + 1 tsp. sour cream

⅔ tsp. vanilla

2–3 fresh peaches, peeled and sliced

⅓ tsp. cinnamon

⅓ tsp. sugar

1. Cream butter and ⅔ cup sugar until light and fluffy.

2. Beat in egg.

3. In a separate bowl, stir together flour and baking powder. Add dry ingredients to wet, stirring just until mixed.

4. Stir in sour cream and vanilla, again stirring until just mixed.

5. Grease interior of four 3-oz. ramekins. Divide batter among ramekins.

6. Top ramekins with sliced peaches. Then sprinkle each ramekin with cinnamon and sugar.

7. Place filled ramekins into slow cooker crock. Cover with cooker lid.

8. Bake on Low 2 hours, or until tester inserted into center of ramekins comes out clean.

9. Put on oven mitts and lift ramekins out of crock, or use a pair of sturdy tongs. Place on wire baking rack to cool.

NOTE These are soft and moist and light, almost like mini peach cobblers.

PINEAPPLE ZUCCHINI CUPCAKES

Makes: 4 large cupcakes
PREP. TIME: 20–30 MINUTES
COOKING TIME: 2–3 HOURS
IDEAL SLOW-COOKER SIZE: 6- OR 7-QUART OVAL

- 1 small egg
- ½ cup sugar
- ½ tsp. vanilla
- ¼ cup cooking oil
- ½ cup grated zucchini
- ¾ cup flour
- ¼ tsp. baking powder
- ¼ tsp. baking soda
- ¼ tsp. salt
- 2 Tbsp. crushed pineapple, undrained
- ¼ cup raisins
- ¼ cup nuts of your choice

Creamy Frosting

- 2 Tbsp. Greek yogurt
- 2 Tbsp. butter, softened
- ½–¾ cup confectioners sugar, sifted

1. In a good-sized bowl, beat egg, sugar, vanilla, and cooking oil together until fluffy.

2. Stir in grated zucchini, flour, baking powder, baking soda, and salt, mixing well.

3. Stir in crushed pineapple, raisins, and nuts, mixing well.

4. Grease interior of four 3-oz. ramekins. Divide cupcake batter among the four.

5. Place ramekins into slow cooker crock. Cover with slow cooker lid.

6. Bake on Low 2–3 hours, or until tester inserted in center of ramekins comes out clean.

7. Lift the ramekins out carefully, using oven mitts to protect your knuckles, or using sturdy tongs. Place on a wire baking rack to cool before frosting.

8. While cupcakes cool, mix frosting ingredients together. Frost when cupcakes are completely cool.

VARIATION

These are wonderful and moist. For more flavor add ¾ tsp. pumpkin spice to one batch. Whichever way you decide to make them, this is one great way to include zucchini in a dish!

BANANA GROVE CUPCAKES

Photo appears in color section.

Makes: 4 large cupcakes
PREP. TIME: 20–30 MINUTES
COOKING TIME: 2 HOURS
IDEAL SLOW-COOKER SIZE: 6- OR 7-QUART OVAL

1⅔ Tbsp. shortening
⅓ cup sugar
1 small egg
¼ tsp. vanilla
¼ cup ripe smooshed bananas
½ cup flour
   dash of salt
   scant ¼ tsp. baking powder
¾ Tbsp. sour milk*
   pinch of baking soda

1. Beat shortening and sugar together until creamed.
2. Add egg, vanilla, and smooshed bananas. Mix together well.
3. In a separate bowl, stir together flour, salt, and baking powder.
4. In a small additional bowl, mix sour milk and baking soda.
5. Add flour mixture and sour milk mixture alternately to shortening mixture. Mix thoroughly.
6. Grease interior of four ramekins.
7. Divide batter among four ramekins, and then place into slow cooker crock.
8. Cover with slow cooker lid.
9. Bake on High 2 hours, or until tester inserted in center of ramekins comes out clean.
10. Put on baking mitts to lift out the ramekins, or use a sturdy pair of tongs. Place on wire baking rack to cool.

* To make sour milk, put 2 teaspoons of lemon juice or vinegar in a ¾-cup measure. Fill the measuring cup with milk. Stir. Let stand for 5 minutes before adding to batter.

TIPS

- All you need is one very ripe banana—and you've got a sweet and tender breakfast or soup go-along.
- These are so good with peanut butter icing (page 250) and a few chopped walnuts.

CHOCOLATE CHIP PIZZA

Photo appears in color section.

Makes: 24 servings
PREP. TIME: 25–30 MINUTES
COOKING TIME: 2–2½ HOURS
IDEAL SLOW-COOKER SIZE: 6-QUART OVAL

1   cup flour
½   tsp. baking powder
⅛   tsp. baking soda
½   tsp. salt
⅓   cup butter, melted
1   cup brown sugar, packed
1   egg
1   Tbsp. hot water
1¼ tsp. vanilla
½   cup chopped nuts, your choice
1   cup chopped M&Ms
1   cup mini marshmallows

> TIP
> To make it seem more like pizza, cut the finished pizza in half the long way. Then cut wedges, zigzag-fashion from the center cut to the outer edge of the crock.

1. In a medium-sized bowl, sift together flour, baking powder, baking soda, and salt. Set aside.

2. In a good-sized bowl, cream together butter and brown sugar until well blended. Add egg, hot water, and vanilla, mixing well.

3. Add dry ingredients to wet, ⅓ at a time, mixing well after each addition.

4. Stir in chopped nuts.

5. Grease interior of slow cooker crock. Spread batter into crock.

6. Sprinkle with chopped M&Ms and mini marshmallows.

7. Cover. Bake on High 2–2½ hours, or until tester inserted in center comes out clean.

8. Uncover, and place crock on baking rack to cool.

9. When room temperature, cut into 20 squares with 4 triangles in the corners.

PHILLY CHIPPERS

Photo appears in color section.

Makes: 24 servings
PREP. TIME: 15–20 MINUTES
COOKING TIME: 2½–3 HOURS
IDEAL SLOW-COOKER SIZE: 6-QUART OVAL

16 Tbsp. (2 sticks) butter, softened

8 oz. pkg. cream cheese, softened

¾ cup sugar

¾ cup brown sugar

1 egg

1 tsp. vanilla

¼ cup milk

2½ cups flour

1 tsp. baking powder

1 tsp. salt

12 oz. pkg., or 2 cups, chocolate chips

1. Grease interior of slow cooker crock.

2. In a large mixing bowl, cream together butter, cream cheese, and sugars.

3. Add egg, vanilla, and milk. Mix well.

4. In a separate bowl, combine flour, baking powder, and salt. Blend dry ingredients into wet.

5. Fold chocolate chips into batter.

6. Pour into crock.

7. Cover. Bake on High 2½–3 hours, or until tester inserted in center of chippers comes out clean.

8. Uncover. Remove crock from cooker. Place on wire baking rack to cool.

9. When chippers reach room temperature, cut into 20 squares and 4 triangles in the corners.

CHOCOLATE PECAN PIE BARS

Photo appears in color section.

Makes: 24 servings
PREP. TIME: 20–30 MINUTES
COOKING TIME: 2–3½ HOURS
IDEAL SLOW-COOKER SIZE: 6-QUART OVAL

8 Tbsp. (1 stick) butter, softened
¼ cup brown sugar, packed
1¼ cups flour
½ tsp. salt
3 large eggs
¾ cup light corn syrup
½ cup sugar
2 Tbsp. (¼ stick) melted butter
12 oz. pkg., or 2 cups, semisweet chocolate chips
2 cups coarsely chopped pecans

> **TIP**
>
> Remember that the crock is hot when you spread the filling over the crust. Don't let your arms get against it.

1. Grease interior of slow cooker crock really well.
2. Cream together 8 Tbsp. butter and brown sugar.
3. Stir in flour and salt until mixture is crumbly.
4. Press mixture into bottom of crock to form crust.
5. Cover. Bake on High 1 hour.
6. Meanwhile, mix eggs, corn syrup, sugar, and 2 Tbsp. melted butter until well blended.
7. Stir in chocolate chips and chopped pecans.
8. When crust is finished baking, uncover. Spread creamy chocolate chip–pecan mixture over crust, being careful not to burn your arms on the hot crock.
9. Cover cooker. Continue baking on High for 1–2½ hours, or until filling is firm in the center.
10. Uncover. Remove crock from cooker. Place on wire baking rack and allow to cool.
11. When bars have reached room temperature, cut into 20 squares and 4 triangles in corners.

COCOA BROWNIES WITH DARK CHOCOLATE FROSTING

Photo appears in color section.

Makes: 12 servings
PREP. TIME: 20 MINUTES
COOKING TIME: 1½–2 HOURS
IDEAL SLOW-COOKER SIZE: 5- OR
5½-QUART

1 cup sugar

8 Tbsp. (1 stick) butter, softened

2 eggs

¼ tsp. salt

1 tsp. vanilla

¼ cup unsweetened cocoa powder

¾ cup flour

½ cup chopped nuts, your favorite

Frosting

1½ cups confectioners sugar

¼ cup unsweetened cocoa powder

4 Tbsp. butter (half a stick), softened

3 Tbsp. cream or milk

½ tsp. vanilla

12 pecan halves

1. To make batter, cream sugar and butter together.

2. Add eggs, salt, vanilla, and cocoa powder.

3. Stir in flour and nuts, blending well.

4. Grease interior of slow cooker crock. Spoon batter into crock.

5. Cover. Bake on High 1½–2 hours, or until tester inserted into center comes out clean.

6. Uncover crock and place it on a baking rack to cool.

7. While brownies are cooling, make frosting. Mix confectioners sugar and cocoa powder together.

8. In a good-sized bowl, cream butter until shiny.

9. Add sugar-cocoa mixture to butter alternately with cream or milk.

10. Stir in vanilla until everything is well mixed. (If you want shiny frosting, heat mixture over very low heat for about 5 minutes, stirring continually. Cool for a minute or two, and then spread over brownies.)

11. Cut into 12 brownies. Top each with a pecan half.

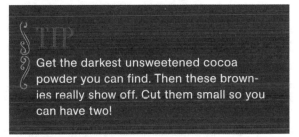

TIP

Get the darkest unsweetened cocoa powder you can find. Then these brownies really show off. Cut them small so you can have two!

DOUBLE CHOCOLATE CRUNCH BARS

Photo appears in color section.

Makes: 24 servings
PREP. TIME: 25 MINUTES
COOKING TIME: 2¾–3½ HOURS
COOLING TIME: 3–4 HOURS
IDEAL SLOW-COOKER SIZE: 6-QUART OVAL

8 Tbsp. (1 stick) butter
¾ cup sugar
2 eggs
1 tsp. vanilla
¾ cup flour
2 Tbsp. unsweetened cocoa powder
¼ tsp. baking powder
¼ tsp. salt
2 cups mini marshmallows
1 cup chocolate chips
1 cup peanut butter, smooth or crunchy
1½ cups crispy rice cereal

TIP

The mini marshmallows may take a little longer than 15 minutes to melt and become spreadable. If you like yours melty, you might want to switch the cooker to Low, so the brownies don't dry out, and give the marshmallows up to 30 minutes.

1. Melt butter. Stir in sugar and blend well.

2. Beat in eggs and vanilla.

3. Add flour, cocoa powder, baking powder, and salt. Mix well.

4. Grease interior of slow cooker crock. Spread batter evenly over the bottom of the crock.

5. Cover. Bake on High 2½–3¼ hours, or until a tester inserted in center of bar comes out clean.

6. Sprinkle mini marshmallows over bars. Cover and bake for 15 minutes more.

7. Turn cooker off and remove crock. Set on a wire baking rack to cool, uncovered.

8. When bars are nearly at room temperature, place chocolate chips and peanut butter in a microwave-safe bowl. Melt on High for 1 minute. Stir. Microwave for 30 seconds more if not completely melted. Stir. Microwave again if needed.

9. Stir cereal into melted chocolate and peanut butter.

10. Spread cereal mixture over bars.

11. Refrigerate for 3–4 hours.

12. Cut into 20 bars (and 4 triangles on the corners) with a silicone or sturdy plastic knife. Your bars will have firm edges, and you'll have preserved the interior of your crock.

TURTLE BARS

Photo appears in color section.

Makes: 24 servings
PREP. TIME: 20–30 MINUTES
COOKING TIME: 3–3½ HOURS
IDEAL SLOW-COOKER SIZE: 6-QUART OVAL

2 cups flour

1¾ cups light brown sugar, divided

20 Tbsp. (2½ sticks) butter, softened and divided

1¼ cups pecan halves

1 cup chocolate chips

1. Grease interior of slow cooker crock.

2. Mix together flour, 1 cup brown sugar, and 8 Tbsp. (1 stick) butter, softened, until crumbly. Pat firmly into bottom of crock.

3. Place pecan halves evenly over crust.

4. Heat remaining ¾ cup brown sugar and remaining 12 Tbsp. (1½ sticks) butter in a saucepan. Boil 1 minute, stirring constantly.

5. Pour over pecan crust.

6. Cover cooker. Bake on High 3–3½ hours, or until mixture is firm.

7. Sprinkle chocolate chips over hot bars. Let stand 2 minutes.

8. Using a knife, swirl chips as they melt, covering the bars as well as you can, but leaving some of the chips whole.

9. Remove crock from cooker and place on a wire baking rack to cool.

10. When room temperature, cut bars into 20 squares and 4 triangles in the corners.

TIP

Parchment paper makes it a snap to lift hot, gooey bars out of the slower cooker.

MAGIC COOKIE BARS

Photo appears in color section.

Makes: 24 servings
PREP. TIME: 20 MINUTES
COOKING TIME: 2–3 HOURS
IDEAL SLOW-COOKER SIZE: 6-QUART OVAL

8 Tbsp. (1 stick) butter, melted
1½ cups graham cracker crumbs
14 oz. can sweetened condensed milk
6 oz. pkg. semisweet chocolate chips
1 cup peanut butter chips
1 cup shredded coconut, sweetened or not
1 cup chopped nuts, your choice

1. Grease interior of slow cooker crock.

2. Pour melted butter into crock.

3. Sprinkle graham cracker crumbs over butter.

4. Gently pour condensed milk over top, being careful not to disturb the crumbs.

5. In a bowl, mix together chocolate and peanut butter chips, coconut, and nuts. Sprinkle evenly over mixture in crock.

6. Cover. Bake on High 2–3 hours, or until firm.

7. Uncover. Lift crock onto wire baking rack and let cool.

8. When room temperature, cut with a silicone or plastic knife into 20 squares and 4 triangles in the corners.

GOOEY OATMEAL JUMBLE BARS

Photo appears in color section.

Makes: 24 servings
PREP. TIME: 20 MINUTES
COOKING TIME: 2 HOURS
IDEAL SLOW-COOKER SIZE: 6-QUART OVAL

3	cups dry oatmeal, quick or old-fashioned
1½	cups flour
1	cup brown sugar
16	Tbsp. (2 sticks) butter, melted
¾	tsp. salt
½	tsp. baking soda
10–12	oz. jar preserves, your choice of flavors

1. Grease interior of slow cooker crock.

2. Combine all ingredients, except preserves, in a big bowl, mixing well.

3. Scoop out 1 cup mixture and reserve.

4. Press remaining mixture into bottom of crock.

5. Spread preserves over crumb crust to within ½" of sides of crock (to prevent burning).

6. Sprinkle everything with reserved crumbs.

7. Cover. Bake on High for 2 hours, or until crust is firm.

8. Uncover and remove crock from cooker. Place on wire baking rack to cool.

9. When room temperature, cut bars into 20 squares and 4 triangles in corners.

VARIATION

Ask the kids in your life what kind of preserves to use. Once they've made their choice, they'll be on board for mixing up the other ingredients. Just give them a big enough bowl so they can really wade in.

RASPBERRY ALMOND BARS

Photo appears in color section.

Makes: 24 servings
PREP. TIME: 20–30 MINUTES
COOKING TIME: 2½–3 HOURS
IDEAL SLOW-COOKER SIZE: 6-QUART OVAL

1 cup flour
¾ cup quick dry oatmeal
½ cup sugar
8 Tbsp. (1 stick) butter, softened
½ tsp. almond extract
½ cup red raspberry preserves
⅓ cup sliced almonds

1. Grease interior of slow cooker crock.

2. In a large bowl, combine flour, oats, and sugar.

3. Cut in butter with a pastry cutter or two knives—or your fingers—until mixture forms coarse crumbs.

4. Stir in extract until well blended.

5. Set aside 1 cup crumbs.

6. Press remaining crumbs into bottom of crock.

7. Spread preserves over crust to within ½" of the edges (the preserves could burn if they touch the hot crock).

8. In a small bowl, combine reserved 1 cup crumbs with almonds. Sprinkle evenly over preserves, pressing down gently to hold the almonds in place.

9. Cover. Bake on High for 2½–3 hours, or until firm in center.

10. Uncover. Lift crock onto wire baking rack to cool.

11. When room temperature, cut bars into 20 squares and 4 triangles in the corners.

CRUNCHY GRANOLA BARS

Makes: 24 servings
PREP. TIME: 20–30 MINUTES
COOKING TIME: 2–3 HOURS
IDEAL SLOW-COOKER SIZE: 6-QUART OVAL

2 cups shredded coconut, sweetened or not

1½ cups old-fashioned dry oats

1½ cups raisins or dried cranberries

2 cups shelled sunflower seeds

½ cup sesame seeds

¾ cup unsalted peanuts or soy nuts

½ cup mini chocolate chips or snipped dried fruit, like apricots or apples

½ tsp. salt

1 cup honey

1 tsp. vanilla

1 cup peanut butter, smooth or crunchy

TIP

Wrap a couple of these and carry them with you if you're going to be squeezed for breakfast or lunch. They'll give you energy for the day.

1. Grease the interior of the slow cooker crock well.

2. In a good-sized bowl, mix together coconut, dry oats, raisins or dried cranberries, sunflower and sesame seeds, peanuts or soy nuts, chocolate chips or dried fruit, and salt.

3. In a separate bowl, blend together honey, vanilla, and peanut butter until smooth.

4. Add wet ingredients to dry ones, then grease your hands and use them to mix everything thoroughly.

5. Press the mixture firmly into the crock.

6. Cover. Bake on Low 2–3 hours, or until firm.

7. Uncover and set crock on baking rack to cool.

8. When room temperature, use a silicone or sturdy plastic knife to cut into 20 squares and 4 triangles.

9. Store in an airtight container.

VIENNESE WALNUT BARS

Photo appears in color section.

Makes: 24 servings
PREP. TIME: 30–35 MINUTES
COOKING TIME: 2½–3 HOURS
IDEAL SLOW-COOKER SIZE: 6-QUART OVAL

Pastry

8 Tbsp. (1 stick) butter, softened

3 oz. pkg. cream cheese, softened

¼ cup sugar

1¼ cups flour

1 cup chopped walnuts

6 oz. pkg., or 1 cup, chocolate chips

Topping

1 cup flour

¼ tsp. baking powder

¼ tsp. salt

1½ cups light brown sugar, packed

4 Tbsp. (half a stick) butter, softened

2 large eggs

1 tsp. instant coffee powder

1 Tbsp. hot water

½ cup chopped walnuts

1. Grease interior of slow cooker crock.

2. Make pastry by creaming together butter, cream cheese, and sugar.

3. Gradually beat in flour.

4. Press mixture evenly into bottom of crock.

5. Sprinkle with walnuts and chocolate chips.

6. Prepare topping by sifting flour, baking powder, and salt together into a medium-sized bowl.

7. Cream together brown sugar, butter, and eggs in a larger bowl.

8. Dissolve coffee in hot water. Add to creamed mixture.

9. Gradually add flour mixture to creamed.

10. Spoon over crust, spreading gently to cover.

11. Sprinkle with walnuts.

12. Cover. Bake on High 2½–3 hours, or until the topping firms up in the middle.

13. Carefully remove crock from cooker. Place on wire baking rack to cool.

14. When room temperature, cut bars into 20 squares and 4 triangles in the corners.

TIP

No, that teaspoon of coffee powder isn't a mistake. It brings a deep richness to the topping of these wonderful bars whose base is a rich shortbread. You will feel like you're on a plaza in a European city when you're eating these!

BANANA PECAN BARS

Photo appears in color section.

Makes: 28 servings
PREP. TIME: 20–30 MINUTES
COOKING TIME: 2–2½ HOURS
IDEAL SLOW-COOKER SIZE: 6-QUART OVAL

½ cup chopped pecans

2 cups flour

2 tsp. baking powder

⅛ tsp. cinnamon

2–3 very ripe bananas, enough to make 1 cup when smooshed

¼ cup shortening at room temperature

1 cup sugar

2 eggs

1 tsp. vanilla

Glaze

½ lb. (rounded 1 cup) confectioners sugar

1 tsp. rum extract

a shy 2 Tbsp. water or orange juice

1. Grease interior of slow cooker crock.

2. Combine pecans, flour, baking powder, and cinnamon.

3. Using a fork, smoosh ripe bananas in a good-sized bowl, enough to equal 1 cup.

4. Cream shortening, sugar, and bananas together.

5. Stir in eggs and vanilla, mixing thoroughly.

6. Add dry ingredients to wet, stirring until just combined.

7. Spread batter into greased crock.

8. Cover. Bake on High 2–2½ hours, or until tester inserted in center of bars comes out clean.

9. Uncover. Remove crock from cooker and place on wire baking rack to cool.

10. While bars are cooling, make glaze. Combine confectioners sugar and rum extract. Stir in just enough water or juice to make glaze pourable.

11. Drizzle glaze over bars. Then cut into 24 squares and 4 triangles in the corners.

NUTTY APRICOT BARS

Photo appears in color section.

Makes: 24 servings
PREP. TIME: 20 MINUTES
COOKING TIME: 2–3 HOURS
IDEAL SLOW-COOKER SIZE: 6-QUART OVAL

  2 eggs, divided
12 Tbsp. (1½ sticks) butter, softened and divided
  1 tsp. baking powder
  1 cup flour
1½ cups sugar, divided
1¼ cups quick oats
  1 cup apricot jam or preserves
  2 cups shredded coconut, sweetened or not
⅓ cup chopped pecans or walnuts
½ tsp. vanilla

1. Combine 1 egg, 8 Tbsp. (1 stick) softened butter, baking powder, flour, ¾ cup sugar, and quick oats until well mixed.

2. Grease interior of slow cooker crock.

3. Press batter into bottom of crock.

4. Spread batter with jam.

5. Mix together remaining egg, 4 Tbsp. (half a stick) softened butter, ¾ cup sugar, coconut, nuts, and vanilla.

6. Drop by spoonfuls over jam. Spread out to cover jam as best you can.

7. Cover. Bake on High for 2–3 hours, or until tester inserted into center of bars comes out clean.

8. Remove crock from cooker. Place, uncovered, on wire baking rack to cool.

9. When room temperature, use a silicone or plastic knife to cut bars into 20 squares, with 4 triangles in the corners.

TIP

Usually the lid of the cooker draws condensation—which you don't want to drip onto the bars or cakes that you're baking. So when you remove the lid, do a fast swoop, turning it quickly upside down away from yourself as you lift it off the cooker.

CHERRY CHEESECAKE BARS

Photo appears in color section.

Makes: 24 servings
PREP. TIME: 20–30 MINUTES
COOKING TIME: 2½–3 HOURS
IDEAL SLOW-COOKER SIZE: 6-QUART OVAL

Crust

6 Tbsp. (¾ stick) butter, softened

½ cup light brown sugar, packed

1 cup flour

¾ cup toasted sliced almonds

Filling

½ cup sugar

8 oz. pkg. cream cheese, softened and cut into chunks

1 egg

2 Tbsp. milk

½ tsp. almond extract

1 cup cherry preserves

1. Grease interior of slow cooker crock.

2. Prepare crust by creaming together butter and brown sugar.

3. Blend in flour and almonds, by hand, until mixture is crumbly.

4. Set aside ½ cup crumbs.

5. Press remaining crumbs into bottom of crock.

6. Cover. Bake on High 1 hour.

7. Uncover. Remove crock from cooker and place on baking rack. Allow crust to cool while you mix up the filling.

8. Cream together sugar and cream cheese.

9. Blend in egg, milk, and almond extract.

10. Spread cherry preserves over crust.

11. Drop filling by spoonfuls over preserves. Spread filling out as well as you can without pulling up the preserves.

12. Sprinkle with reserved ½ cup crumbs.

13. Return crock to cooker. Cover. Continue cooking on High for 1½–2 hours, or until filling is set.

14. Uncover. Remove crock to baking rack to cool.

15. When bars are room temperature, cut into 20 squares and 4 triangles. Refrigerate until ready to serve.

TIP

You can do amazing things in a slow cooker, especially if you add ingredients in stages. The filling doesn't need to bake as long as the crust, so you add it later. You have the convenience of the slow cooker, but the ability to do more delicate dishes by staging the addition of ingredients that don't need to cook as long.

FROSTY LEMON BARS

Photo appears in color section.

Makes: 24 servings
PREP. TIME: 20–30 MINUTES
COOKING TIME: 2½–3 HOURS
IDEAL SLOW-COOKER SIZE: 6-QUART OVAL

Crust

2¼ cups flour
½ cup confectioners sugar
16 Tbsp. (2 sticks) butter

Filling

4 eggs
¼ cup lemon juice
2 cups white sugar
¼ cup flour
1 tsp. baking powder
3–4 Tbsp. confectioners sugar

1. Grease interior of slow cooker crock.
2. Make the crust by combining flour and confectioners sugar in a good-sized mixing bowl.
3. Cut the butter into chunks. Work into dry ingredients with your hands until well mixed.
4. Press mixture into bottom of crock.
5. Cover. Bake on High 1 hour.
6. Meanwhile, prepare filling. Beat eggs in the bowl where you made the crust.
7. Add lemon juice and mix well.
8. In a separate bowl, combine sugar, flour, and baking powder. Stir into wet ingredients and beat well.
9. Pour filling over crust.
10. Cover and bake on High 1½–2 more hours, or until filling sets up and is firm.
11. Uncover. Remove crock from cooker and place on wire baking rack to cool.
12. When bars have reached room temperature, sprinkle with confectioners sugar. Cut into 20 squares and 4 triangles.
13. Refrigerate until ready to serve.

NOTE It's the classic lemon bars, done in a slow cooker. Your kitchen has stayed cool, and you've been able to run a quick errand while they were baking.

BANANA CHOCOLATE CHIP BARS

CAROL HUBER, AUSTIN, TX

Makes: 12–15 servings
PREP. TIME: 20 MINUTES
COOKING TIME: 2–3 HOURS
IDEAL SLOW-COOKER SIZE: 6- OR 7-QT., *OVAL*

¾ cup (1½ sticks) butter, softened

⅔ cup granulated sugar

⅔ cup brown sugar

2 eggs

1 tsp. vanilla

3 ripe bananas, mashed

2 cups flour

2 tsp. baking powder

½ tsp. salt

12 oz. pkg. semisweet chocolate chips

1. Grease a loaf pan that will either hang on the edges of your oval slow-cooker crock, or will sit down in the slow-cooker crock on metal jar rings or small trivet.

2. In a good-sized mixing bowl, cream together butter and sugars.

3. Add eggs and vanilla. Mix well.

4. Stir in mashed bananas and stir well.

5. In a medium bowl, sift together flour, baking powder, and salt.

6. Stir dry ingredients into creamed mixture.

7. Stir in chocolate chips.

8. Pour into greased loaf pan.

9. Suspend pan on edges of slow-cooker crock, or place on trivet or jar rings on bottom of crock.

10. Vent slow-cooker lid at one end by propping it open with a wooden spoon handle or chopstick.

11. Cook on High 2–3 hours, or until toothpick inserted in center comes out clean.

12. Uncover pan and remove from cooker. Let cool before slicing into bars.

NOTE ≫–♥–▷ Whenever I have a really ripe banana, I mash it and put it in a labeled box in the freezer. I add to it when another too-ripe banana turns up on the counter. When I've got three, I make this recipe, knowing that these bars provide some nutrition along with their matchless flavor!

Pies AND Crisps

CHOCOLATE PECAN PIE

Photo appears in color section.

Makes: 8 servings
PREP. TIME: 25 MINUTES
COOKING TIME: 2–3 HOURS
STANDING TIME: 2 HOURS
IDEAL SLOW-COOKER SIZE: 6-QUART

pastry for a 9" pie

4 oz. bittersweet chocolate, chopped

6 oz. bag chopped pecans, about 1⅓ cups

3 eggs

1 cup sugar

6 Tbsp. butter, melted

½ cup dark corn syrup

¼ cup maple syrup

1 tsp. vanilla

¼ tsp. salt

1. Take rolled out pastry and fit it into slow cooker as you would line a pie plate, bringing it up the sides 1–2" and gently pushing it into the bottom.

2. In a small bowl, toss together chocolate and pecans. Sprinkle evenly in pie crust.

3. In a medium bowl, whisk eggs and sugar. Add butter, corn syrup, maple syrup, vanilla, and salt. Whisk again.

4. Pour filling over chocolate/pecans in crust.

5. Cover and cook on High for 2–3 hours, until filling is set and crust is getting browned.

6. Remove crock from electrical unit, remove lid, and set pie aside to cool to room temperature, about 2 hours, before slicing and serving.

MOCHA PIE

Photo appears in color section.

Makes: 8 servings
PREP. TIME: 20 MINUTES
COOKING TIME: 2–3 HOURS
STANDING TIME: 2 HOURS
IDEAL SLOW-COOKER SIZE: 6-QUART

pastry for a 9" pie

2 eggs

⅔ cup heavy whipping cream

1½ cups sugar

3 Tbsp. unsweetened cocoa powder

1 Tbsp. instant coffee granules

4 Tbsp. (½ stick) butter, melted

1 tsp. vanilla

¼ tsp. salt

1. Take rolled out pastry and fit it into slow cooker as you would line a pie plate, bringing it up the sides 1–2" and gently pushing it into the bottom.

2. In a mixing bowl, beat eggs and cream until mixture no longer clings to whisk.

3. Add rest of ingredients and whisk well.

4. Pour filling into prepared crust.

5. Cover and cook on High for 2–3 hours, until filling is set in the middle and crust is browning.

6. Remove crock from electrical unit, uncover, and set aside to cool for 2 hours before slicing and serving.

VARIATION

Take out the coffee, and put a layer of peanut butter between the filling and the crust . . . add some cinnamon and cayenne for a Mexican flair . . . or chop up some leftover Halloween candy bars and sprinkle them in the crust before pouring in the filling.

FAMOUS PA DUTCH SHOOFLY PIE

Makes: 8 servings
PREP. TIME: 30 MINUTES
COOKING TIME: 1½–2 HOURS
STANDING TIME: 30–60 MINUTES
IDEAL SLOW-COOKER SIZE: 6-QUART

pastry for a 9" pie

1 cup all-purpose flour

½ cup brown sugar

2 Tbsp. butter, room temperature

⅓ cup blackstrap molasses

⅔ cup mild baking molasses

1 egg

⅔ cup cold water

1 tsp. baking soda

¼ cup hot water

TIP

Serve this the traditional Pennsylvania Dutch way: for breakfast! But it's also delicious with a glass of cold milk and a peach on the side in the middle of summer.

1. Take rolled out pastry and fit it into slow cooker as you would line a pie plate, bringing it up the sides 2" and gently pushing it into the bottom.

2. In a mixing bowl, cut together flour, brown sugar, and butter to make fine crumbs. Measure and set aside ½ cup crumbs.

3. In another mixing bowl, combine both molasses, egg, and cold water. Whisk.

4. Separately, dissolve baking soda in hot water and then add it to mixture. Whisk again.

5. Add crumbs to molasses mixture. Pour into pie shell in cooker. Sprinkle with reserved ½ cup crumbs.

6. Cover, adding 3–4 sheets of paper towels under the lid to catch condensation.

7. Cook on High for 1½–2 hours, until pie is puffed a bit and center is not jiggly.

8. Uncover slow cooker and remove crock from electrical unit. Set aside for 30–60 minutes before slicing and serving pie.

MAGIC COCONUT CUSTARD PIE

Makes: 8 servings
PREP. TIME: 10 MINUTES
COOKING TIME: 2–3 HOURS
STANDING TIME: 30–60 MINUTES
IDEAL SLOW-COOKER SIZE: 5-QUART

4 eggs
6 Tbsp. butter, room temperature
½ cup all-purpose flour
2 cups 2% or whole milk
¾ cup sugar
1 tsp. vanilla
1 cup unsweetened shredded coconut

1. In a blender, combine eggs, butter, flour, milk, sugar, and vanilla. Whip.

2. Stir in coconut.

3. Pour mixture into greased slow cooker.

4. Cover and cook on High for 2–3 hours, until set in the middle.

5. Uncover slow cooker and remove crock from electrical unit. Set aside for 30–60 minutes before slicing and serving pie, or allow to cool to room temperature for a totally firm pie.

TIP

The "magic" here is that the pie forms its own crust! Serve slices of this pie with some fresh berries or fruit salad.

DOUBLE-CRUST CHERRY PIE

Photo appears in color section.

Makes: 8 servings
PREP. TIME: 20 MINUTES
COOKING TIME: 1½–2 HOURS
STANDING TIME: 30–60 MINUTES
IDEAL SLOW-COOKER SIZE: 6-QUART

    pastry for two 9" pies
2 21-oz. cans cherry pie filling
1 tsp. almond extract

1. Take one of the rolled out pastries and fit it into slow cooker as you would line a pie plate, bringing it up the sides 1–2" and gently pushing it into the bottom.

2. Separately, stir together pie filling and almond extract. Spoon into crust in slow cooker.

3. Cut remaining crust in 1" strips. Lay half the strips ½" apart on top of the pie filling, pinching the ends gently to the bottom crust and removing excess length. Lay the rest of the strips the opposite direction in the same manner.

4. Cover and cook on High for 1½–2 hours, until crust is firm and getting brown and filling is hot.

5. Remove hot crock from electrical unit and set aside to cool for 30–60 minutes before cutting. For a totally firm pie, allow to cool to room temperature before serving.

Cherry pie is a classic because it's straightforward and delicious, especially served with vanilla ice cream.

OPEN-FACE PEACH PIE

Photo appears in color section.

Makes: 8 servings
PREP. TIME: 30 MINUTES
COOKING TIME: 1½–2½ HOURS
STANDING TIME: 30–60 MINUTES
IDEAL SLOW-COOKER SIZE: 6-QUART

1 cup all-purpose flour

⅓ cup whole wheat flour

¼ tsp. baking powder

½ tsp. salt

2 Tbsp. confectioners sugar

4 Tbsp. (½ stick) butter, room temperature

3 cups sliced fresh peaches, any juice drained off

¼ cup sugar

1 tsp. ground cinnamon

1 egg

1 cup plain Greek yogurt

1. In a mixing bowl, combine both flours, baking powder, salt, and confectioners sugar. Cut in butter with a pastry cutter or 2 knives to make fine crumbs.

2. Press crumb mixture in slow cooker to make crust that covers bottom and comes up 1–2" on the sides.

3. Distribute peaches over crust. Sprinkle evenly with sugar and cinnamon.

4. In a small mixing bowl, beat egg. Add yogurt and stir.

5. Pour yogurt mixture evenly over peaches.

6. Cover and cook on High for 1½–2½ hours, until yogurt topping is firm and crust is slightly browned.

7. Carefully remove hot crock from electrical unit and remove lid. Allow pie to rest for 30–60 minutes before cutting and serving. For a totally firm pie, allow to cool to room temperature.

VARIATION

You may use canned peaches in place of fresh ones, but drain them very well.

RHUBARB CUSTARD PIE

Makes: 8 servings
PREP. TIME: 30 MINUTES
COOKING TIME: 1½–2 HOURS
STANDING TIME: 30–60 MINUTES
IDEAL SLOW-COOKER SIZE: 6-QUART

    pastry for a 9" pie
2   eggs
1   cup sugar
    pinch salt
¼   tsp. ground nutmeg
2   Tbsp. flour
⅔   cup heavy cream
2½ cups diced rhubarb

1. Take rolled out pastry and fit it into slow cooker as you would line a pie plate, bringing it up the sides 1–2" and gently pushing it into the bottom.

2. In a mixing bowl, whisk eggs until they no longer cling to the whisk.

3. Add sugar, salt, nutmeg, flour, and cream. Whisk again until no lumps remain.

4. Place rhubarb in crust.

5. Pour egg mixture over rhubarb.

6. Cover and cook on High for 1½–2 hours or until knife blade inserted in center comes out clean.

7. Uncover slow cooker and remove crock from electrical unit. Set aside for 30–60 minutes before slicing and serving pie, or allow to cool to room temperature for a totally firm pie.

LEMON SPONGE PIE

Photo appears in color section.

Makes: 8 servings
PREP. TIME: 25 MINUTES
COOKING TIME: 1½–2½ HOURS
STANDING TIME: 1–2 HOURS
IDEAL SLOW-COOKER SIZE: 6-QUART

pastry for a 9" pie

3 eggs, separated

¼ tsp. cream of tartar

2 Tbsp. butter

1 cup sugar

finely grated zest of 2 lemons

juice of 2 lemons

3 Tbsp. all-purpose flour

½ tsp. salt

1⅓ cups milk

1. Take rolled out pastry and fit it into slow cooker as you would line a pie plate, bringing it up the sides 1–2" and gently pushing it into the bottom.

2. Beat egg whites and cream of tartar with an electric mixer until they stand up in stiff peaks. Set aside.

3. In a mixing bowl, cream butter, sugar, and egg yolks.

4. Add lemon zest, lemon juice, flour, salt, and milk. Beat again.

5. Fold in beaten egg whites.

6. Pour mixture in pastry-lined slow cooker.

7. Cover and cook on High for 1½–2½ hours, until middle is set and lightly browned.

8. Remove crock from electrical unit and uncover. Allow to cool for 1–2 hours before slicing and serving.

NOTE This is much easier to make than a classic lemon meringue pie, and you get the fluffy top and the wonderful gooey lemon part.

BLUEBERRY GINGER TART

Photo appears in color section.

Makes: 8 servings
PREP. TIME: 30 MINUTES
COOKING TIME: 1½–2 HOURS
STANDING TIME: 30–60 MINUTES
IDEAL SLOW-COOKER SIZE: 6-QUART

1 cup whole wheat pastry flour

¾ cup all-purpose flour

¼ cup brown sugar

⅛ tsp. salt

⅔ cup butter, chilled

2 Tbsp. fresh lemon juice, divided

3½ cups fresh or thawed and drained frozen blueberries

⅔ cup sugar

4 tsp. cornstarch

1 Tbsp. finely grated lemon zest

2 tsp. minced fresh ginger root

TIPS

This is a wonderful combination of flavors. Be warned, however, that the slices will be gooey and tender, so don't expect perfect presentation. But the flavor will win you over!

1. In a mixing bowl, stir together both flours, brown sugar, and salt.

2. Cut in cold butter with 2 knives or a pastry blender.

3. Remove 1 cup of crumbs and set aside for topping. To remainder in the bowl, add 1 Tbsp. lemon juice.

4. Press lemon crumb mixture into slow cooker to make a tart crust that comes 1" up the sides.

5. Separately, stir together blueberries, sugar, cornstarch, remaining 1 Tbsp. lemon juice, lemon zest, and ginger.

6. Pour filling into tart crust. Sprinkle with reserved 1 cup crumbs.

7. Cover slow cooker, venting lid at one end with wooden spoon handle or chopstick.

8. Cook on High for 1½–2 hours, until blueberry filling is thickened and bubbling at edges.

9. Remove crock from electrical unit and uncover. Allow to cool for 30–60 minutes before slicing and serving.

CHOCOLATE PECAN PIE BARS ♥ page 287

COCOA BROWNIES WITH DARK CHOCOLATE FROSTING ♥ page 288

DOUBLE CHOCOLATE CRUNCH BARS ♥ page 290

TURTLE BARS ♥ page 291

MAGIC COOKIE BARS
page 292

CRUNCHY GRANOLA BARS ♥ page 295

GOOEY OATMEAL JUMBLE BARS
page 293

RASPBERRY ALMOND BARS ♥ page 294

VIENNESE WALNUT BARS
page 296

BANANA PECAN BARS
page 298

NUTTY APRICOT BARS ♥ page 299

CHERRY CHEESECAKE BARS
page 300

FROSTY LEMON BARS
page 302

CHOCOLATE PECAN PIE
page 306

MOCHA PIE
page 307

DOUBLE-CRUST CHERRY PIE ♥ page 310

OPEN-FACE PEACH PIE ♥ page 311

LEMON SPONGE PIE ♥ page 313

BLUEBERRY GINGER TART ♥ page 314

BLUEBERRY CRINKLE
page 321

STRAWBERRY CRISP
page 324

BLUEBERRY CRISP ♥ page 325

DEEP DISH FRUITY DELIGHT

Makes: 12–15 servings
PREP. TIME: 15 MINUTES
COOKING TIME: 3½–4 HOURS
IDEAL SLOW-COOKER SIZE: 5- OR 6-QUART

20 oz. can crushed pineapple, drained
21 oz. can cherry, apple, or blueberry pie filling
18¼ oz. box yellow cake or angel food cake mix
8 Tbsp. (1 stick) butter, melted
½–1 cup chopped nuts

1. Grease interior of slow cooker crock.

2. Spread drained pineapple over bottom of crock.

3. Spoon pie filling evenly over pineapple.

4. Sprinkle dry cake mix over pie filling.

5. Drizzle melted butter over dry cake mix.

6. Sprinkle with nuts.

7. Cover. Bake on High 3½–4 hours, or until tester inserted into center of cobbler comes out clean.

8. Uncover, being careful not to let water from inside of lid drip on cobbler. Remove crock from cooker and place on wire baking rack to cool.

9. When warm or room temperature, slice or spoon out to serve.

VARIATION

Add 1 cup flaked or grated coconut to Step 6 if you wish.

ANY-FRUIT-THAT-MAKES-YOU-HAPPY COBBLER

Makes: 6–8 servings
PREP. TIME: 15–20 MINUTES
COOKING TIME: 1½–3 HOURS
IDEAL SLOW-COOKER SIZE: 3- TO 5-QUART

8 Tbsp. (1 stick) butter

1 cup flour

1 cup milk

1 cup sugar, or less, depending on the sweetness of the fruit you're using

2 tsp. baking powder

dash of salt

3–4 cups cut fresh fruit

1. Grease interior of slow cooker.

2. Melt butter in a microwave-safe bowl. Stir in all other ingredients except fruit. Mix thoroughly.

3. Spoon batter into crock, spreading it out evenly.

4. Arrange cut-up fruit, pitted cherries, or berries on top of batter.

5. Cover. Bake on High 1½–3 hours, depending on the fruit. It's finished when the middle is set and juice is bubbling at the edges.

6. Uncover, being careful not to let the condensation on the interior of the cooker lid drip on the cobbler.

7. Let cool until it's the temperature you like.

VARIATION

Use whatever fruit is in season. Use more than is called for if you wish. You may need to cook it a bit longer, but this recipe is highly flexible.

PEACH COBBLER

Makes: 8 servings
PREP. TIME: 20 MINUTES
COOKING TIME: 3–4 HOURS
IDEAL SLOW-COOKER SIZE: 5-QUART

3–4 cups sliced peaches
⅓ cup + ½ cup sugar
¼ cup brown sugar
dash nutmeg
dash cinnamon
8 Tbsp. (1 stick) butter
¾ cup flour
2 tsp. baking powder
¾ cup milk

1. Grease interior of slow cooker crock.
2. Mix together in a good-sized bowl the peaches, ⅓ cup sugar, brown sugar, nutmeg, and cinnamon. Set aside to macerate.
3. Melt butter, or place in slow cooker crock turned on High, and let it melt there.
4. Meanwhile, stir together remaining ingredients in a bowl—½ cup sugar, flour, baking powder, and milk until smooth.
5. When butter is melted, make sure it covers the bottom of the crock. Spoon batter evenly over butter in crock, but don't stir.
6. Spoon sugared peaches over batter.
7. Cover. Bake on High 3–4 hours, or until firm in middle and bubbly around the edges.
8. Uncover carefully so condensation from inside of lid doesn't drip on the cobbler. Remove crock from cooker. Serve when warm with milk or ice cream.

VARIATION

This cobbler is also good with canned or frozen peaches. Drain canned peaches or thaw frozen ones before adding them to the crock. The cobbler won't firm up well if you add that extra moisture.

COBBLER WITH FRESH CHERRIES

Makes: 6 servings
PREP. TIME: 20 MINUTES
COOKING TIME: 2½–3½ HOURS
STANDING TIME: 1 HOUR
IDEAL SLOW-COOKER SIZE: 4-QUART

4 cups (about 2 lbs.) pitted fresh cherries, sweet or sour

⅓–¾ cup sugar, depending on how sweet the cherries are

1 Tbsp. instant tapioca

⅓ cup water

1 Tbsp. butter

Cobbler Batter

8 Tbsp. (1 stick) butter

1¼ cups flour

1 cup sugar

2 Tbsp. baking powder

½ tsp. salt

1 cup milk

1. Grease interior of slow cooker crock.

2. In a good-sized saucepan, combine pitted cherries, ⅓ cup sugar, tapioca, and water.

3. Let stand for an hour, stirring now and then. Test the mixture to see if it's the sweetness you like. Now's the time to add more sugar if you want.

4. Cook over medium heat until boiling, stirring continually to prevent sticking and scorching. Simmer for 5–10 minutes, stirring constantly.

5. Remove from heat. Stir in 1 Tbsp. butter.

6. To make batter, cut up stick of butter into slow cooker crock. Turn cooker onto High so butter melts.

7. Meanwhile, combine flour, sugar, baking powder, and salt in a good-sized bowl. When well mixed, stir in milk until batter is smooth.

8. Drop batter by spoonfuls evenly over melted butter in crock. Do not stir.

9. Spoon the thickened cherry mixture over batter. Do not stir.

10. Cover. Cook on High for 2–3 hours, or until firm in middle and bubbly around edges.

11. Remove lid carefully and swiftly so no drops of water from the lid drip onto the cobbler. Continue baking on High 30 more minutes so cobbler becomes drier on top.

12. Remove crock from cooker and place on baking rack to cool. When warm or room temperature, serve.

VARIATION

You can use canned or frozen cherries for this. If canned, cut the sugar back and use the juice instead of the water that's called for. Sour cherries create a delicious tart-sweet combination!

RHUBARB CRUNCH

Makes: 6–8 servings
PREP. TIME: 30 MINUTES
COOKING TIME: 1½–2 HOURS
IDEAL SLOW-COOKER SIZE: 3-QUART

1 cup flour, sifted (use ½ cup whole wheat and ½ cup white if you wish)
¼ cup dry oats, quick or rolled
1 cup brown sugar, packed
8 Tbsp. butter (1 stick), melted
1 tsp. cinnamon
1 cup sugar
2 Tbsp. cornstarch
1 cup water
1 tsp. vanilla
2 cups diced rhubarb

1. In a good-sized bowl, stir together flour, dry oats, brown sugar, melted butter, and cinnamon until crumbly.

2. Set aside half the crumbs. Pat remaining crumbs over bottom of slow cooker crock.

3. Combine sugar, cornstarch, water, and vanilla in a 2-qt. microwave-safe bowl, stirring until smooth.

4. Add rhubarb to water/sugar mixture. Microwave, covered, on High for 2 minutes. Stir. Cook another minute, or until mixture becomes thick and clear, stirring frequently.

5. Pour rhubarb sauce over crumbs in crock.

6. Crumble remaining crumbs over top of sauce.

7. Cover. Bake on High 1 hour.

8. Uncover. (Make sure the lid doesn't drip water on top of crunch when removing it.) Bake on High an additional 30–60 minutes, or until crunch is crunchy on top.

9. Remove crock from cooker. Allow crunch to cool until it's warm or room temperature before digging in.

BLUEBERRY CRINKLE

Photo appears in color section.

Makes: 6–8 servings
PREP. TIME: 15–20 MINUTES
COOKING TIME: 2–3 HOURS
IDEAL SLOW-COOKER SIZE: 3- OR 4-QUART

½ cup brown sugar

¾ cup dry quick oats

½ cup flour, white or whole wheat

½ tsp. cinnamon

   dash of salt

6 Tbsp. (¾ stick) butter

4 cups blueberries, fresh or frozen

2 Tbsp. sugar

2 Tbsp. instant tapioca

2 Tbsp. lemon juice

½ tsp. lemon zest

1. Grease interior of slow cooker crock.

2. In a large bowl, combine brown sugar, dry oats, flour, cinnamon, and salt.

3. Using 2 knives, a pastry cutter, or your fingers, work butter into dry ingredients until small crumbs form.

4. In a separate bowl, stir together blueberries, sugar, tapioca, lemon juice, and lemon zest.

5. Spoon blueberry mixture into slow cooker crock.

6. Sprinkle crumbs over blueberries.

7. Cover. Cook 2–3 hours on Low, or until firm in the middle with juice bubbling up around the edges.

8. Remove lid with a giant swoop away from yourself so condensation on inside of lid doesn't drip on the crumbs.

9. Lift crock out of cooker. Let cool until either warm or room temperature before eating.

VARIATION

When blueberries are in season, buy a large amount, pour the berries into pint-sized containers, and freeze them. No need to thaw them for this recipe. Of course, fresh can't be beat in this crinkle. Eat this with dollops of Greek yogurt for a new twist.

STRAWBERRY RHUBARB CRISP

Makes: 8 servings
PREP. TIME: 30 MINUTES
COOKING TIME: 3–4 HOURS
IDEAL SLOW-COOKER SIZE: 5-QUART

4 cups sliced rhubarb

4 cups sliced strawberries

¾ cup sugar

½ cup orange marmalade

3 Tbsp. flour

2 Tbsp. (¼ stick) butter, melted

Topping

½ cup chopped nuts of your choice

¼ cup dry oats, quick or rolled

½ cup flour

1 tsp. cinnamon

6 Tbsp. (¾ cup) butter

1. Grease interior of slow cooker crock.

2. In a good-sized bowl, mix together sliced rhubarb and strawberries, sugar, orange marmalade, and flour.

3. Pour into crock.

4. Drizzle melted butter over fruit mixture.

5. In a separate bowl, make topping by mixing together chopped nuts, dry oats, flour, and cinnamon.

6. Blend butter into dry ingredients either with your fingers, 2 knives, or a pastry cutter until crumbs form.

7. Sprinkle crumbs evenly over fruit.

8. Cover cooker. Bake on High 2½–3½ hours, or until firm in middle and bubbly around edges.

9. Quickly remove lid, swooping it away from yourself so drops on inside of lid don't drip on the crisp. Continue baking 30 more minutes to allow crisp to dry on top.

10. Remove crock from cooker and place on wire baking rack to cool.

11. Serve crisp when warm or at room temperature.

VARIATION

Frozen strawberries are fine for this crisp—but it's best to thaw them first and drain them well before adding them to the crock. The berries and rhubarb will still turn juicy as they bake.

STRAWBERRY CRISP

Photo appears in color section.

Makes: 6 servings
PREP. TIME: 30 MINUTES
COOKING TIME: 2½–3½ HOURS
IDEAL SLOW-COOKER SIZE: 4-QUART

1 cup dry oats, quick or rolled

1 cup flour

1 cup brown sugar, packed

8 Tbsp. (1 stick) butter

4 cups sliced fresh strawberries

½ cup sugar, or less

1. Grease interior of slow cooker crock.

2. In a good-sized bowl, combine dry oatmeal, flour, and brown sugar. Cut butter into chunks and work into dry ingredients with your fingers, 2 knives, or a pastry cutter until crumbly.

3. In a separate bowl, gently mix together sliced strawberries and sugar.

4. Divide crumbs in half. Place half into bottom of slow cooker crock. Press down to form crust.

5. Spoon strawberries evenly over crust.

6. Scatter remaining half of crumbs over strawberries.

7. Cover. Bake on High 2–3 hours, or until firm in center and bubbly around edges.

8. Remove lid carefully with a swift swoop away from yourself to keep condensation on inside of lid from dripping onto crisp. Continue baking on High another 30 minutes to allow crisp to dry on top.

9. Remove crock from cooker and place on wire baking rack to cool. Serve warm or at room temperature.

VARIATION

Frozen strawberries work in this recipe, too. It's best to let them thaw and then drain them well before spooning them over the crust.

BLUEBERRY CRISP

PHYLLIS GOOD, LANCASTER, PA
Photo appears in color section.

Makes: 6–8 servings
PREP. TIME: 15–20 MINUTES
COOKING TIME: 2 HOURS
IDEAL SLOW-COOKER SIZE: 4-QUART

½ cup brown sugar
¾ cup dry rolled oats
½ cup whole wheat flour, or all-purpose flour
½ tsp. cinnamon
  salt
6 Tbsp. butter, at room temperature
4 cups blueberries, fresh or frozen
2–4 Tbsp. sugar, depending on how sweet you like things
2 Tbsp. quick-cooking tapioca
2 Tbsp. lemon juice
½ tsp. grated lemon peel

1. In a large bowl, combine brown sugar, oats, flour, cinnamon, and salt. Cut in butter using a pastry cutter or two knives to make crumbs. Set aside.

2. In a separate bowl, stir together blueberries, sugar, tapioca, lemon juice, and lemon peel.

3. Spoon blueberry mixture into greased slow cooker. Sprinkle crumbs over blueberries.

4. Cover and cook on High for 1½ hours. Remove lid and cook an additional 30 minutes on High.

OLD-TIMEY RAISIN CRISP

Makes: 12 servings
PREP. TIME: 20 MINUTES
COOKING TIME: 2½–3½ HOURS
STANDING TIME: 1 HOUR
IDEAL SLOW-COOKER SIZE: 5-QUART

1 lb. raisins

2 Tbsp. cornstarch

½ cup sugar

1 cup water

2 Tbsp. lemon juice

Crumbs

1¾ cups flour

½ tsp. baking soda

1 cup brown sugar

¼ tsp. salt

1½ cups dry oats, quick or rolled

12 Tbsp. (1½ sticks) butter

1. Grease interior of slow cooker crock.

2. In a saucepan, combine raisins, cornstarch, sugar, and water. Cook until slightly thickened, stirring continually.

3. Remove from heat, stir in lemon juice, and let cool for an hour.

4. Prepare crumbs by combining flour, baking soda, brown sugar, salt, and dry oats in a good-sized bowl until well mixed.

5. Cut butter into chunks. Work into dry ingredients with your fingers, 2 knives, or a pastry cutter until fine crumbs form.

6. Divide crumbs in half. Spread half into bottom of slow cooker crock. Press down to form crust.

7. Spoon raisin mixture over crumb crust.

8. Cover with remaining half of crumbs.

9. Cover. Bake on High 2–3 hours, or until firm in middle and bubbly around the edges.

10. Remove lid carefully and quickly so drops of water from inside the lid don't drip on the crisp.

11. Continue baking 30 more minutes to allow the crisp to dry on top.

12. Remove crock from cooker and place on baking rack.

13. Cut into squares, or spoon out of crock, to serve when warm or at room temperature.

Don't skip the lemon juice. It makes sure the crisp isn't super-sweet. Add a little more if you'd like to really taste it.

APRICOT CRISP

Makes: 5 servings
PREP. TIME: 20–30 MINUTES
COOKING TIME: 3½–4 HOURS
IDEAL SLOW-COOKER SIZE: 4-QUART

2¼ lbs. fresh apricots

1¼ cups flour

¼ cup chopped walnuts or pecans

1¼ cups sugar

pinch ground cloves

pinch cardamom

1 tsp. cinnamon

12 Tbsp. (1½ sticks) butter

1. Grease interior of slow cooker crock.

2. Cut apricots in half, remove stone, and place fruit evenly into crock.

3. In a good-sized bowl, mix together flour, chopped nuts, sugar, cloves, cardamom, and cinnamon until well blended.

4. Cut butter into chunks. Using either your fingers, 2 knives, or a pastry cutter, work butter into dry ingredients.

5. When crumbly, scatter over apricot halves.

6. Cover. Bake on High 3–3½ hours, or until fruit is tender.

7. Remove lid carefully and quickly, tilting it away from yourself to prevent condensation on inside of lid from dripping onto crisp. Continue baking uncovered for another 30 minutes so crisp dries on top.

8. Remove crock and place on wire baking rack to cool. Serve crisp warm or at room temperature.

VARIATION

Try these with canned apricots, too. But drain them well before using. Cut the sugar in half if the syrup is sweetened.

SPICY SWEET APPLE CRISP

Makes: 6 servings
PREP. TIME: 20 MINUTES
COOKING TIME: 3½–4 HOURS
IDEAL SLOW-COOKER SIZE: 5-QUART

9 crisp baking apples, peeled or not
1 cup flour
1 cup sugar
1 tsp. baking powder
   pinch of salt
1 egg
4 Tbsp. (half a stick) butter
   several shakes of roasted, or other gourmet, cinnamon
   dash or two of cardamom

1. Grease interior of slow cooker crock.

2. Slice apples into crock, spreading them out evenly.

3. In a good-sized bowl, mix together flour, sugar, baking powder, and salt.

4. Break egg into dry ingredients and mix together.

5. Cut butter into chunks. Using your fingers, or 2 knives, or a pastry cutter, work into dough until small chunks form.

6. Scatter chunks over apples.

7. Sprinkle liberally with roasted cinnamon. Add a dash or two of cardamom.

8. Cover with cooker lid. Bake on High 3–3½ hours, or until firm in the middle and juices bubble up around the edges.

9. Remove lid carefully, tilting it quickly away from yourself so no condensation drips on the crisp. Continue baking 30 more minutes to allow the topping to crisp up.

10. Let cool until warm or room temperature before serving.

NOTE If you'd like to shake up the traditional apple crisp just a little bit, this is a winner.

APPLE PEAR CRISP

Makes: 8–10 servings
PREP. TIME: 15–20 MINUTES
COOKING TIME: 2–4 HOURS
IDEAL SLOW-COOKER SIZE: 5-QUART

3–4 large apples, unpeeled and sliced

3–4 large pears, unpeeled and sliced

½ cup sugar, or less, depending on how naturally sweet the apples are

1 Tbsp. lemon juice

1 Tbsp. flour

Topping

1 cup flour

1 cup brown sugar

⅔ cup dry oats, quick or rolled (rolled have more texture)

½ tsp. cinnamon

6 Tbsp. (¾ stick) butter

1. Grease interior of slow cooker crock.

2. In a big bowl, mix together apple and pear slices, sugar, lemon juice, and 1 Tbsp. flour.

3. Pour into crock.

4. In the same bowl, mix topping ingredients: flour, brown sugar, dry oats, and cinnamon. Then cut in butter with 2 knives, a pastry cutter, or your fingers. When crumbs the size of small peas form, sprinkle over fruit mixture.

5. Cover crock. Bake on High 2–3 hours, or on Low 4 hours, or until fruit is bubbly.

6. Thirty minutes before end of cooking time, remove lid (don't let condensation from inside of lid drip on the crisp), so the topping can dry.

7. Serve as is, or topped with ice cream or in a bowl with milk.

NOTE This is year-round versatile. Eat it for breakfast, for a quick supper, or for a late afternoon or evening snack. Also, it's delicious warm or cold.

PEACHES AND PUDDING CRISP

Photo appears in color section.

Makes: 8 servings
PREP. TIME: 20 MINUTES
COOKING TIME: 3–4 HOURS
IDEAL SLOW-COOKER SIZE: 5-QUART

5–6 cups peaches, fresh or canned
½ cup peach juice or syrup
2 small pkgs. instant vanilla pudding, divided
½ cup brown sugar

Topping
1 cup flour
1½ cups dry oatmeal, quick or rolled
½ cup brown sugar
8 Tbsp. (1 stick) butter, melted
¾ tsp. salt
2 tsp. cinnamon
reserved dry instant vanilla pudding

TIP This crisp gets crunchy, but it won't get brown on top in a slow cooker. Run the finished dish under the broiler for just a minute or two until it's properly brown and crunchy. That, against the soft peaches—yum!

1. Grease interior of slow cooker crock.

2. Combine peaches, their syrup, 2 Tbsp. dry pudding mix, and brown sugar in good-sized mixing bowl. Set aside remaining dry pudding mix.

3. Place in slow cooker crock.

4. Combine all topping ingredients until well blended and crumbly. Sprinkle over peach mixture.

5. Cover. Bake on High 2½–3½ hours, or until firm in middle and bubbly around the edges.

6. Remove lid carefully, tilting it quickly away from yourself so that water from the inside of the lid doesn't drip on the crisp.

7. Continue baking 30 more minutes so crisp dries out on top.

8. Remove crock from cooker and place on baking rack to cool. Serve when warm or at room temperature.

Puddings AND Custards

CHOCOLATE BREAD PUDDING

Photo appears in color section.

Makes: 10 servings
PREP. TIME: 15 MINUTES
COOKING TIME: 2–3 HOURS
IDEAL SLOW-COOKER SIZE: 5-QUART

1	Tbsp. butter
10	cups cubed white bread, preferably hearty and preferably stale
3½	cups whole milk
5	eggs
2	tsp. vanilla
¼	cup sugar
½	cup brown sugar
3	Tbsp. unsweetened cocoa powder
½	cup semisweet chocolate chips

1. Grease slow cooker with butter.

2. Place bread cubes in buttered slow cooker.

3. In a mixing bowl, beat together milk, eggs, and vanilla. Add both sugars and cocoa. Whisk again.

4. Pour milk mixture over bread. Push any floating cubes down into the mixture.

5. Sprinkle with chocolate chips.

6. Cover and cook on High for 2–3 hours until puffy and liquid is absorbed.

7. Serve hot, warm, or chilled. The puffiness will subside as the pudding cools.

> **TIP**
>
> Stale, or even toasted, bread makes a better texture in bread pudding. It soaks up the custard more nicely and gives a better flavor. If you're starting with fresh bread, either allow it to sit uncovered at room temperature overnight, or toast it lightly. Serve with caramel sauce or fresh berries.

CLASSIC BREAD PUDDING

Photo appears in color section.

Makes: 10 servings
PREP. TIME: 25 MINUTES
COOKING TIME: 2–3 HOURS
IDEAL SLOW-COOKER SIZE: 5-QUART

4 Tbsp. (½ stick) butter, melted
10 cups diced white bread, stale
⅔ cup raisins
5 eggs
3½ cups whole milk
⅓ cup sugar
½ tsp. vanilla
1 tsp. cinnamon
½ tsp. salt

1. Pour butter in slow cooker and swirl it around to grease the bottom and up the sides several inches.

2. Add bread cubes and raisins to slow cooker. Mix gently.

3. In a mixing bowl, whisk eggs until they no longer cling to the whisk. Add milk, sugar, vanilla, cinnamon, and salt.

4. Pour milk mixture over bread mixture. Push floating cubes down into the mixture so they get a coating.

5. Cover and cook on High for 2–3 hours, until liquid is absorbed and the pudding is puffy and browning at the edges.

6. Serve hot, warm, or chilled. Expect the puff to sink down as the pudding cools.

TIP
Eat classic bread pudding as it is, or serve a caramel sauce and fruit on top.

CROCKERY CHOCOLATE PUDDING

Photo appears in color section.

Makes: 4 servings
PREP. TIME: 15 MINUTES
COOKING TIME: 3–4 HOURS
CHILLING TIME: 4 HOURS
IDEAL SLOW-COOKER SIZE: 3-QUART

½ cup sugar

3 Tbsp. cornstarch

3 Tbsp. unsweetened cocoa powder

1 cup half-and-half

1¼ cups milk

1 tsp. vanilla

1 Tbsp. salted butter

1. Combine all ingredients in greased slow cooker. Whisk well.

2. Cover and cook on Low for 3–4 hours, whisking thoroughly twice, until pudding is thickened.

3. Pour into serving dish and chill at least 4 hours, covered, before serving.

VARIATION

If you prefer a less sweet pudding, use ⅓ cup sugar.

VANILLA BEAN RICE PUDDING

Photo appears in color section.

Makes: 8 servings
PREP. TIME: 20 MINUTES
COOKING TIME: 2–4 HOURS
STANDING TIME: 10 MINUTES
IDEAL SLOW-COOKER SIZE: 4-QUART

- 6 cups milk, 2% or whole
- 1½ cups white rice, uncooked
- 1 cup sugar
- 2 Tbsp. butter, melted
- ½ tsp. salt
- ½ tsp. ground cinnamon
- 1 vanilla bean
- 1 egg

1. Combine milk, rice, sugar, butter, salt, and cinnamon in slow cooker.
2. Split vanilla bean in half and scrape seeds into milk mixture. Drop in split bean as well.
3. Cover and cook on High for 2–4 hours, until rice is tender and most of the milk is absorbed.
4. Whisk egg in a small bowl.
5. Slowly add ½ cup hot rice mixture to beaten egg, whisking constantly.
6. Slowly pour rice/egg mixture back into slow cooker, whisking constantly. Whisk an additional minute.
7. Cover and allow to stand 10 minutes.
8. Pour hot pudding into serving dish. Serve warm, or chill first before serving.

VARIATION

Add 1 cup raisins in step 1.

TIP

Steps 4–6 are called "tempering" the egg. This gentle introduction of the egg to the hot pudding helps to thicken the pudding while keeping the silky texture of the egg. Putting the egg straight into hot pudding would create scrambled egg!

BANANA BREAD PUDDING WITH BUTTERSCOTCH SAUCE

Makes: 10 servings
PREP. TIME: 30 MINUTES
COOKING TIME: 2–3 HOURS
STANDING TIME: 10 MINUTES
IDEAL SLOW-COOKER SIZE: 5-QUART

 5 ripe bananas, peeled and sliced in coins
10 cups diced white French bread, stale
 5 eggs
3½ cups whole milk
 ¾ cup brown sugar, divided
 ¼ tsp. ground nutmeg
 ¾ tsp. salt, divided
 2 tsp. vanilla, divided
 2 Tbsp. dark spiced rum, divided
 4 Tbsp. (½ stick) salted butter
 ½ cup heavy cream

TIP

Use this butterscotch sauce for other desserts as well—ice cream, tapioca pudding, plain chocolate cake, and so on. Keep it in the fridge and warm it slightly before using so you can stir and recombine the sauce.

1. In a greased slow cooker, make 2 or 3 layers of banana slices and bread, starting with banana slices.

2. In a mixing bowl, whisk eggs until they no longer cling to the whisk.

3. Add milk, ¼ cup brown sugar, nutmeg, ½ tsp. salt, 1 tsp. vanilla, and 1 Tbsp. rum.

4. Pour milk mixture gently over layers in crock. Be sure bread cubes are submerged.

5. Cover and cook on High for 2–3 hours, until bread pudding is set in the middle and edges are browning.

6. Set aside with lid off to firm up while you make the butterscotch sauce. The puffiness will sink down a bit.

7. In a medium saucepan, combine butter, remaining ½ cup brown sugar, cream, remaining ¼ tsp. salt, and remaining 1 Tbsp. rum.

8. Cook and stir over medium heat until sauce is just coming to a gentle boil. Lower heat to keep at a low boil for 5 minutes, stirring occasionally.

9. Add remaining 1 tsp. vanilla to sauce. Serve warm over warm bread pudding.

APPLE WALNUT BREAD PUDDING WITH WHISKEY SAUCE

Photo appears in color section.

Makes: 10 servings
PREP. TIME: 30 MINUTES
COOKING TIME: 2–3 HOURS
STANDING TIME: 30 MINUTES
IDEAL SLOW-COOKER SIZE: 5-QUART

- 10 cups diced stale bread, a mixture of kinds is fine
- 2 cups peeled, chopped apples
- 5 eggs
- 3½ cups whole milk
- ½ cup brown sugar, divided
- 1 tsp. ground cinnamon
- ½ tsp. vanilla
- ½ tsp. salt
- ½ cup chopped walnuts, toasted
- 3 Tbsp. salted butter
- ¼ cup heavy cream
- 2 Tbsp. whiskey

1. Place half the bread in a greased slow cooker. Add all the apples as a layer. Cover with remaining bread.

2. In a mixing bowl, whisk eggs until they no longer cling to the whisk. Add milk, ¼ cup brown sugar, cinnamon, vanilla, and salt.

3. Pour milk mixture gently over layers in crock. Push bread cubes down so they are completely submerged.

4. Cover and cook on High for 2–3 hours until slightly puffy and liquid is absorbed.

5. Sprinkle with walnuts, pressing gently into the tender top.

6. Set aside with lid off to firm up while you make the whiskey sauce. Expect the puff to sink down as the pudding sits.

7. In a saucepan, combine butter, remaining ¼ cup brown sugar, cream, and whiskey.

8. Stir and cook over medium heat until it reaches a gentle boil. Remove from heat and serve warm over warm bread pudding.

RASPBERRIOCA

Makes: 8–10 servings
PREP. TIME: 10 MINUTES
COOKING TIME: 3–6 HOURS
IDEAL SLOW-COOKER SIZE: 3-QUART

4 cups water

½ cup pearl tapioca

3 oz. box raspberry gelatin

⅓ cup sugar

2 cups frozen red raspberries

1 cup heavy whipping cream

1. In slow cooker, combine water and tapioca.

2. Cover and cook on Low for 6 hours or High for 3 hours, stirring twice.

3. Stir in gelatin and sugar until dissolved.

4. Gently stir in raspberries.

5. Pour into bowl and refrigerate until chilled.

6. Use an electric mixer to beat cream into soft peaks in chilled bowl. Stir into chilled tapioca. Serve.

VANILLA TAPIOCA

Makes: 8 servings
PREP. TIME: 5 MINUTES
COOKING TIME: 3–6 HOURS
STANDING TIME: 30 MINUTES
IDEAL SLOW-COOKER SIZE: 3- OR 4-QUART

4 cups milk, preferably 2%

2 eggs

⅔ cup sugar

½ cup pearl tapioca

¼ tsp. salt

1 tsp. vanilla

1. In slow cooker, whisk milk and eggs together until eggs no longer cling to whisk.

2. Add sugar, tapioca, and salt. Mix again.

3. Cover and cook on Low for 6 hours or on High for 3 hours, whisking thoroughly twice.

4. Add vanilla.

5. Remove crock from electric cooker and allow to sit uncovered for 30 minutes before serving warm. Alternatively, transfer pudding to serving dish and refrigerate for several hours before serving cold.

TIP

Great with fresh fruit on top, or any toppings you enjoy on ice cream.

TROPICAL PINEAPPLE PUDDING

Makes: 8 servings
PREP. TIME: 15 MINUTES
COOKING TIME: 3–4 HOURS
STANDING TIME: 30 MINUTES
IDEAL SLOW-COOKER SIZE: 3-QUART

20 oz. can crushed pineapple, undrained
11 oz. can mandarin oranges, undrained
 2 eggs, beaten
½ cup coconut milk
 3 Tbsp. cornstarch
½ cup sugar
¼ tsp. salt
    zest and juice of 1 lime

1. Combine pineapple and oranges in slow cooker.
2. Separately, whisk eggs, coconut milk, cornstarch, sugar, salt, lime zest, and lime juice until totally smooth.
3. Add egg mixture to fruit in slow cooker, mixing to combine thoroughly.
4. Cover and cook on Low for 3–4 hours, whisking thoroughly twice, until thick.
5. Allow to sit with lid off for 30 minutes before serving warm. Or transfer to serving dish and chill for several hours in fridge before serving.

VARIATION

Make tropical parfaits by layering chilled pudding in pretty glasses with vanilla wafers or similar cookies, whipped cream, toasted grated coconut, and sliced bananas.

PUMPKIN CUSTARD

Photo appears in color section.

Makes: 6 servings
PREP. TIME: 15 MINUTES
COOKING TIME: 2–3 HOURS
IDEAL SLOW-COOKER SIZE: 3-QUART

1 Tbsp. butter
1½ cups cooked, pureed pumpkin
⅔ cup dark brown sugar
3 eggs, beaten
1 cup heavy cream
1 Tbsp. flour
1 tsp. ground cinnamon
½ tsp. ground ginger
½ tsp. ground nutmeg
¼ tsp. ground cloves
½ tsp. salt

1. Use butter to grease slow cooker.

2. Combine rest of ingredients, whisking well.

3. Pour into buttered crock.

4. Cover and cook on High for 2–3 hours until set in the middle. Serve warm.

> **TIP**
>
> Make this into a pumpkin pie by lining a 6-quart oval crock with pastry for a 9" pie. Bring the pastry up the sides 1–2". Pour in the custard. Cover and cook on High for 2–3 hours until set. Allow to cool for easier slicing and serving.

RASPBERRY CUSTARD

Photo appears in color section.

Makes: 6 servings
PREP. TIME: 15 MINUTES
COOKING TIME: 3–4 HOURS
STANDING TIME: 30–60 MINUTES
IDEAL SLOW-COOKER SIZE: 4-QUART

5 eggs
½ cup sugar
½ tsp. salt
¾ cup all-purpose flour
12 oz. can evaporated milk
1 tsp. vanilla extract
   pinch cinnamon
2 Tbsp. butter
2 cups red raspberries, fresh or frozen, thawed and drained

1. Beat eggs, sugar, and salt in mixing bowl until eggs no longer cling to whisk.

2. Add flour in three portions, whisking well after each addition until no lumps remain.

3. Whisk in evaporated milk, vanilla, and cinnamon.

4. Use butter to generously grease slow cooker.

5. Pour egg mixture into cooker. Sprinkle evenly with raspberries.

6. Cover and cook on Low for 3–4 hours, until set.

7. Remove lid and allow to cool for 30–60 minutes before serving. May chill before serving as well.

VARIATION

Of course you can use other berries in this custard, whatever you have in the freezer or find to pick.

SIMPLE EGG CUSTARD

Makes: 6 servings
PREP. TIME: 20 MINUTES
COOKING TIME: 2–3 HOURS
CHILLING TIME: 4 HOURS
IDEAL SLOW-COOKER SIZE: 6-QUART

2 cups whole milk

4 eggs

⅓ cup sugar

½ tsp. salt

1 tsp. vanilla

1. Place ingredients in blender. Whip well.

2. Divide between 4–6 ramekins, or 6 ¼ pint canning jars.

3. Space the ramekins/jars out in slow cooker.

4. Pour water in slow cooker, being careful to avoid ramekins, so water comes up halfway up the sides of the ramekins.

5. Cover and cook on High for 2–3 hours, until custard is set.

6. Carefully remove hot ramekins from slow cooker—a canning jar lifter works perfectly for this—and set on wire rack to cool to room temperature. Chill, covered, for at least 4 hours before serving.

VARIATION

Add a few berries or some sliced peaches in the bottom of the ramekins before pouring in the egg/milk mixture.

If you can get your hands on really nice eggs with the deep yellow-orange yolks (usually straight from the farm!), your custard will show that lovely buttery color. But of course, any eggs will work. If you use ¼ pint canning jars for making this recipe, you can easily take this delicious dessert with you. Just screw on a canning lid and ring and go! Perfect for picnics and packed lunches.

SPANISH FLAN

Photo appears in color section.

Makes: 6 servings
PREP. TIME: 20 MINUTES
COOKING TIME: 3–5 HOURS
COOLING TIME: 30 MINUTES
IDEAL SLOW-COOKER SIZE: 5-QUART

1 cup sugar

¼ tsp. lemon juice

3 eggs

14 oz. can sweetened condensed milk

12 oz. can evaporated milk

1 tsp. vanilla

pinch salt

1. Place sugar and lemon juice in slow cooker.

2. With lid off, cook on High for 1–2 hours, occasionally tilting the slow cooker to move sugar around as it caramelizes. When the sugar has browned into liquid caramel, turn setting to Low.

3. In a mixing bowl, whisk together eggs, both milks, vanilla, and salt.

4. Pour gently and evenly over caramel in slow cooker.

5. Cover and cook on Low for an additional 2–3 hours until set.

6. Remove lid from cooker and allow flan to cool for 30 minutes.

7. Run a knife around the edge of the flan. Invert crock over rimmed platter. Caramel should pool around the edges of the flan. Cut into slices and serve with extra caramel drizzled on top.

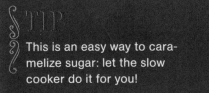

TIP

This is an easy way to caramelize sugar: let the slow cooker do it for you!

MAPLE POT DE CRÈME

Photo appears in color section.

Makes: 4–6 servings
PREP. TIME: 10 MINUTES
COOKING TIME: 2–3 HOURS
CHILLING TIME: AT LEAST 2 HOURS
IDEAL SLOW-COOKER SIZE: 6-QUART

2 egg yolks

2 eggs

1 cup heavy cream

½ cup whole milk

1 Tbsp. dark brown sugar

⅓ cup grade B (dark) maple syrup

pinch salt

1 tsp. vanilla

¼ tsp. ground nutmeg

whipped cream, for garnish, optional

> **TIP**
> Serve this up with whipped cream and berries or a drizzle of chocolate sauce.

1. In a mixing bowl, beat egg yolks and eggs until light and frothy.

2. Add cream, milk, brown sugar, maple syrup, salt, vanilla, and nutmeg. Mix well.

3. Use a baking dish that fits in your slow cooker.

4. Pour maple mixture in baking dish and set it in slow cooker.

5. Carefully pour water around the baking dish until the water comes halfway up the sides.

6. Cover cooker. Cook on High for 2–3 hours, until pot de crème is set but still a little bit jiggly in the middle.

7. Wearing oven mitts to protect your knuckles, carefully remove hot dish from cooker. Set on wire rack to cool to room temperature.

8. Cover tightly and chill for at least 2 hours before serving. Garnish with whipped cream if you wish.

STRAWBERRY RHUBARB SAUCE

Makes: 6 servings
PREP. TIME: 20 MINUTES
COOKING TIME: 3–4 HOURS
CHILLING TIME: 2 HOURS
STANDING TIME: 1 HOUR
IDEAL SLOW-COOKER SIZE: 4-QUART

1½ lbs. rhubarb, cut in ½" pieces
     pinch salt
⅓ cup water
½ cup sugar
2 cups diced strawberries

1. Combine rhubarb, salt, water, and sugar in slow cooker.

2. Cover and cook on Low for 3–4 hours.

3. Pour sauce into serving dish. Allow to cool to room temperature.

4. Stir strawberries gently into sauce. Chill at least 2 hours before serving.

TIP

Serve as is in small dessert dishes, or serve as a sauce over pound cake, angel food cake, or ice cream.

HOT FUDGE SAUCE

BETH NAFZIGER, LOWVILLE, NY

Makes: 1½ cups
PREP. TIME: 15 MINUTES
IDEAL SLOW-COOKER SIZE: 1-QT.

¾ cup semisweet chocolate chips

4 Tbsp. (½ stick) butter

⅔ cup sugar

5 oz. can (⅔ cup) evaporated milk

1. In a small heavy saucepan melt chocolate and butter together.

2. Add sugar. Gradually stir in evaporated milk.

3. Bring mixture to a boil, and then reduce heat. Boil gently over low heat for 8 minutes, stirring frequently.

4. Remove pan from heat. Pour sauce into slow cooker.

5. Set cooker control to Warm—the ideal temperature for serving.

NOTE I have served this for many years as part of our family Christmas Eve celebration.

TIP
Use as a dipping sauce for angel food cake cubes, banana chunks, pineapple chunks, and mini-pretzels.

Breads and Muffins

PEACHES AND PUDDING CRISP ♥ page 331

CHOCOLATE BREAD PUDDING ♥ page 334

CROCKERY CHOCOLATE PUDDING
page 336

CLASSIC BREAD PUDDING
page 335

APPLE WALNUT BREAD PUDDING
WITH WHISKEY SAUCE
page 339

PUMPKIN CUSTARD
page 343

VANILLA BEAN RICE PUDDING
page 337

RASPBERRY CUSTARD
page 344

SPANISH FLAN ♥ page 346

MAPLE POT DE CRÈME ♥ page 347

CROCKERY OATMEAL BREAD ♥ page 336

DARK RYE BREAD
page 355

IRISH OATMEAL BREAD
page 360

GLAZED POPPYSEED BREAD
page 364

LITTLE BOSTON BROWN LOAVES
page 361

BANANA PEANUT BUTTER BREAD page 366

STRAWBERRIES AND CREAM BREAD
page 367

CORNBREAD FROM SCRATCH
page 371

SAVORY CHEESE MUFFINS ♥ page 373

DOUBLE CHOCOLATE MUFFINS ♥ page 374

MORNING GLORY MUFFINS ♥ page 377

APPLE CRANBERRY MUFFINS ♥ page 383

DAILY BREAD

Makes: one 9" loaf
PREP. TIME: 30 MINUTES
COOKING TIME: 2–3 HOURS
RISING TIME: 1 HOUR
IDEAL SLOW-COOKER SIZE: 6-QUART

1½ cups whole wheat flour, divided
2 tsp. instant yeast
1 tsp. salt
3 Tbsp. honey
1 Tbsp. oil, plus a little more for the bowl
¾ cup warm water
1½ cups unbleached all-purpose flour

1. In mixing bowl, combine 1 cup whole wheat flour, yeast, salt, honey, oil, and warm water. Beat well for 1 minute.

2. Stir in remaining ½ cup whole wheat flour and gradually add the all-purpose flour until a thick dough is forming.

3. Knead by hand for 5 minutes.

4. Pour a little oil over the dough and bowl, turning ball of dough to grease all sides. Cover with damp kitchen towel and set in warm place to rise until doubled, about 1 hour.

5. On counter or board, press dough flat with hands or rolling pin. Roll up into loaf, tucking ends under and pinching bottom seam securely.

6. Place loaf in greased loaf pan, seam-side down. Set pan on metal trivet or jar ring in slow cooker.

7. Cover and cook on High for 2–3 hours, or until top is firm, bread is pulling away from the sides of the pan, and an instant-read thermometer inserted in middle of loaf registers 200°F.

8. Wearing oven gloves to protect your knuckles, remove pan from cooker. Turn loaf out onto wire rack and allow to cool before slicing.

VARIATION

This is a basic whole wheat bread with excellent flavor. You can increase the amount of whole wheat flour and decrease the white flour, but consider adding 1–2 tsp. vital wheat gluten to keep the bread light and willing to rise.

CROCKERY OATMEAL BREAD

Photo appears in color section.

Makes: one 9" loaf
PREP. TIME: 30 MINUTES
COOKING TIME: 2–3 HOURS
STANDING TIME: 30 MINUTES
RISING TIME: 1 HOUR
IDEAL SLOW-COOKER SIZE: 6 QUART

½ cup rolled oats
1¼ cups whole wheat flour, divided
¼ cup brown sugar
1½ tsp. salt
1 Tbsp. butter
1 cup boiling water
1½ tsp. instant yeast
1½ cups unbleached all-purpose flour, divided
1 Tbsp. oil

1. In a mixing bowl, combine oats, ¼ cup whole wheat flour, brown sugar, salt, butter, and boiling water. Set aside to cool to room temperature, about 30 minutes.

2. Stir yeast into lukewarm mixture. Stir in remaining 1 cup whole wheat flour.

3. Add 1 cup all-purpose flour. Begin to knead, adding remaining ½ cup gradually as needed to make dough. Knead for 5 minutes.

4. Pour oil over dough and bowl, turning dough ball to grease all sides. Cover with damp kitchen towel and set in warm place to rise until doubled, about 1 hour.

5. On counter or board, press dough flat with hands or rolling pin. Roll up into loaf, tucking ends under and pinching bottom seam securely.

6. Place loaf in greased loaf pan. Set pan on metal trivet or jar ring in slow cooker.

7. Cover and cook on High for 2–3 hours, or until top is firm, loaf is pulling away from sides of pan, and instant-read thermometer inserted in middle of loaf registers 200°F.

8. Wearing oven gloves to protect your knuckles, remove pan from cooker. Turn loaf out onto wire rack and allow to cool before slicing.

NOTE This bread is wonderful toasted for breakfast.

ARTISAN BREAD IN THE CROCK

PHYLLIS GOOD, LANCASTER, PA

Makes: one 9" loaf
PREP. TIME: 30 MINUTES
COOKING TIME: 2–3 HOURS
RISING TIME: 14–27 HOURS
IDEAL SLOW-COOKER SIZE: 6-QUART

2 cups whole wheat flour

2 cups unbleached all-purpose flour

1¼ tsp. salt

¼ tsp. instant yeast

2 cups warm water, divided

3 Tbsp. coarse cornmeal, divided

1. In a large bowl with a tight-fitting lid (or use plastic wrap) mix flours, salt, and yeast.

2. Add 1½ cups water. Mix. Add more water gradually, up to 2 cups, until a wet dough is formed, like very thick mud.

3. Cover tightly and set in a dark place at room temperature for at least 12 hours and not more than 24 hours.

4. Grease a large square of parchment paper and place in slow cooker. Sprinkle with 2 Tbsp. cornmeal.

5. Pour and prod the dough out of the bowl onto the cornmeal-sprinkled parchment in the cooker.

6. Sprinkle with remaining 1 Tbsp. cornmeal.

7. Cover and allow to rest for 2–3 hours.

8. Turn slow cooker on to High and bake for 2–3 hours, until top is firm and instant-read thermometer inserted in middle of loaf registers 200°F.

9. Wearing oven gloves to protect your knuckles, lift parchment with loaf out of slow cooker. Set on wire rack to cool before slicing.

VARIATION

You can experiment with adding olives, dried tomatoes, or herbs before placing in the slow cooker.

TIP

The long rise replaces the kneading and the small pinch of yeast gives the loaf a less yeasty taste, that "artisan" flavor, and holes that I love. Using the slow cooker means that the loaf will be a bit flatter than one baked in a traditional oven, but it's worth the trade for the convenience.

DARK RYE BREAD

Photo appears in color section.

Makes: one 9" loaf
PREP. TIME: 30 MINUTES
COOKING TIME: 2–3 HOURS
RISING TIME: 1 HOUR
IDEAL SLOW-COOKER SIZE: 6-QUART

- 1 Tbsp. instant yeast
- 2 Tbsp. unsweetened cocoa powder
- 1 tsp. caraway seeds
- 2 Tbsp. blackstrap molasses
- 1 Tbsp. sugar
- ½ tsp. salt
- 1 Tbsp. oil, plus more for bowl
- 1 cup water
- 2 cups all-purpose unbleached flour, + 1 Tbsp., optional, for sprinkling
- 1½ cups whole-grain rye flour

1. In mixing bowl, combine yeast, cocoa powder, caraway seeds, molasses, sugar, salt, oil, water, and all-purpose flour. Beat for 1 minute.

2. Add rye flour gradually, first stirring and then using hands to make a stiff dough.

3. Knead for 5 minutes.

4. Pour some oil over dough and bowl, turning dough ball to grease all sides. Cover with damp kitchen towel and set in warm place to rise until doubled, about 1 hour.

5. On counter or board, press dough flat with hands. Roll up into a loaf. Tuck edges under to form a round or oblong loaf.

6. Place loaf in center of large square of parchment paper and gently lift it into the slow cooker.

7. With a sharp knife, slash an X in the loaf about ½" deep. Sprinkle with 1 Tbsp. flour if you wish.

8. Cover and cook on High for 2–3 hours, until top is firm and instant-read thermometer inserted in middle of loaf registers 200°F. The X will have dramatically opened up to make a rustic-looking loaf.

9. Wearing oven gloves to protect your knuckles, remove paper with loaf from cooker. Set on wire rack and allow to cool before slicing.

NOTE

Dark rye bread makes excellent grilled reuben sandwiches. It also is nice as part of Sunday supper: a platter of sliced meat and cheese, some pickles, and bread for making open-faced sandwiches.

ENGLISH MUFFIN LOAF

Makes: one 9" loaf
PREP. TIME: 20 MINUTES
COOKING TIME: 2–3 HOURS
RISING TIME: 1 HOUR
IDEAL SLOW-COOKER SIZE: 6-QUART

2½ cups unbleached all-purpose flour, divided

1 Tbsp. instant yeast

1 Tbsp. sugar

1 tsp. salt

¼ tsp. baking soda

1 cup warm milk

1 Tbsp. coarse cornmeal

1. In a mixing bowl, combine 1 cup flour, yeast, sugar, salt, baking soda, and warm milk.

2. Beat with electric mixer for 3 minutes, scraping bowl occasionally.

3. Stir in remaining 1½ cups flour to make a stiff batter.

4. Grease loaf pan. Sprinkle with cornmeal.

5. Pour batter in prepared pan. Cover with kitchen towel and set aside for 1 hour to rise.

6. Place risen loaf on metal trivet or jar ring in slow cooker.

7. Cover and cook on High for 2–3 hours, until loaf is firm on top and instant-read thermometer inserted in middle of loaf registers 200°F.

8. Wearing oven gloves to protect your knuckles, remove pan from cooker. Turn loaf out onto wire rack and allow to cool before slicing.

NOTE This is a great starting recipe for beginning bread bakers because the mixer does the kneading. Treat slices of this bread just like store-bought English muffins.

TOMATO HERB BREAD

Makes: one 9" loaf
PREP. TIME: 30 MINUTES
COOKING TIME: 2–3 HOURS
RISING TIME: 1 HOUR
IDEAL SLOW-COOKER SIZE: 6-QUART

¾ cup peeled, chopped tomatoes (canned are fine)
1 tsp. dried dill weed
½ tsp. dried basil
¼ tsp. dried oregano
1 tsp. salt
1 Tbsp. honey
1 Tbsp. melted butter
2 tsp. instant yeast
2½ cups unbleached all-purpose flour
   a little oil for the bowl

1. In food processor or blender, puree tomatoes, dill, basil, oregano, salt, honey, and 1 Tbsp. butter.

2. Pour mixture into mixing bowl. Add yeast. Stir.

3. Gradually add flour, stirring and then kneading by hand to form a smooth dough.

4. Knead for 5 minutes. Pour a little oil on dough and bowl, turning ball of dough to grease all sides.

5. Cover with a damp kitchen towel and set aside in a warm spot to rise for 1 hour or until doubled.

6. On counter or board, press dough flat with hands or rolling pin. Roll up into loaf, tucking ends under and pinching bottom seam securely.

7. Place loaf in greased loaf pan. Set pan on metal trivet or jar ring in slow cooker.

8. Cover and cook on High for 2–3 hours, or until top is firm, loaf is pulling away from sides of pan, and instant-read thermometer inserted in middle of loaf registers 200°F.

9. Wearing oven gloves to protect your knuckles, remove pan from cooker. Turn loaf out onto wire rack and allow to cool before slicing.

NOTE This bread is perfect to use in grilled cheese sandwiches. And this is definitely a summer-friendly recipe since the slow cooker won't heat up the house like the oven would!

ZUCCHINI SANDWICH BUNS

Makes: 12 rolls
PREP. TIME: 30 MINUTES
COOKING TIME: 1½–3 HOURS
RISING TIME: 1 HOUR
IDEAL SLOW-COOKER SIZE: 6-QUART

1½ cups shredded zucchini

⅓ cup warm water

⅓ cup warm milk

3 Tbsp. oil, plus a little for the bowl

2 Tbsp. instant yeast

⅓ cup sugar

2 tsp. salt

1 cup whole wheat flour

3 cups unbleached all-purpose flour, divided

TIP
Separate rolls and keep tightly covered at room temperature for 2 days, or wrap tightly and freeze. They are excellent for hamburgers, sloppy joes, or sandwiches.

1. In a mixing bowl, combine zucchini, water, milk, oil, yeast, sugar, salt, and whole wheat flour. Do not pour off any liquid from zucchini.

2. Add unbleached flour a cup at a time, stirring until soft dough forms.

3. Knead 5 minutes. The dough will be sticky, but persevere!

4. Pour a little oil on dough and bowl, turning dough ball to grease it. Cover with damp kitchen towel and set aside to rise until doubled, about 1 hour.

5. Divide dough into 12 pieces. Press and roll them into balls.

6. Grease a large square of parchment paper and tuck it into the slow cooker.

7. Place rolls inside slow cooker.

8. Cover and cook on High for 1½–3 hours, checking at 1½ hours by gently pulling apart two rolls in the middle and checking to make sure they are not doughy yet.

9. Wearing oven gloves to protect your knuckles, lift parchment with rolls out of cooker. Set it on wire rack to cool.

GRANNY'S POTATO ROLLS

Makes: 8 servings
PREP. TIME: 30 MINUTES
COOKING TIME: 1½–2½ HOURS
RISING TIME: 1½ HOURS
IDEAL SLOW-COOKER SIZE: 6-QUART

1 small potato, to make ½ cup mashed potato

1 cup warm milk

4 Tbsp. (½ stick) butter, room temperature

⅓ cup sugar

1 cup whole wheat flour

1 Tbsp. instant yeast

1 tsp. salt

1 egg, beaten

3 cups unbleached all-purpose flour, divided

a little oil for the bowl

1. Peel the potato and dice. Cook in microwave or in saucepan on stove top with 2–3 Tbsp. water until soft. Beat and mash well to make very smooth mashed potato.

2. Combine warm mashed potato with milk, butter, sugar, whole wheat flour, and yeast. Cover with kitchen towel and set aside for 30 minutes.

3. Stir in salt, egg, and 1 cup all-purpose flour. Gradually add up to 2 cups more of unbleached flour, stirring to make soft dough.

4. Knead dough for 3–5 minutes. It will be sticky and soft, but that will make tender rolls, so be patient!

5. Pour a little oil on dough and bowl, turning ball of dough until all sides are greased. Cover with damp kitchen towel and set aside to rise until doubled, about 1 hour.

6. Divide dough into 8–10 pieces. Shape into balls.

7. Grease a large square of parchment and tuck it into slow cooker. Space rolls evenly on parchment in cooker.

8. Cover and cook on High for 1½–2½ hours, checking to see if rolls are done by pulling apart two in the center to make sure they are not doughy yet.

9. Wearing oven gloves to protect your knuckles, remove parchment with rolls from slow cooker. Set on wire rack to cool.

IRISH OATMEAL BREAD

Photo appears in color section.

Makes: one 9" loaf
PREP. TIME: 25 MINUTES
STANDING TIME: 6–10 HOURS
COOKING TIME: 3–4 HOURS
COOLING TIME: 10 MINUTES
IDEAL SLOW-COOKER SIZE: 6-QUART

1 cup plain full-fat yogurt
⅔ cup milk
1 cup rolled oats
2 eggs
2 Tbsp. oil
¾ cup dark brown sugar
1 cup whole wheat flour
⅔ cup all-purpose flour
1 tsp. baking soda
1 tsp. salt

TIP

The overnight soak gives a delicious flavor and texture to the bread; it's surprisingly light for its hearty ingredients. Serve it with butter, marmalade, or mild cheese.

1. Combine yogurt, milk, and oats in bowl with lid. Refrigerate for 6–10 hours.

2. Add eggs, oil, and sugar to yogurt mixture. Mix well.

3. Separately, combine both flours, baking soda, and salt.

4. Stir flour mixture gently into yogurt mixture.

5. Pour batter into greased and floured loaf pan that fits into cooker.

6. Set loaf pan on a jar lid or trivet on the floor of the cooker. Prop lid open at one end with a wooden spoon handle or chopstick.

7. Cook on High for 3–4 hours, until edges of bread are pulling away from sides and tester inserted in middle of loaf comes out clean. Bread will not brown as much as oven-baked bread!

8. Wearing oven gloves to protect your knuckles, remove hot pan from hot cooker. Allow to cool 10 minutes. Run a knife around the loaf and turn loaf out onto a cooling rack to finish cooling. Slices most easily when cool if you can wait that long.

LITTLE BOSTON BROWN LOAVES

Photo appears in color section.

Makes: four 16–oz. loaves
PREP. TIME: 30 MINUTES
COOKING TIME: 5–6 HOURS
COOLING TIME: 10 MINUTES
IDEAL SLOW-COOKER SIZE: 6-QUART

1 cup whole wheat flour
½ cup rye flour
½ cup stone-ground cornmeal
2 tsp. baking soda
1 tsp. salt
¼ tsp. allspice
¾ cup chopped raisins
1½ cups buttermilk
½ cup blackstrap molasses
2 Tbsp. butter, room temperature

TIP
Serve with a traditional New England supper of baked beans, or eat as breakfast toast with cream cheese.

1. In a mixing bowl, combine flours, cornmeal, baking soda, salt, and allspice. Stir in raisins.

2. Separately, mix buttermilk and molasses.

3. Add buttermilk mixture to flour mixture. Stir until just combined. Set aside while you prepare the cans and cooker.

4. Use 4 clean 15- or 16-oz. cans. Grease insides generously with butter.

5. Divide batter between the 4 cans to fill cans ⅔ full. Grease squares of tin foil with butter and use to make tight lids on each can.

6. Set cans in slow cooker. Pour in water to come halfway up the sides of the cans.

7. Cover and cook on Low for 5–6 hours, until skewer inserted through foil lid into bread comes out clean.

8. Carefully remove hot cans (a jar lifter is helpful), uncover, and allow to rest for 10 minutes. Run a knife around the edge of each loaf and turn loaves out onto cooling rack to cool. Slices easily when cool if you can wait that long.

BUTTERY BEER BREAD

Makes: one 9" loaf
PREP. TIME: 15 MINUTES
COOKING TIME: 3–4 HOURS
STANDING TIME: 20 MINUTES
IDEAL SLOW-COOKER SIZE: 6-QUART

1 cup whole wheat flour

2 cups all-purpose flour

2 Tbsp. sugar

3 tsp. baking powder

1 tsp. salt

12 oz. beer, any kind, room temperature

¼ cup melted butter

1. In a mixing bowl, combine flours, sugar, baking powder, and salt.

2. Add beer and mix.

3. Pour batter in greased and floured loaf pan that fits in your slow cooker. Drizzle top of loaf with melted butter.

4. Set pan on jar lid or metal trivet in slow cooker. Place lid on slow cooker, venting at one end with a wooden spoon handle or chopstick.

5. Cook on High for 3–4 hours, until edges of bread are pulling away from sides and tester inserted in middle of loaf comes out clean. Bread will not brown as much as oven-baked bread!

6. Wearing oven gloves to protect your knuckles, remove hot pan from cooker and allow to cool 10 minutes. Run a knife around the loaf and turn it out onto cooling rack, waiting 10 more minutes for easiest slicing.

NOTE This savory bread is less fuss than yeast bread, but seems extra-special with its buttery top.

RASPBERRY ALMOND BREAD

Makes: one 9" loaf
PREP. TIME: 20 MINUTES
COOKING TIME: 3–4 HOURS
STANDING TIME: 20 MINUTES
IDEAL SLOW-COOKER SIZE: 6-QUART

- 1 cup whole wheat flour
- 1 cup all-purpose flour
- ¼ cup rolled oats
- ⅔ cup sugar
- 2 tsp. baking powder
- 1 tsp. baking soda
- ½ tsp. salt
- 1 cup fresh or unsweetened frozen raspberries (do not thaw)
- ½ cup sliced almonds, lightly toasted
- 1 egg, lightly beaten
- ½ cup plain yogurt
- ⅓ cup canola oil
- ½ tsp. almond extract

TIP

Wonderful sliced and spread with Nutella.

1. In large bowl, mix flours, oats, sugar, baking powder, baking soda, and salt. Gently stir in raspberries and almonds.

2. Separately, mix egg, yogurt, oil, and almond extract.

3. Gently stir wet ingredients into dry until just barely mixed—streaks of flour are fine.

4. Pour batter into greased and floured loaf pan that fits in your slow cooker.

5. Place pan of batter into crock on jar lid or metal trivet. Cover and place wooden chopstick or spoon handle under lid to vent at one end.

6. Cook on High for 3–4 hours, until edges of bread are pulling away from sides and tester inserted in middle of loaf comes out clean. Bread does not brown as much as oven-baked bread!

7. Wearing oven mitts to protect your knuckles, remove hot pan from cooker.

8. Allow bread to cool 10 minutes. Run a knife around the edge, and turn loaf out onto cooling rack for 10 more minutes before slicing. Serve warm.

GLAZED POPPYSEED BREAD

Photo appears in color section.

Makes: one 9" loaf
PREP. TIME: 20 MINUTES
COOKING TIME: 3–4 HOURS
STANDING TIME: 30 MINUTES
IDEAL SLOW-COOKER SIZE: 6-QUART

2 cups all-purpose flour

½ cup sugar

½ tsp. salt

1 tsp. baking powder

½ tsp. baking soda

2 Tbsp. poppy seeds

⅓ cup vegetable oil

¼ cup buttermilk

1 egg

juice and zest of 1 lemon

Glaze

1 cup confectioners sugar

¼ tsp. butter extract

¼ tsp. almond extract

pinch salt

2–3 Tbsp. milk

1. In a mixing bowl, combine flour, sugar, salt, baking powder, baking soda, and poppy seeds.

2. Separately, mix oil, buttermilk, egg, lemon zest, and lemon juice.

3. Add wet ingredients to flour mixture and mix just until combined.

4. Pour batter into greased and floured loaf pan that fits in your slow cooker.

5. Place pan of batter into crock on jar lid or metal trivet. Cover and place wooden chopstick or spoon handle under lid to vent at one end.

6. Cook on High for 3–4 hours, until edges of bread are pulling away from sides and tester inserted in middle of loaf comes out clean. Bread will not brown as much as oven-baked bread!

7. Wearing oven mitts to protect your knuckles, remove hot pan from cooker.

8. Allow bread to cool 10 minutes while you make the glaze.

9. To make glaze, combine ingredients in small bowl, using lesser amount of milk. Add more milk as needed to make thick, pourable glaze.

10. Run a knife around edge of loaf and turn out onto cooling rack.

11. Poke holes in top of loaf with a skewer or chopstick. Pour glaze slowly and evenly over top of loaf. Allow to rest for 10–20 minutes before slicing.

VARIATION

The glaze is optional—the bread will still be delicious and moist without it.

BANANA PEANUT BUTTER BREAD

Photo appears in color section.

Makes: one 9" loaf
PREP. TIME: 20 MINUTES
COOKING TIME: 3–4 HOURS
STANDING TIME: 10 MINUTES
IDEAL SLOW-COOKER SIZE: 6-QUART

1   cup all-purpose flour

1   cup whole wheat flour

1   tsp. baking soda

½   tsp. salt

1   cup mashed ripe banana (about 2 medium)

½   cup creamy peanut butter

½   cup sugar

⅓   cup plain yogurt

⅓   cup vegetable oil

2   eggs

1   tsp. vanilla extract

1   cup semisweet chocolate chips

1. In a mixing bowl, combine flours, baking soda, and salt.

2. Separately, mix banana, peanut butter, sugar, yogurt, oil, eggs, and vanilla. When thoroughly mixed, stir in chocolate chips.

3. Add wet ingredients to dry ingredients, stirring just until combined.

4. Pour batter in greased and floured loaf pan.

5. Set pan on jar lid or metal trivet in slow cooker. Place lid on slow cooker, venting at one end with a wooden spoon handle or chopstick.

6. Cook on High for 3–4 hours, until edges of bread are pulling away from sides and tester inserted in middle of loaf comes out clean. Bread will not brown as much as oven-baked bread!

7. Wearing oven gloves to protect your knuckles, remove hot pan from cooker and allow to cool 10 minutes. Run a knife around the loaf and turn it out onto cooling rack. Slices best when cool, if you can wait that long!

NOTE Serve this bread for breakfast, snacks, or dessert—it's always welcome!

STRAWBERRIES AND CREAM BREAD

Photo appears in color section.

Makes: one 9" loaf
PREP. TIME: 30 MINUTES
COOKING TIME: 3–4 HOURS
STANDING TIME: 20 MINUTES
IDEAL SLOW-COOKER SIZE: 6-QUART

1½ cups diced strawberries

2 tsp. lemon juice

2 cups all-purpose flour

1 cup sugar

½ tsp. salt

2 tsp. baking powder

½ cup vegetable oil

½ cup orange juice

1½ tsp. vanilla

1 egg

8 oz. pkg. cream cheese, room temperature, diced

> **TIP**
> Sprinkle loaf with confectioners sugar before serving.

1. In a small bowl, combine strawberries and lemon juice. Set aside.

2. In a mixing bowl, combine flour, sugar, salt, and baking powder.

3. Separately, combine oil, orange juice, vanilla, and egg. Whisk. Stir in cream cheese.

4. Add strawberries to oil mixture.

5. Combine wet and dry mixtures, stirring gently just until combined.

6. Pour batter in greased and floured loaf pan that fits in your slow cooker.

7. Set pan on jar lid or metal trivet in slow cooker. Place lid on slow cooker, venting at one end with a wooden spoon handle or chopstick.

8. Cook on High for 3–4 hours, until edges of bread are pulling away from sides and tester inserted in middle of loaf comes out clean. Bread will not brown as much as oven-baked bread!

9. Wearing oven gloves to protect your knuckles, remove hot pan from cooker and allow to cool 10 minutes. Run a knife around the loaf and turn it out onto cooling rack. Wait 10 more minutes before slicing.

ROSEMARY RAISIN BREAD

Makes: one 9" loaf
PREP. TIME: 20 MINUTES
COOKING TIME: 3–4 HOURS
STANDING TIME: 20 MINUTES
IDEAL SLOW-COOKER SIZE: 6-QUART

1¼ cups whole wheat flour
1¼ cups all-purpose flour
½ cup sugar
½ tsp. baking soda
½ tsp. baking powder
½ tsp. salt
1½ tsp. dried rosemary
1 cup raisins
1½ cups buttermilk

1. In a mixing bowl, combine flours, sugar, baking soda, baking powder, salt, and rosemary. Stir in raisins.

2. Add buttermilk and mix gently, just until combined.

3. Pour batter into greased and floured loaf pan that fits in your slow cooker.

4. Place pan of batter into crock on jar lid or metal trivet. Cover and place wooden chopstick or spoon handle under lid to vent at one end.

5. Cook on High for 3–4 hours, until edges of bread are pulling away from sides and tester inserted in middle of loaf comes out clean. Bread will not brown as much as oven-baked bread!

6. Wearing oven mitts to protect your knuckles, remove hot pan from cooker.

7. Allow bread to cool 10 minutes. Run a knife around the edge, and turn loaf out onto cooling rack for 10 more minutes before slicing. Serve warm.

NOTE This bread is lovely toasted and then spread with butter or lemon curd.
≫—♥—⇨

VARIATIONS
❧ Substitute 1 cup plain yogurt mixed with ½ cup milk for the buttermilk.
❧ May substitute more all-purpose flour for the whole wheat flour.

THANKSGIVING BREAD

Makes: one 9" loaf
PREP. TIME: 30 MINUTES
COOKING TIME: 3–4 HOURS
STANDING TIME: 10 MINUTES
IDEAL SLOW-COOKER SIZE: 6-QUART

1¾ cups flour
¼ cup stone-ground cornmeal
¾ cup sugar
1½ tsp. baking powder
½ tsp. salt
⅓ cup oil
1 Tbsp. grated orange zest
½ cup orange juice
1 egg
1 cup chopped fresh cranberries
½ cup chopped walnuts

TIP

Buy a few extra bags of cranberries and stash them in the freezer for later—just thaw a cup, drain well, and chop.

1. In a mixing bowl, combine flour, cornmeal, sugar, baking powder, and salt.

2. Separately, mix oil, zest, juice, and egg. Beat. Stir in cranberries and walnuts.

3. Add wet ingredients to dry ingredients, stirring just until combined.

4. Pour batter in greased and floured loaf pan.

5. Set pan on jar lid or metal trivet in slow cooker. Place lid on slow cooker, venting at one end with a wooden spoon handle or chopstick.

6. Cook on High for 3–4 hours, until edges of bread are pulling away from sides and tester inserted in middle of loaf comes out clean. Bread will not brown as much as oven-baked bread!

7. Wearing oven gloves to protect your knuckles, remove hot pan from cooker and allow to cool 10 minutes. Run a knife around the loaf and turn it out onto cooling rack. Slices best when cool, if you can wait that long!

VARIATION

You may substitute more all-purpose flour for the whole wheat flour.

JUST CORNBREAD

Makes: 4–6 servings
PREP. TIME: 20 MINUTES
COOKING TIME: 2–3 HOURS
IDEAL SLOW-COOKER SIZE: 6-QUART

1   cup all-purpose flour

1   cup stone-ground yellow cornmeal

4   tsp. baking powder

1   tsp. salt

2   Tbsp. brown sugar

1   egg

1   cup milk

⅓   cup oil

1   Tbsp. butter

 TIP
You may also put the batter in a loaf pan and bake per directions given with Buttery Beer Bread on page 362.

1. In a mixing bowl, combine flour, cornmeal, baking powder, salt, and brown sugar.

2. Make a well in the dry ingredients. Add egg, milk, and oil.

3. Whisk wet ingredients lightly, drawing in the dry ingredients until ingredients are just mixed with streaks of flour remaining.

4. Grease slow cooker with butter.

5. Pour batter in slow cooker. Smooth top.

6. Cover. Cook on High for 2–3 hours until edges are pulling away from the sides and tester inserted in middle comes out clean. Bread will not brown as much as oven-baked bread!

VARIATIONS

If you want more than just cornbread:

❧ Add ½ cup grated sharp cheese, 1 tsp. paprika, and ½ tsp. dried oregano for Cheesy Cornbread.

❧ Add ¼ cup chopped fresh cilantro, ½ cup corn, ½ tsp. chili powder, and 4-oz. can green chilies, well-drained, for Mexican Cornbread.

❧ Replace part of the oil with bacon drippings, and replace the brown sugar with ¼ cup maple syrup. Reduce milk to ¾ cup, and add ¼ tsp. baking soda. Sprinkle top of batter with chopped, cooked bacon bits. This is Maple-Bacon Cornbread.

CORNBREAD FROM SCRATCH

DOROTHY M. VAN DEEST, MEMPHIS, TN

Photo appears in color section.

Makes: 6 servings
PREP. TIME: 15 MINUTES
COOKING TIME: 2–3 HOURS
IDEAL SLOW-COOKER SIZE: 6-QUART.

1¼ cups flour

¾ cup yellow cornmeal

¼ cup sugar

4½ tsp. baking powder

1 tsp. salt

1 egg, slightly beaten

1 cup milk

5⅓ Tbsp. (⅓ cup) butter, melted, or oil

1. In mixing bowl sift together flour, cornmeal, sugar, baking powder, and salt. Make a well in the center.

2. Pour egg, milk, and butter into well. Mix into the dry mixture until just moistened.

3. Pour mixture into a greased 2-quart mold. Cover with a plate. Place on a trivet or rack in the bottom of slow cooker.

4. Cover. Cook on High 2–3 hours.

CORNY CORNMEAL MUFFINS

Makes: 4 large muffins
PREP. TIME: 20 MINUTES
COOKING TIME: 2 HOURS
IDEAL SLOW-COOKER SIZE: 6- OR 7-QUART
OVAL

½   cup flour
½   cup yellow cornmeal
2¾ Tbsp. sugar
1½ tsp. baking powder
½   tsp. salt
1   Tbsp. finely chopped onion
½   cup cream-style corn
¼   cup mayonnaise
1½ Tbsp. vegetable oil
1   small egg

1. In a good-sized bowl, mix together all dry ingredients—flour, cornmeal, sugar, baking powder, and salt.

2. Make a well in the middle of the dry ingredients and add chopped onion, corn, mayo, oil, and egg. Stir just until lightly mixed.

3. Grease interior of four 3-oz. ramekins. Divide batter evenly among the ramekins.

4. Place filled ramekins into slow cooker crock. Cover with slow cooker lid.

5. Bake on High 2 hours, or until tester inserted into center of ramekins comes out clean.

6. Put on oven mitts and lift ramekins out of crock and onto wire baking rack to cool. Or use a sturdy pair of tongs to lift them out.

7. Serve muffins warm or at room temperature.

NOTE A lot of cornbread turns out dry. But this one, because of the creamed corn and mayonnaise, is lusciously moist. The chopped onion adds to its savory flavor.

SAVORY CHEESE MUFFINS

Photo appears in color section.

Makes: 4 large muffins
PREP. TIME: 20–30 MINUTES
COOKING TIME: 2 HOURS
IDEAL SLOW-COOKER SIZE: 6- OR 7-QUART
OVAL

1 cup flour

1 Tbsp. baking powder

¼ tsp. salt

4 Tbsp. (½ stick) butter, softened

2 Tbsp. sugar

1 egg

½ cup milk

½ cup grated sharp cheddar cheese

½ tsp. dried basil, or 1½ tsp. chopped fresh basil

TIP

Savory muffins are so good. But you might want to tip off the people eating them so they aren't expecting a bite of sweetness!

1. Sift flour, baking powder, and salt into a bowl.

2. In a separate, good-sized, bowl, beat together butter and sugar until creamy and light.

3. Add egg and beat well.

4. Add dry ingredients to wet, alternating with milk.

5. Quickly fold in grated cheese and basil, just until blended.

6. Grease interior of four 3-oz. ramekins. Divide batter equally among them.

7. Place ramekins into slow cooker crock. Cover with slow cooker lid.

8. Bake on High 2 hours, or until tester inserted into center of ramekins comes out clean.

9. Wearing oven mitts, lift ramekins out of crock and place on wire baking rack to cool. Or use a pair of sturdy tongs to get them out.

10. Serve muffins warm or at room temperature.

DOUBLE CHOCOLATE MUFFINS

Photo appears in color section.

Makes: 4 large muffins
PREP. TIME: 20–30 MINUTES
COOKING TIME: 2 HOURS
IDEAL SLOW-COOKER SIZE: 6- OR 7-QUART OVAL

¼ cup dry quick oats
2¾ Tbsp. milk
½ cup all-purpose flour
¼ cup whole wheat flour
1 Tbsp. wheat or oat bran
¼ cup sugar
2 Tbsp. brown sugar
2¾ Tbsp. unsweetened cocoa powder
⅛ tsp. salt
rounded ½ tsp. baking powder
1 small egg
2 Tbsp. vegetable oil
½ cup milk
1½ tsp. vanilla
⅓ cup chocolate chips

Glaze
½–1 Tbsp. peanut butter, creamy or crunchy
¾ cup confectioners sugar
tiny bit of water

1. In a microwave-safe container, combine quick oats and 2¾ Tbsp. milk. Microwave on High 1 minute. Set aside.

2. In a good-sized bowl, combine flours, bran, sugars, cocoa powder, salt, and baking powder.

3. To the bowl with the oats mixture, add the egg, oil, ½ cup milk, vanilla, and chocolate chips.

4. Gently add wet ingredients to dry, mixing just until moistened.

5. Grease interior of four 3-oz. ramekins. Divide batter equally among them.

6. Place ramekins into slow cooker crock. Cover with slow cooker lid.

7. Bake on High 2 hours, or until tester inserted into center of ramekins comes out clean.

8. Pull on oven mitts and lift ramekins out of cooker and onto wire baking rack to cool. Or use a sturdy pair of tongs to lift them out.

9. When the muffins are cooled, make the glaze. Combine peanut butter and confectioners sugar in a bowl. Stir together gently. When well mixed, stir in a tsp. of water. You want to drizzle the glaze, so add only a little bit of water at a time, until you can drizzle it onto the muffins without it sliding off to the edges.

NOTE Good texture, deep down chocolate flavor, light on calories—what more can you ask for from a muffin? Oh, and the peanut butter, too.

PECAN MUFFINS

Makes: 4 large muffins
PREP. TIME: 15 MINUTES
COOKING TIME: 1½–2 HOURS
IDEAL SLOW-COOKER SIZE: 6- OR 7-QUART OVAL

½ cup brown sugar

¼ cup flour

½ cup chopped pecans

⅓ cup melted butter

1 egg

1. Combine brown sugar, flour, and pecans in a good-sized mixing bowl.

2. In a separate smaller bowl, combine butter and egg.

3. Stir wet ingredients into dry, just until moistened.

4. Grease interior of four 3-oz. ramekins. Divide batter evenly among the ramekins.

5. Place filled ramekins into slow cooker crock. Cover with slow cooker lid.

6. Bake on High 1½–2 hours, or until tester inserted into center of ramekins comes out clean.

7. Wearing oven mitts, lift out ramekins and place on wire baking rack to cool. Or use a sturdy pair of tongs to lift them out.

8. Serve warm or at room temperature.

These freeze well and thaw in a minute or less in the microwave.

MORNING GLORY MUFFINS

Photo appears in color section.

Makes: 4 large muffins
PREP. TIME: 20–30 MINUTES
COOKING TIME: 2–3 HOURS
IDEAL SLOW-COOKER SIZE: 6- OR 7-QUART
OVAL

1 small egg
¼ cup vegetable oil
½ tsp. vanilla
  scant ⅓ cup sugar
½ cup + 1½ tsp. flour
½ tsp. baking soda
½ tsp. cinnamon
⅛ tsp. salt
½ cup grated carrots
¼ cup raisins
2 Tbsp. chopped nuts of your choice
2 Tbsp. grated unsweetened coconut
¼ apple, peeled and grated or finely chopped

1. In a good-sized mixing bowl, beat egg. Then add oil, vanilla, and sugar and combine well.

2. In a separate mixing bowl, stir together flour, baking soda, cinnamon, and salt. When well mixed, add grated carrots, raisins, chopped nuts, grated coconut, and grated or chopped apple. Stir together well.

3. Add dry ingredients mixed with fruit and nuts into creamed ingredients. Blend just until everything is moistened.

4. Grease interior of four 3-oz. ramekins. Divide batter equally among the ramekins.

5. Place ramekins into slow cooker crock. Cover with slow cooker lid.

6. Bake on Low 2–3 hours, or until tester inserted into center of ramekins comes out clean.

7. Put on oven mitts and lift ramekins onto wire baking rack to cool. Or use a sturdy pair of tongs to lift them out.

8. Serve warm or at room temperature.

NOTE These muffins have a great texture. And because there are so many different ingredients, the texture's different with every bite. They are similar to carrot cake without the icing, and they certainly don't need it. Add a dab of cream cheese or butter if you want.

TASTY, CRUNCHY BRAN MUFFINS

Makes: 4 large muffins
PREP. TIME: 15–20 MINUTES
COOKING TIME: 2 HOURS
IDEAL SLOW-COOKER SIZE: 6- OR 7-QUART OVAL

⅓ cup all-bran cereal

2 Tbsp. + 2 tsp. whole wheat flour

2 Tbsp. + 2 tsp. wheat germ, toasted or not

2 Tbsp. + 2 tsp. sunflower seeds

⅓ cup raisins

1 tsp. baking powder

1 small egg

⅓ cup milk

1¾ Tbsp. vegetable oil

2 tsp. molasses

⅓ tsp. vanilla

TIP

Use whatever strength and sweetness of molasses you like best. You can always drizzle some over your muffin halves before eating them, too.

1. Combine dry cereal, flour, wheat germ, sunflower seeds, raisins, and baking powder in a good-sized bowl, mixing well.

2. In a separate bowl, combine egg, milk, vegetable oil, molasses, and vanilla until well mixed.

3. Pour wet ingredients over dry. Mix only until moistened throughout.

4. Grease interior of four 3-oz. ramekins. Divide batter among ramekins.

5. Place ramekins into slow cooker crock. Cover with slow cooker lid.

6. Bake on High 2 hours, or until tester inserted into center of ramekins comes out clean.

7. Wearing oven mitts, lift out ramekins and place on wire baking rack to cool. Or use a pair of sturdy tongs to lift them out.

8. Serve warm or at room temperature.

BLUEBERRY OAT MUFFINS

Makes: 4 large muffins
PREP. TIME: 20 MINUTES
COOKING TIME: 2 HOURS
IDEAL SLOW-COOKER SIZE: 6- OR 7-QUART
OVAL

⅓ cup uncooked rolled oats
⅓ cup schmierkase or buttermilk*
⅓ cup flour
⅓ tsp. baking powder
    rounded ¼ tsp. baking soda
¼ tsp. salt
¼ cup brown sugar, lightly packed
1⅓ Tbsp. vegetable oil or butter, melted
 1 small egg
⅓ cup fresh or frozen blueberries

TIP

Make these ahead of time and freeze them. Take them out of the freezer and heat them in the microwave before serving.

1. Combine oats and schmierkase or buttermilk in a good-sized bowl.

2. In another bowl, combine flour, baking powder, baking soda, salt, and brown sugar. Stir, blending well.

3. Add oil or butter and egg to oat mixture. Mix well.

4. Add dry ingredients to oat mixture. Stir just until ingredients are moistened.

5. Gently fold in blueberries.

6. Grease interior of four 3-oz. ramekins. Divide batter evenly among ramekins.

7. Place ramekins into slow cooker crock. Cover with slow cooker lid.

8. Bake on High 2 hours, or until tester inserted into center of ramekins comes out clean.

9. Pull on oven mitts and lift ramekins onto wire baking rack to cool. Or use a sturdy pair of tongs.

10. Serve warm or at room temperature.

VARIATION

You can substitute ⅓ cup chopped apples (no need to peel them), plus 1 tsp. cinnamon, for blueberries.

* If you don't have schmierkase or buttermilk, place 1 tsp. lemon juice or vinegar in ⅓ cup measure. Fill cup with milk. Let stand for 3–4 minutes. Stir, then add to batter.

RASPBERRY STREUSEL MUFFINS

Makes: 4 large muffins
PREP. TIME: 20–30 MINUTES
COOKING TIME: 2–3 HOURS
IDEAL SLOW-COOKER SIZE: 6- OR 7-QUART
OVAL

4 Tbsp. (half a stick) butter, softened
¼ cup sugar
small egg
1 cup flour
¼ tsp. baking soda
¼ tsp. baking powder
¼ tsp. cinnamon
⅛ tsp. salt
¼ cup milk
¼ cup sour cream
½ tsp. vanilla
½ cup raspberries, black or red

Topping
¼ cup flour
¼ cup quick oats
2 Tbsp. + 1 tsp. sugar
¼ tsp. cinnamon
dash of salt
3 Tbsp. butter, softened
confectioners sugar

1. Beat butter and sugar together in good-sized bowl until light and creamy. Add egg and beat until well blended.

2. In a separate bowl, combine flour, baking soda, baking powder, cinnamon, and salt.

3. In another bowl, combine milk, sour cream, and vanilla.

4. Add flour mixture to butter-sugar-egg mixture, alternating with milk mixture. Fold mixtures together gently, until ingredients are just combined.

5. Carefully fold in raspberries so as not to damage the berries or over-mix the batter.

6. In the dry bowl you've used, mix together the dry topping ingredients—flour, quick oats, sugar, cinnamon, and salt.

7. When well mixed, work in the butter with your fingers until mixture is crumbly.

8. Grease interior of four 3-oz. ramekins. Divide muffin batter equally among the ramekins. Sprinkle tops with topping. (If you have any streusel topping left over, freeze it for future use.)

9. Place filled ramekins into slow cooker crock. Cover with slow cooker lid.

10. Bake on Low 2–3 hours, or until tester inserted into centers of ramekins comes out clean.

11. Wearing oven mitts, lift ramekins out of crock and place on wire baking rack to cool. Or use a pair of sturdy tongs to lift out the ramekins.

12. When the muffins are completely cool, sprinkle with confectioners sugar.

VARIATION

The season for fresh raspberries is so short that sometimes you completely miss it. Then you end up using frozen raspberries to make these muffins. If you do that, don't thaw the raspberries. Just toss the still frozen berries in a separate bowl with a Tbsp. of flour, right before folding them into the batter.

LIGHT BANANA RAISIN MUFFINS

Makes: 4 large muffins
PREP. TIME: 20 MINUTES
COOKING TIME: 2 HOURS
IDEAL SLOW-COOKER SIZE: 6- OR 7-QUART OVAL

⅓ cup flour
⅓ cup dry rolled oats
1 tsp. baking powder
   rounded ¼ tsp. cinnamon
⅓ cup skim milk
⅓ cup smooshed ripe bananas
⅓ cup raisins
1 Tbsp. + 1 tsp. vegetable oil
1 Tbsp. + 1 tsp. brown sugar, packed
   small egg white

1. Combine flour, dry oats, baking powder, and cinnamon in a good-sized bowl. Set aside.

2. Combine remaining ingredients in a separate bowl until well mixed.

3. Add wet ingredients to dry, mixing just until dry ingredients are moistened.

4. Grease interior of four 3-oz. ramekins. Divide batter among ramekins.

5. Place filled ramekins into slow cooker crock. Cover with slow cooker lid.

6. Bake on High 2 hours, or until tester inserted into center of ramekins comes out clean.

7. Wearing oven mitts, lift ramekins out of cooker and place on wire baking rack to cool. Or use a sturdy pair of tongs to do the lifting.

8. Serve warm or at room temperature.

TIP

These are a quick and easy breakfast. And they're a good way to use a ripe banana! The sugar content is low (remember—"Light"), so bring out some marmalade for those who like a little more sweetness.

APPLE CRANBERRY MUFFINS

Photo appears in color section.

Makes: 4 large muffins
PREP. TIME: 20 MINUTES
COOKING TIME: 2 HOURS
IDEAL SLOW-COOKER SIZE: 6- OR 7-QUART OVAL

½ cup + 1¼ Tbsp. flour
1 Tbsp. + 1 tsp. sugar
  rounded ¾ tsp. baking powder
¼ tsp. salt
  rounded ⅛ tsp. cinnamon
1 small egg
¼ cup milk
1¾ Tbsp. vegetable oil
⅓ cup apple, unpeeled and finely chopped
3 Tbsp. chopped fresh or frozen cranberries

> **TIP**
> Choose a tart baking apple for the best flavor.

1. In a good-sized mixing bowl, stir together flour, sugar, baking powder, salt, and cinnamon. When well mixed, make a well in the center of the dry ingredients.

2. In a separate bowl, blend together egg, milk, oil, apples, and cranberries.

3. Add wet ingredients all at once to dry. Stir just until moistened.

4. Grease interior of four 3-oz. ramekins.

5. Divide batter equally among four ramekins.

6. Place filled ramekins into slow cooker crock. Cover with slow cooker lid.

7. Bake on High for 2 hours, or until tester inserted into center of ramekins comes out clean.

8. Wearing oven mitts, lift ramekins out of cooker and onto wire baking rack to cool. Or use a sturdy pair of tongs to lift them out.

VARIATION

If you don't have fresh or frozen cranberries, or if you want a little different flavor and texture, use 3 Tbsp. dried cranberries. They work well and add good flavor.

APPLE PUMPKIN MUFFINS

PHYLLIS GOOD, LANCASTER, PA

Makes: 4 large muffins
PREP. TIME: 20–30 MINUTES
COOKING TIME: 2 HOURS
IDEAL SLOW-COOKER SIZE: 6- OR 7-QUART OVAL

½ cup + 2 Tbsp. flour
½ cup sugar
¾ tsp. pumpkin pie spice
¼ tsp. baking soda
⅛ tsp. salt
1 small egg
¼ cup canned or cooked pumpkin
2 Tbsp. vegetable oil
½ cup finely chopped unpeeled apples

Streusel

1¾ Tbsp. sugar
¾ tsp. flour
⅛ tsp. cinnamon
1 tsp. butter, softened

1. In a good-sized mixing bowl, combine flour, sugar, pumpkin pie spice, baking soda, and salt.

2. In a separate bowl, combine egg, pumpkin, and oil. Stir into dry ingredients, just until moistened.

3. Fold in apples.

4. Grease interior of four 3-oz. ramekins.

5. Divide batter among four ramekins.

6. In a small bowl, combine sugar, flour, and cinnamon for streusel topping. Work in butter with your fingers until mixture becomes crumbly. Sprinkle evenly over tops of filled ramekins.

7. Place ramekins in slow cooker crock. Cover with slow cooker lid.

8. Bake on High 2 hours, or until tester inserted into center of ramekins comes out clean.

9. Put on oven mitts to lift ramekins out of cooker and onto wire baking rack to cool. Or use a sturdy pair of tongs to lift them out.

10. Let cool to warm or room temperature before serving.

> ## TIP
>
> I used to peel apples whenever they went into a recipe, until a friend gave me her recipe for apple muffins, which I loved. I had no idea that the apples weren't peeled before going into the batter. That was the end of my peeling apples for most apple dishes I make (except apple pie, but one of these days, I'm going to use unpeeled apples in a pie and see what happens)!

LEMON NUT MUFFINS

Makes: 4 large muffins
PREP. TIME: 20–30 MINUTES
COOKING TIME: 2 HOURS
IDEAL SLOW-COOKER SIZE: 6- OR 7-QUART OVAL

¾ cup + 2 Tbsp. flour

½ cup chopped walnuts

2¾ Tbsp. sugar

1 tsp. baking powder

½ tsp. lemon zest

¼ tsp. salt

small egg

¼ cup milk

2¾ Tbsp. butter, melted

2 Tbsp. sour cream

Streusel Topping

1½ Tbsp. flour

1½ Tbsp. brown sugar

1½ Tbsp. wheat germ, toasted or not

1 Tbsp. butter, softened

½ tsp. lemon zest

1. Mix flour, chopped walnuts, sugar, baking powder, lemon zest, and salt together in a good-sized bowl.

2. In a smaller bowl, beat egg with fork. Stir in milk, butter, and sour cream.

3. Stir wet ingredients into dry, just until blended.

4. Grease interior of four 3-oz. ramekins. Divide batter evenly among the four ramekins.

5. Place filled ramekins into slow cooker crock.

6. Prepare streusel topping by combining flour, brown sugar, and wheat germ in bowl. Using your fingers, work in butter and lemon zest until mixture is crumbly.

7. Scatter topping evenly over filled ramekins.

8. Cover crock with slow cooker lid.

9. Bake on High 2 hours, or until tester inserted into center of ramekins comes out clean.

10. Put on oven mitts and lift ramekins out of crock. Place them on a wire baking rack to cool. Or use sturdy tongs to lift out ramekins.

11. Serve warm or at room temperature.

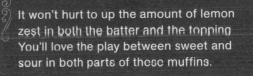

TIP

It won't hurt to up the amount of lemon zest in both the batter and the topping. You'll love the play between sweet and sour in both parts of these muffins.

INDEX

Underscored page references indicate boxed texts and notes. An asterisk (*) indicates recipe photos are shown in the color-inserts.